An Introduction to Karl Marx's *Das Kapital*

A STUDY IN FORMALISATION

An Introduction to Karl Marx's *Das Kapital*

A STUDY IN FORMALISATION

Gérard Maarek

Preface by *W. J. Baumol*

Translated by *Mansel Evans*

OXFORD UNIVERSITY PRESS
New York

This edition first published in 1979 by Martin Robertson & Co. Ltd.

Published in the U.S.A. by
Oxford University Press, New York

ISBN 0 19 520156-6

Typeset by Santype Ltd., Salisbury
Printed and bound by Richard Clay Ltd.,
at The Chaucer Press, Bungay, Suffolk.

Contents

Preface by W. J. Baumol vii
Acknowledgements xi
Foreword xiii

PART I

THE LABOUR THEORY OF VALUE AND THEORY OF GENERAL EQUILIBRIUM

Introduction 3
1 **The Concept of Value** 5
2 **The Concept of Equilibrium** 12
3 **A First Validation of the Theory** 26
4 **Limitation of the Field of Validity of the Theory: a Static Analysis** 44
5 **Limitation of the Field of Validity of the Theory: a Dynamic Analysis** 64

PART II

THE MARXIAN THEORY OF PROFIT AND EXPLOITATION

Introduction 85
6 **The Main Hypotheses** 87
7 **Marxian Equilibria** 101
8 **Materials for a Theory of Exploitation** 114
9 **Simple Reproduction** 135
10 **The Conversion of Values into Production Prices** 144

PART III

THE DEVELOPMENT OF THE CAPITALIST ECONOMY ACCORDING TO MARX

Introduction 161
11 **A Short Description of the Theory of Capitalist Development** 163
12 **The General Law of Capitalist Accumulation** 173

13 **The Law of the Falling Tendency of the Rate of Profit** **185**
14 **Extended Reproduction** **199**
Notes **215**
Appendices **219**
References **229**
Analytical Index **231**

Preface

It is a pleasure to welcome to the English literature Gérard Maarek's significant contribution to Marxian mathematical economics. The timing is just right. Intense interest in this sort of analysis has manifested itself almost simultaneously in various quarters representing a variety of political and economic persuasions. Work in the area has been offered by economists of outstanding technical skill and scholarly ability, using the sophisticated tools of modern mathematical economics either to shed light upon Marxian analysis or to see what new directions the Marxian literature can suggest for neoclassical research.

The basic approach employed by these writings is an attempted marriage between the neoclassical and Marxian theories of value and distribution. They employ the tools of modern general equilibrium analysis which, as is well known, trace part of their ancestry from the Marxian schemes of simple and expanded reproduction. The common element in almost all of these writings is the premise that Marx's analysis of the determination of the price of a commodity takes its labour content, direct and indirect, as its fundamental underlying datum. This provides the entrée for the analysis of the modern mathematical economists who use their formal tools to investigate whether there exist particular production relationships under which this would be strictly correct. As I have indicated in another paper,[1] there is clear evidence that this approach involves a misinterpretation of Marx to whom value was a concept fundamentally different from price, and who did *not* consider prices to be determined by the labour content of commodities. Nevertheless, the mathematical analyses which take off from the contrary position have proved to be fruitful, offering new insights into the theories of growth, distribution and a variety of other subjects.

Though preceded in this literature by writers as outstanding as Paul Samuelson and Michio Morishima, Maarek is nevertheless able to provide us with some significant and innovative materials, particularly on the issue of the determination of the share of wages out of the total product of the economy. Maarek is among those readers of Marx, surprisingly small in number, who recognize that Engels' concept of the reserve army of the unemployed does not constitute a model of wage determination, which yields a wage equal to physical subsistence. Not only is this *non sequitur* in the folklore of Marxism pointed out by Maarek, but he also provides a clever model of wage determination which makes use of game theoretic concepts, and which, the author suggests, is consistent with the spirit of the Marxian analysis. Indeed, in its discussion of the division of total product between wages and profits (or between the value of wages and surplus value), Maarek's analysis comes off far better as a representation of Marx than perhaps the author realizes himself.

The Marxian distribution model, in the common view of the matter, works something as follows: labour power, like all other commodities, has its value determined by some equilibrating mechanism which makes it equal to '... the labour-time necessary for the production, and consequently also the reproduction, of this special article' [Volume I, p. 189]. Wages, then, are driven toward a rigidly fixed subsistence level leaving the remainder of the value of the product of the labour power over as surplus value to be divided into profit, interest and rent.

The mechanism that drives wages to a bare subsistence level is generally taken to be variation in the size of the reserve army of the unemployed. As soon as wages rise above subsistence, capitalists are motivated to adopt techniques that are more labour-saving, and the resulting reduction in demand for labour (the expansion of the reserve army of the unemployed) will force wages back to their miserable level.

There is something to this view, but far less than is widely supposed. In the argument it has never been quite clear why the equilibrium level of wages should fall *precisely* at subsistence; why the adoption of more or less labour intensive equipment should not drive it to some other level.[2]

As a matter of fact, as I have shown elsewhere,[3] Marx denied repeatedly and violently that wages under capitalism tend toward a physical subsistence level. He denied it in *Capital*, and denounced such an iron law of wages in *Wages, Price and Profit* and *Critique of the Gotha Programme*.

Maarek recognizes very clearly that there is a problem here (pp. 167–69), noting Marx's emphatic rejection of the Malthusian population model which *is* capable of driving wages to subsistence. Indeed, he offers a substitute solution to the problem of the wage determination in Marx. Treating the issue as a game expressed for expository purposes as a process of rivalry (between Robinson Crusoe and Friday), Maarek uses Malinvaud's model of bilateral monopoly to conclude that there will in fact be a range of possible wage levels for Friday, corresponding to the core of the game and occupying the interval specified by the following four conditions:

a) Friday's utility must exceed minus infinity since he always has the choice (!) of refusing to work for Crusoe and starving to death;
b) Crusoe's utility must exceed what he can obtain by using his inputs and doing all the work himself;
c) Friday's utility must be maximal for whatever utility level is achieved by Crusoe;
d) Crusoe's utility must be maximal for whatever utility is achieved by Friday.

This is spelled out elegantly in graphic form, and Maarek argues that within the limits set by conditions a)–d) the division of the product between Friday and Crusoe, i.e. between wages and surplus value, is indeterminate.

It is very interesting that Marx also comes to the conclusion that theory can only describe a range within which the actual wage level must fall and, indeed, that we can only determine the lower bound of this range *a priori*. In the key concluding pages of *Wages, Price and Profit* Marx summarizes his views on the subject:

> ... although we can fix the *minimum* of wages, we cannot fix their *maximum*. We can only say that, the limits of the working day being given, the *maximum* of profit corresponds to the *physical minimum of wages*; and that wages being given, the *maximum of profit* corresponds to such a prolongation of the working day as is compatible with the physical forces of the labourer. The maximum of profit is, therefore, limited by the physical minimum of wages and the physical maximum of the working day. It is evident that between the two limits of this *maximum rate of profit* an immense scale of variations is possible. The fixation of its actual degree is only settled by the continuous struggle between capital and labour, the capitalist constantly tending to reduce wages to their physical minimum, and to extend the working day to its physical maximim, while the working man constantly presses in the opposite direction.

> The matter resolves itself into a question of the respective powers of the combatants. [pp. 51–2, Marx's italics]

The relative powers of the combatants, it may be noted, were taken to be heavily dependent on the supply and demand for labour. Thus, the Marxian analysis of wages is very far from being a rigid subsistence model, in Marx there is no semblance of an 'iron law of wages'. Maarek does offer us a flexible-wage model, as we have seen.

Maarek's wage analysis illustrates the three points about his book: first, the author's originality and ingenuity; second, the wide variety of analytical tools of which he is able to make good use in his work; and, finally, his careful reading of Marx's writings. While, as already suggested, I cannot agree with all his interpretations, unlike some other writers Maarek has been unwilling to write about Marx without first getting to know him well.

The title of Maarek's book suggests that it is designed primarily to help readers trained in neoclassical economics to obtain some grasp of Marxian economics. But I suggest it will also be useful to a Marxian economist who comes to the book to find out what bourgeois economics is all about. In short, there are many people who can profit from a reading of Maarek, and so the decision to provide an English edition will surely represent a most valuable addition to the literature.

William J. Baumol
Princeton and New York Universities

Acknowledgements

The French edition of the present work was published by Calmann-Lévy in 1976. It has however, had a long and chequered history, an early roneotyped version appearing as long ago as 1969, at the University of Tunis, where I was then teaching.

In this first version the pleasure taken in the formalisation of concepts tended to overshadow the economic analysis, so that the essay presented only a feeble reflection of my reading of *Das Kapital.*

E. Malinvaud, who had been kind enough to take an interest in my research, encouraged me to improve the text, by cutting out irrelevant passages and supporting my arguments, wherever possible, by detailed reference to *Das Kapital.* This I proceeded to do, and I can only hope that I approached in some slight measure the probity and intellectual rigour which are so characteristic a feature of the widely acclaimed writings of my guide and mentor. However, the work would have been abandoned yet again, had not those who had read the second draft helped me to overcome the reluctance of the Paris publishers, in whose view the book was too non-conformist: Morishima had not yet published his *Marx's Economics,* and it had not yet become fashionable to subject Marxist doctrine to severe critical appraisal.

I am further indebted to E. Malinvaud for having kindly consented to write the preface to the French edition. It is only fitting that his name should figure prominently in this foreword to the English edition, since his role in the publication of the work was decisive.

I should also like to express here my thanks to Christian Schmidt, consultant to Calmann-Lévy; as a specialist in this field he proved to be an invaluable ally in getting the book into print.

Nor can I forget the valuable advice given to me so unstintingly by my friends P.-M. Larnac, C. Morrisson, of Paris University, and J.-C. Milleron, of the National School of Statistics. My thanks go out to them, and to all those who, directly or indirectly, helped and encouraged me in the task of writing this book.

Foreword

Amicus Plato, sed magis amica veritas

Yet another 'reading' of Das Kapital ...

The following pages are based upon notes made in the course of my reading and later reassembled.

The starting point of this reading was the desire to learn about a world unknown and yet so close to us, the world of the Marxist economist, similar to us physically, but so different psychologically. I was also anxious to penetrate the mysteries of Marxist economic jargon, which, although written in ordinary everyday language, bore all the hall-marks of a foreign tongue. To this end I considered it preferable to go straight to Marx rather than to Marxists, in other words to address myself directly to the text of *Das Kapital*, rather than to the host of commentaries it has provoked, in the hope that this would provide the key that would open the door to this strange universe.

The act of reading is a drama involving two characters: the author, the slave of the lines he has written, and the reader, whose good will alone enables the author to unburden himself. However, this struggle is an unequal one, because the reader's unformulated thoughts usually come up against the well structured system of the writer. The result of such a confrontation is usually that the work is either acknowledged as a masterpiece, or sinks rapidly into oblivion. But *Das Kapital* has neither triumphed nor been sunk without trace; a hundred years after its publication it is still being discussed. Adam Smith's *Wealth of Nations* and Ricardo's *Principles of Political Economy and Taxation* are universally recognised as having made a great contribution to the economic sciences, but *Das Kapital* creates dissension not only among economists, but also among historians and philosophers, in fact throughout humanity in general.

Since all methods are valid if they enable us to discover the truth I shall not relive the old battles fought at the time of the book's publication, but quite simply treat the author as if he were one of our contemporaries; in other words, I shall interpret the text with the aid of all the tools that economic analysis today makes available to us.

Such an approach will, it is hoped, be useful to those who, although brought up on the neoclassical economists and familiar with the abstract formal models of mathematical analysis, are puzzled, concerned even, by the attacks made against their discipline with such vigour by Marxist economists. If the present work succeeds in guiding them through the maze of *Das Kapital*, with its 106 chapters, I shall be more than satisfied.

In the course of my own reading of the work, it became more and more obvious that Marx's economic doctrines could be reduced by the analytical instruments that modern economics uses, and could even be quite faithfully restated in modern terms. I would therefore hope that the present work is not only a guide to a reading of *Das Kapital*, but a demonstration of the underlying similarity that exists between Marx's methods and those used by present-day economists, going beyond formal ideological differences. I am fully aware that such a demonstration has already been attempted, but I have preferred not to place the multitude of interpretations of Marx's work between the work itself and the reader. Such an approach is not to be taken as lack of modesty but rather as fear when faced with the awesome task of sifting through the immense volume of literature on the subject.

Is such an exercise legitimate?

However, even as one writes one can hear the objections of Marxists – from the lowest to the highest – who protest at such an undertaking. First, it is contended that such an approach is inadequate, since it is the one to which Marx, throughout his life, objected violently: why try to encapsulate Marx's economic thinking in categories that claim to be permanent, when Engels points out that

> although, in general terms one would expect to find in his writings ready-made definitions, valid once and for all, since objects and their reciprocal relationships are conceived as being, not fixed but variable, it is clear that

> their mental reflections, concepts, are also subject to variation and change; thus they will not be locked into a rigid definition but developed according to the historical process of their formation. [Engels, preface to Book III of *Das Kapital*, vol. III, p. 17][1]

My only response to such a profoundly philosophical idea is to pose the doubtless naive question: how can I be aware of being on a storm-tossed sea, if I am not at the same time aware of its opposite, calm waters?

I shall then be accused of being merely 'a bourgeois economist whose narrow mind is unable to separate the form of appearance from the thing that appears' (I, 533); 'that in their appearance things often represent themselves in inverted form is pretty well known in every science except political economy', (I, 503); that it is necessary to distinguish between 'phenomena and their hidden substratum' (I, 507).

Unfortunately, modern science has given up seeking hidden causes, concerning itself only with phenomena, and there is only a good way and a bad way of dealing with these; the Marxist fraternity is well behind the times, so much so that the very severe judgement of Marx could fairly be levelled at their heads:

> It is only too typical of vulgar political economy that it resurrects ideas which at an earlier stage of development were original, profound and true, only to repeat them at a time when they have become flat, out of date, and false. [III, 150]

In the attacks made on modern economic science in the name of Marx, it is often alleged that the modern discipline simplifies reality far too much, presenting a foreshortened and therefore incomplete picture of it; far better for it to fuse with the neighbouring sciences like sociology, psychology, etc., and create a vast anthropology of which Marx, it is claimed, is the real founder. That is why isolating the contribution of Marx the economist, as is proposed here, is considered an improper exercise. But even if it were agreed that such a conception can be attributed to him, our critics must admit that Marx chose to take issue with the economists of his age on their own ground, and did not launch vague attacks of an epistemological nature. As far as one is aware, *Das Kapital* is a book on political economy, and, with their proletarian good sense, all librarians classify it as such.

Marx, the scientific economist

To counter such objections we have only to go to Marx himself, for in my opinion the overall spirit of his work (not the isolated quotation) completely justifies his rehabilitation as a scientific economist.

First, there is the fact that Marx did not live cut off from his fellow men, and did not produce an original and worked-out theory completely on his own. He is a direct descendant of the classical and pre-classical economists – Adam Smith, Quesnay, Ricardo – and does not fail to point out what he owes to those illustrious predecessors; nearly all the concepts he uses, nearly all the problems he deals with, appear already in their works. Furthermore, he is particularly concerned with economic ideas current at the time, even if he does not always agree with them. It is true that Malthus, J. B. Say and John Stuart Mill are the favourite targets of his diatribes, but it is also true that a careful reading of their work stimulated his thinking.

There are in *Das Kapital* few traces of his famous dialectical method, which consists of placing oneself alternately on the crest, then in the hollow, of the wave. Of this method he himself said: 'If applied to economics it would provide the logic and metaphysics of economics – in other words the universal economic categories would be clothed in esoteric language known to very few' (Marx [13][2], p. 118). It is true that some slight concession is made to the notion of dialectical method in the repeated use of the word 'contradiction' (e.g., the title of Chapter XV in Book III, p. 188), or images such as: 'For example, it is a contradiction to depict one body as falling towards another, and, at the same time, constantly flying away from it. The ellipse is a form of motion which, while allowing this contradiction to go on, at the same time reconciles it' (I, 106).

Notwithstanding Engels's remark in the previous section, Marx has clearly stated concepts sufficiently general in scope to be useful for the understanding of any type of society. Labour, for example, is given a universal definition:

> Labour is, in the first place, a process in which both man and Nature participate, and in which man of his own accord starts, regulates and controls the material re-actions between himself and Nature. He opposes himself to Nature as one of her own forces. [I, 173]

The notion of the function of production is likewise made clear: 'Whatever the social forms of production, labourers and means of production always remain factors of it' (II, 36); and the universal nature of 'monetary laws' (II, 336), and of the concept of 'capital' (I, 703). Finally the modes of production, and in particular the capitalist mode, are defined by their predominant characteristic – which implies that this predominant characteristic, capital for example, may be perceived as a secondary characteristic in modes of production predating capitalism. And, of course, pure economics tries to fuse these fundamental characteristics in an a-historical model, without weighting each one. Though Marx is very careful to avoid saying so, this notion of pure economics underlines each of his analyses. The function of this present study is to bring it to the surface.

As for Marx's method, it is that used in all forms of scientific inquiry: he constructs a formal model wherein abstract concepts are related to one another. This model claims to be an image of the real world, and when it is put into action is considered as simulating its workings. If the conclusions drawn are close to the facts noted in the real world, the model or theory may be considered as valid, until such time as a more complex model, going beyond the previous one and corresponding even more closely to the facts of the real world, takes its place.

These briefly outlined phases of modern scientific method are all to be found in every chapter of Marx's work. He begins by limiting the area of his researches, in the interests of simplicity: thus, for example, he argues within the context of an economy that has no system of credit, until the fifth section of Book III, and right up to the end of the work the notion of the State as an economic agent is practically absent. Then too, he passes over the numerous complexities of real life, restricting himself to 'fundamental forms'. 'We see here that ... it is absolutely necessary to view the process of reproduction in its basic form – in which obscuring minor circumstances have been eliminated' (II, 461). He often favours the use of averages (II, 180). His favourite method is to construct simple arithmetical models (e.g., his study of simple and extended reproduction in vol. II), which illustrate and even guide his argument (cf. the highly detailed fashion in which he explores the 'relationship between the rate of profit and the rate of surplus-value!' (III, 60–80). It is to be regretted that he did not use algebra (in which he was considered proficient by Engels), rather than arithmetic, in which he was far less so.

Marx accepts, and even seeks out, confrontation with the facts. He is very aware of the important part to be played by statistical information and deplores the scarcity of such information in countries other than Great Britain (I, 230, n. 2). However, a considerable proportion of his work is taken up with the presentation of statistical data used to confirm the conclusions drawn from his models (cf. his study of the cycles of the cotton industry, III, 141–53). Finally, his scientific scruples had him absorb an enormous amount of technical information relating to various sectors of industry; few economists, whether Marxist or not, can claim to have done this.

Plan and content of the present work

The above lines will have shown pretty clearly that this Introduction to *Das Kapital*

1. will not study any changes in Marx's thinking on any particular subject that may have taken place during the long period when he was writing his work: *Das Kapital* will be considered as a whole, without any internal contradictions;
2. will not attempt to place *Das Kapital* in relation to the rest of Marx's work;
3. will not contain any commentary on the historical or sociological analyses contained in *Das Kapital*;
4. will not describe the reactions and interpretations of the multitude of commentators of *Das Kapital*;
5. will not subject any of Marx's theoretical propositions to empirical verification, so that they will be neither confirmed nor invalidated.

It would have been impossible to include here a discussion of these topics, each of which could provide enough material for a full-length study.

The only aim, therefore, of this Introduction is to 'dissect' *Das Kapital*, considered as a work of pure economic theory, or a collection of propositions of economic analysis.

The present work could have followed the same plan as *Das Kapital* itself,[3] a commentary running parallel to Marx's text. Such is the technique adopted, for example, by A. Hansen in his *Introduc-*

tion to the Thought of J. M. Keynes. However, what proved to be possible for *The General Theory* appeared unrealistic for *Das Kapital*, both on account of the far greater dimensions of the latter work, and because of the enormous complexity of its plan.

This Introduction takes rather the form of an inquiry into the Marxian theory of profit. The first part is taken up with what in Marx's work is the *negation* of profit, i.e., the Theory of Labour Value; while the second, on the contrary, deals with the *affirmation* of profit in the exploitation of the working class. The third part considers profit *in motion*, i.e., the dynamics of the capitalist economy. The reader will, it is hoped, forgive the – quite unintentional – dialectical pattern of this plan.

Where a parallel exists between chapters of the present work and those of *Das Kapital*, this will be pointed out in Appendix 2.

The area studied does not cover the whole of Marx's work. Apart from the many theoretical details that are omitted, it has also been decided to eliminate the monetary aspect from the analysis; although indissolubly linked in Marx's mind to the 'real' aspects, the underlying monetary theory seemed too elementary and too fragmented to deserve consideration on the same basis as the other elements of the model. Separate research would enable this question to be more adequately dealt with.

Form and content

Before entering on a discussion on the matter proper, it may not be out of place to say a little on the form of *Das Kapital* and its 'atmosphere', which contributed not a little to its success. The form is, in any event, inseparable from the content, for Marx had placed his theory at the service of a cause, whose justification he was attempting to prove scientifically. Very often the most violent attacks, the harshest judgements on certain contemporaries, are to be found in the middle of paragraphs dealing with points of pure theory.

In this connection, pride of place must be given to the 'corporation' of economists, who are not spared. It should not be forgotten that *Das Kapital* bears the sub-title: *A Critique of Political Economy*: Marx castigates first and foremost 'Vulgar Political Economy' (vol. III), accusing it consecutively – and concurrently – of imbecility, of bad faith and of being in the pay of the capitalists. He speaks of the 'Insipidities of J. B. Say' (I, 415); of the 'pretentious cretinism of MacCulloch' (I, 416); of Malthus, of whom he says: 'The whole of his population theory is a shameless plagiarism' (I, 475, n.). With regard to classical economics, for which he has rather more respect, he describes it as 'being on its deathbed' (III, 650).

It is almost impossible to count his attacks against capitalists as a whole and their 'ideologists', his anti-Semitic remarks, his diatribes against religion – he even goes so far as to fulminate against 'the inexpressibly narrow-minded point of view of a bank clerk' (II, 231). His spleen erupts on nearly every page, against civil servants ('bugetivores' – I, 240), protestantism (I, 675), and Holy Russia (I, 229).

He does not disdain the use of slang expressions, and assumes in turn a gruff and doctrinal tone. But above all he has the gift of thundering like Zeus, of delivering a flood of grandiloquent and brilliant formulae which will later be used as slogans for the members of his sect. Does not every Marxist economist consider himself in honour bound to imitate the style of the Master? However, exaggerated language can be forgiven only when it clothes thought so rich and so profound, as in Marx's case.

Part I
THE LABOUR THEORY OF VALUE AND THE THEORY OF GENERAL EQUILIBRIUM

Introduction

As already stated in the Foreword, this study of the Marxian theory of profit begins with a consideration of something that is the very negation of profit in *Das Kapital*, i.e., the Labour Theory of Value, for we shall find, as is only natural, that, in an economy where this Theory is valid, no commercial or manufacturing operations can now produce a profit.

For many years the Theory has been consigned to the repository of now-discredited economic theories, and in one sentence it is described – and dismissed. The question of the Theory's validity is nowadays touched upon – on the rare occasions when economics textbooks[1] *do* touch upon it – in a rather disparaging fashion.

Our own approach will be less dismissive and more objective; we shall attempt rather to set limits to the area of the Theory's validity, and to indicate the hypotheses on the working of the economy for which the Theory can be shown to be valid. However, since such research cannot be carried out in a vacuum, we have decided to study it within the framework of the modern Theory of General Equilibrium. Hence the title of this first part.

We shall therefore begin with a detailed consideration of the two key words of the title, 'value' and 'equilibrium' (Chapters 1 and 2), after which an elementary model validating the Labour Theory of Value will be presented (Chapter 3). Finally we shall attempt to extend this model in both static and dynamic terms.

1 The Concept of Value

1.1 The enunciation of the Labour Theory of Value

Das Kapital opens with a description of the two classical concepts, use-value and exchange-value.

'The utility of a thing makes it a use-value' (I, 44). The world of use-value is none other than the neoclassicists' world of goods.

'Exchange-value at first sight presents itself as a quantative relation, as the proportion in which values in use of one sort are exchanged for those of another sort, a relation constantly changing in time and place' (I, 44). Even the phrase 'exchange relation' is used here with exactly the same meaning that it has for Walras ([20], Lecture 11, 87).

The Labour Theory of Value is considered as determining these exchange-values: 'The value of one commodity is to the value of any other, as the labour time necessary for the production of the one is to that necessary for the production of the other' (I, 47).

It is, of course, understood that this labour time is obtained by adding together all the periods of time spent directly and indirectly in producing this commodity. Marx is quite explicit on this point: 'The quantity of labour expended in the production of the consumed article, forms a portion of the quantity of labour necessary to produce the new use-value' (I, 194).

1.2 A curious meaning of the word 'value'

Exceptions to the Theory (the word 'Theory', written with a capital letter, will henceforth be used instead of the phrase 'Labour Theory of Value') immediately spring to mind, not only to ours but also to

Marx's (III, 504). But for Marx, as for Ricardo, such objects form only 'an insignificant part of the commodities which are exchanged every day in the market' ([16], 14).

Furthermore, Marx is also aware that even for reproducible goods the exchange relations actually observed in the market do not verify the Theory, and that in capitalist countries non-observance of the Theory is the rule rather than the exception.

Therefore, for Marx, the term 'value of a commodity' takes on a subtle change of meaning until it signifies only 'the labour-time required for its manufacture' (III, 29). Initially the expression of a relationship only, value has become an absolute quantity that can be measured in hours or days of labour. If misunderstanding in interpreting *Das Kapital* is to be avoided, the reader would do well to bear in mind this rather odd definition of the word.

As if to confuse the reader even further, Marx usually gives the word 'value', as thus defined, a 'monetary expression'. For example,

> Suppose two equal quantities of socially necessary labour to be respectively represented by one quarter of wheat and £2 (nearly ½ oz of gold), £2 is the expression in money of the magnitude of the value of the quarter of wheat, or its price. [I, 104]

For Marx, the expression: 'such an article is worth £2 sterling' merely means that, since the extraction of a certain number of grammes of gold, valued at £1 sterling, needs, directly or indirectly, T hours of labour, the production of that article needs $2T$ hours of labour. The unit of money is thus advanced to the rank of a unit of measure of labour time. It is quite clear, therefore, that in an economy where the Theory does not function, values (in Marx's sense) expressed in money – Marx merely says 'prices' – may quite easily differ from the money prices noted in the market, i.e., from the real exchange relations between commodities and money.

1.3 The paternity of the law

Marx is in no way the discoverer of the Theory, having merely inherited it from the classical economists, and even from older writers. Among its earliest advocates Marx mentions (I, 85 n.), William Petty (1623–1687), Benjamin Franklin (1706–1790) and especially David Ricardo (1772–1823). The latter, who is often considered to be the originator of the Theory – when it is not wrongly attributed to Marx himself – asserted that Adam Smith (1723–1790) was the inventor (cf. [16], 14).

Marx discusses this question of the origin of the Theory at considerable length in his *Contribution to a Critique of Political Economy*, a trial run for *Das Kapital*, mentioning not only Adam Smith among his predecessors but also Boisguillebert (1646–1714) and Steuart (1712–1780) (cf. [14], 29). And in his *History of Economic Doctrines* [15], which is nothing more than the Fourth Book of *Das Kapital* left unfinished, he continues to analyse the thought of these writers and to point out their shortcomings in their interpretations of the Theory.

The point of these few remarks is to show that, when Marx was writing his *Critique of Political Economy*, nearly all economists were agreed in considering the Labour Theory of Value as the foundation of all economic science. Marx had of course perceived the faults that had developed in the classical structure built by the classical economists, announcing, quite rightly, that classical theory was 'on its last legs', 'on its death-bed' (III, 650). But he was quite unperturbed by the attacks of the post-Ricardians (Senior, Bailey, John Stuart Mill) on the Theory; indeed, he often ridiculed such attacks. It was as if he had demolished the old edifice, but retained the old foundations. Little did he realise that at the very time when *Das Kapital* was being published economic thought was beginning to undergo a profound transformation; no longer would the question of labour occupy the centre of the economic stage. The English, French and Austrian schools, later described as marginalist, or neoclassical, would no longer consider the Theory as sacrosanct. With their arrival, and after their departure from the scene, the Theory was no longer discussed or even mentioned.

Marx thus comes at a period of transition, between the new economic thinking which remained a closed book to him and the classical doctrines for whose last representatives he had nothing but scorn. Confronted by such a theoretical void, he was forced to create. From the classical economists he salvaged a few bits and pieces (including the Theory), from socialist thought he took the generous impulses, while German philosophy added genuine depth to his thinking. The result never ceases to astonish.

1.4 An outline proof

Is the Theory a theorem or a postulate? That is the question. Marx never doubted that it was a demonstrable truth, and yet felt towards it rather as a religious believer toward his credo, so profoundly convinced was he.

> The recent scientific discovery, that the products of labour, so far as they are values, are but material expressions of the human labour spent in their production, marks, indeed, an epoch in the history of the development of the human race. [I, 79]

The fact that 'value in general might have an entirely different source than labour would mean that political economy would be without a rational basis' (III, 114). And Marx goes even further: when he goes on to consider the question of ground rent he writes that 'to abandon the concept of value' is to give up 'any hope of scientific knowledge in this field' (III, 600).

Sadly, it must be stated that the proof of the Theory that Marx puts forward is much too unconvincing to justify such enthusiastic and uncritical praise, and the reason why he develops it so sketchily can only be that for him the Theory is an irrefutable truth which has already been revealed to his readers by the early fathers of political economy.

His demonstration takes the form of this simple sophism:

> Let us take two commodities, e.g., corn and iron. The proportions in which they are exchangeable, whatever those proportions may be, can always be represented by an equation in which a given quantity of corn is equated to some quantity of iron: e.g., one-quarter of corn = x cwt iron. What does this equation tell us? It tells us that in two different things – in one quarter of corn and x cwt of iron, there exists in equal quantities something common to both … . This common 'something' cannot be either a geometrical, a chemical, or any other natural property of commodities …. If, then, we leave out of consideration the use-value of commodities, they have only one common property left, that of being products of labour. [I, 45]

Quod erat demonstrandum! Aristotle's Physics and Descartes' Physiology are also based on such verbal sleight of hand!

However, an unsatisfactory proof does not necessarily invalidate a theorem: only a correct demonstration of its invalidity can do that. In the following chapters we shall see how far the Theory is valid – surely an exercise worth carrying out, since such intelligent men as Ricardo and Marx would not have accepted it if it had been completely false.

1.5 The role and place of the Theory in *Das Kapital*

Marx therefore proclaims his belief in the Theory on purely rational grounds. However, he realises – to do otherwise would be to fly in the face of the facts – that the Theory is not observed; that, in his own words, 'goods are not sold at their value'.

Das Kapital, indeed, consists of a desperate effort to explain away this flagrant contradiction between the facts and the Theory – with Marx putting the blame on the Theory, or more precisely on the capitalist mode of production. For two-thirds of the work – Volumes I and II – he will refuse to base his arguments on the exchange relations that really take place, positing that the Theory is fully operative. He thus favours a system of notional prices, which we shall call 'value prices', as against real prices, which he calls 'production prices'. He considers it quite legitimate to do this because for him the Theory 'goes further than it seems to', and continues to determine values 'unbeknownst to' both theorist and 'practical capitalist' alike. (cf. III, 130.) It is not until Volume III that he shows how the transition from value prices to production prices can be made.

For Marx it is the existence of competition in capitalist countries that creates the illusion that the Theory has ceased to be valid, and forces it to work indirectly. Such an eclipse is, however, merely temporary, for just as in earlier modes of production, the primitive, the feudal, etc., the Theory determined exchange relations, so it will in the communist society which will follow capitalism, and which he defines as a 'community of free individuals, carrying on their work with the means of production in common' (I, 82–3). The Golden Age is both behind us and before us. As for Engels, he is even more precise, stating that the Theory has held sway for between 5000 and 7000 years (III, 10). More importantly, and in spite of his strong dislike for this type of analysis, Marx sees the Theory as being valid in terms of pure economics: it will come into play to guide the choices that Robinson Crusoe makes all alone on his desert island (cf. I, 81).

The Theory is thus placed in an anomalous position: whereas it is a demonstrable and inevitable truth in every other system of production, yet in the capitalist system it fails to function properly; in this case Marx insists on presenting it as a *hidden truth* – hidden from the proletariat by the mystifications of the capitalists. Unfortunately, science cannot accept the concept of hidden truths .... If Marx is saying merely that labour productivity is a key parameter in the determination of prices, he is making a big mystery out of nothing. But if he is trying to confer upon the Theory a metaphysical dignity, the status of an 'inner essence' (III, 130), then we must say: 'No!'

There are therefore grounds for thinking that Marx's faith in the Theory is, at least in part, sentimental; and indeed, it fits in perfectly with his socialist leanings, since it makes all income derive from labour only. Marx could not but accept from his classical predecessors such a precious weapon in the fight against industrialists and landowners. In the teaching of the Theory his natural antipathy for these two classes of society found an apparently objective justification.

1.6 The modern conception of value

Let us suppose *n* commodities are exchanged upon the market. One unit of commodity *i* is exchanged against r_{ij} units of commodity *j*, r_{ij} representing the exchange relation between commodities *i* and *j*. One of these commodities, *k* for example, is used as money – it may be gold, or silver, or any other acceptable commodity. The r_{ik}, the exchange relation of *i* in money terms, are their *money prices*. All exchange relations and monetary prices are obviously linked by the formula:

$$r_{ij} = \frac{r_{ik}}{r_{jk}}$$

which expresses the impossibility for those carrying out the exchanges to make any profit from a series of sales and purchases. Money prices are equal to the quantity of money, grammes of gold for example, exchanged for a unit of each commodity. However, instead of grammes, one can use a conventional unit measuring the weight of gold, the pound sterling equal to g grammes of gold, or the French franc equal to g' grammes of gold. In that case, money prices are multiplied by the same constant: $1/g$ if the new unit of weight is the pound sterling, $1/g'$ if it is the franc. Only the price of the commodity that is money, r_{kk}, remains equal to unity. If $p_1, p_2, \ldots, p_i, \ldots$ represent such a price system, the exchange relations are expressed as the relation between two prices, and are unaffected by any change in the choice of the unit of weight.

$$r_{ij} = \frac{r_{ik}}{r_{jk}} = \frac{p_i}{p_j}$$

In an economy where there is no standard commodity, a barter economy for example, these notions are easily generalised. Exchange relationships are ratios verifying the circular relations seen above: $r_{ij} = r_{ik}/r_{jk}$ for any three commodities (i, j, k); but k can be any one of the commodities considered. The $n(n-1)/2$ exchange relations depend in fact on $(n-1)$ of them, for example, $r_{1k}, r_{2k}, \ldots, r_{kk} = 1, \ldots, r_{nk}$. (By extension these numbers will still be called the *prices* of the n commodities, k being chosen as the standard commodity.) It may even be decided to abandon any particular standard commodity, in which case prices will be expressed in conventional units (called units of account), which are quite arbitrary. Only the exchange relations, i.e., the price relations, and not the prices themselves, will then have any economic meaning. According to such a point of view, which is the one prevailing in Walras's work, any 'absolute' notion of value has disappeared. Nothing, be it labour or anything else, has any absolute value. A commodity has value only relative to another commodity. Its money price is only the expression of this value linked to that of money. More generally, prices (money or otherwise) are merely numbers enabling us to make rapid calculations of the exchange relationships.

If in certain circumstances the exchange relation of two commodities is precisely equal to the relation of the amount of labour directly or indirectly involved in their production, then the problem is quite different. Such a property of exchange relations – in other words the existence of the Theory – although most attractive, is not one of their 'essences', and remains fortuitous. It can be established only by theoretical demonstration and subsequent verification.

2 The Concept of Equilibrium

2.1 An illustrative model

In the course of this chapter an elementary model of general equilibrium will be presented, within which the Theory will be verified. Our general approach will be very different from the concrete style employed by Marx to develop his theory. The concepts considered, long used by the neoclassical economists, and familiar to any 'bourgeois' economist, are assumed to be valid, and will be criticised from a Marxist viewpoint only in the second half of this study.

The author will, it is hoped, be excused for the rather esoteric treatment accorded certain themes – an impression that may well be confirmed by the model's characteristics: a highly developed aggregate of goods and economic agents, rather simplistic hypotheses regarding techniques of production and consumer habits, and an economy described in static terms.

This model merely provides a starting point for the discussion of the validity of the Theory. Suitably amended, it will in Part II provide a formal model respecting very faithfully the text of *Das Kapital.*

Finally, it should be added that it differs from Leontief's 'closed' model only on minor points of detail (cf. [8], Part II).

2.2 Goods and agents

In the economy under consideration two factors are present: goods and agents. Among the $(n + 1)$ commodities, we may distinguish between:

1. labour, written as T;
2. n material commodities, written $B_1, B_2, B_i, \ldots, B_n$.

Each agent is a person or a group of persons, either real or in the form of a company, partnership, etc. It is assumed that each agent's stock of goods can be clearly defined, just as it is assumed that the only consideration is the quantity of goods flowing in and out of his possession. Those commodities flowing inwards are called inputs; those flowing outwards, outputs. Furthermore, it is considered that the inputs are consumed, and the outputs produced, by each agent, of whom there are $(n + 1)$, divided into:

1. n firms, $E_1, E_2, E_j, \ldots, E_n$;
2. households, written M.

There is a one-for-one correspondence between the $(n + 1)$ goods and the $(n + 1)$ agents: each agent is considered as producing one, and only one, commodity, whereas each commodity is considered as being produced by one and only one agent. Thus households M produce (or provide) the labour T, and each firm E_j produces commodity B_j.

It will however be evident that firms and households consume different quantities of these commodities, which implies that exchanges take place between the different agents, resulting in the redistribution necessary for their needs.

Finally it should be noted that none of the commodities considered above plays the part of money, a hypothesis maintained, as already indicated in the Foreword, virtually throughout this study.

2.3 The structural characteristics of the economy

Our analysis will deal with a definite period of time, a week, a month or a year, for example. It will be appreciated that the inputs and outputs flowing from one agent to another cannot be arbitrarily fixed. More precisely, the outputs will be a function of the inputs consumed, the relations between the two being termed 'the structural characteristics of the economy'.

This is made clear in Table 2.1, showing the quantities consumed by each agent.

The column vector on the right of this consumption table has as its ith component $(i = 1, 2, \ldots, n)$ the amount produced of commo-

TABLE 2.1

	E_1	E_2	$\cdots$	E_j	$\cdots$	E_n	M		
B_1	c_{11}	c_{12}	$\cdots$	c_{1j}	$\cdots$	c_{1n}	y_1		x_1
B_2	c_{21}	c_{22}	$\cdots$	c_{2j}	$\cdots$	c_{2n}	y_2		x_2
$\vdots$	$\vdots$	$\vdots$		$\vdots$		$\vdots$	$\vdots$		
B_i	c_{i1}	c_{i2}	$\cdots$	c_{ij}	$\cdots$	c_{in}	y_i		x_i
$\vdots$	$\vdots$	$\vdots$		$\vdots$		$\vdots$	$\vdots$		
B_n	c_{n1}	c_{n2}	$\cdots$	c_{nj}	$\cdots$	c_{nn}	y_n		x_n
T	w_1	w_2	$\cdots$	w_j	$\cdots$	w_n	0		W

c_{ij}: quantity of commodity B_i consumed by firm E_j;
w_j: quantity of labour consumed by firm E_j;
y_i: quantity of commodity B_i consumed by households M.

dity B_i (produced by E_i). Its $(n+1)$th component is equal to the sum of all the labour W supplied by households during the period under consideration.

Techniques of production

The form chosen to express the relationship between a firm's inputs and outputs is very simple: it is supposed that the quantity of inputs required is strictly proportional to the quantity of outputs it is desired to produce. Thus:

$$c_{ij} = a_{ij} \cdot x_j \tag{1}$$

$$w_j = v_j \cdot x_j \tag{2}$$

where the constants a_{ij} are termed *technical coefficients*, and the v_j are the *employment coefficients* (being inverse to labour productivity in each firm).

Reference to this hypothesis on the techniques of production has become sufficiently frequent in contemporary economic literature to warrant a few words of commentary (cf. Koopmans [7], Dorfman, Samuelson and Solow [3], Leontief [8], Gale [4], etc.).

There is strict complementarity (or its opposite, total absence of substitutability) between the factors of production; i.e., an increase in production can be obtained only by the simultaneous adding of all these factors in determined proportions. It is further assumed that productivity is constant in relation to the scale of production, so that increasing a firm's inputs by a given factor would increase its outputs by the same factor.

Although he does not describe these hypotheses in such detail, it is quite clear that Marx follows them throughout *Das Kapital*, and there are many quotations indicating this. Thus, regarding complementarity:

> The quantity of means of production must suffice to absorb the amount of labour, to be transformed by it into products. If the means of production at hand were insufficient, the excess labour at the disposal of the purchaser could not be utilised; his right to dispose of it would be futile. If there were more means of production than available labour, they would not be saturated with labour, would not be transformed into products. [II, 27]

This is what Marx has to say about constant productivity: 'Assuming all other circumstances to be equal and a certain quantity a of some commodity to cost b hours' labour-time, a quantity na of the same commodity will cost nb hours' labour-time' (III, 144).

Sometimes constant productivity and strict complementarity are mentioned together. Thus: 'If now our spinner, by working for one hour, can convert $1\frac{2}{3}$ lbs of cotton into $1\frac{2}{3}$ lbs of yarn, it follows that in six hours he will convert 10 lbs of cotton into 10 lbs of yarn' (I, 185).

Consumer habits

It is assumed that, during the time period, consumption per head of each commodity is known, being written α_i $(i = 1, 2, \ldots, n)$. The α_i are positive, and may even be nil in the case of certain commodities that are not required by households, although they enter into the process of production.

If N represents the total population, consumption (y_i) will be:

$$y_i = \alpha_i N. \tag{3}$$

But these consumption levels may either not be reached, or be exceeded, depending upon known techniques of production and the amount of labour available $W = \bar{W}$. Overall domestic consumption may conveniently be considered as undergoing homothetic variations, i.e., which leave its structure unchanged; this will be written:

$$y = \lambda \alpha_i N \tag{4}$$

where λ is the homothetic ratio being considered.

This equation requires some explanation.

1. The parameter λ is an *index of the standard of living* (and will represent this throughout the rest of the text).
2. λ is only defined to within a constant multiplier. It can be replaced by λ/u provided that individual consumption α_i is replaced by $u\alpha_i$, (u being > 0).
3. This hypothesis regarding homothetic growth in consumption implies consumer elasticity, compared to the scale of production, this elasticity being equal to 1 for all commodities. Price elasticities are nil.
4. Marx's text does not explicitly support this hypothesis. However, its extreme rigidity would seem *a priori* compatible with the low levels of consumption he normally has in mind. In any case this hypothesis plays a small part in the subsequent argument.

2.4 Feasible states of a static economy

A *state of the economy* consists of a specification of the production and consumption of all firms, the consumption of households, and the level of employment W, during a stated period of time; in other words, it is a specification of the

n variables (x_i)

n^2 variables (c_{ij}) and n variables (w_j)

n variables (y_i)

1 variable W.

The only condition is that these quantities must be positive or zero. It is also to be assumed that we are dealing with a static economy, with neither future nor past; i.e., apart from labour, we neglect any other stocks of commodities that the agents might have available to them at the beginning of the period and that might have increased or decreased during the period. To take account of stocks would lead to a much more complicated model, and need not concern us for the moment.

These stocks are therefore considered as being nil at the beginning and end of the period. Nor shall we consider for the present the problem created by the possible appearance at the end of the period of surplus commodities, which are not used but destroyed or thrown away.

The essential characteristic of a static economy is therefore the fact that all commodities produced are consumed; which implies that the values given to the different variables must verify:

$$\sum_{j=1}^{n} c_{ij} + y_i = x_i \qquad (i = 1, 2, \ldots, n) \tag{5}$$

$$\sum_{j=1}^{n} w_j = W. \tag{6}$$

A state of the economy is said to be feasible if the different variables are compatible with the structural relationships (production techniques and consumer habits) given in (1), (2) and (4), and if, in addition, production and the standard of living index are positive, and the constraint with regard to labour is respected:

$$\begin{aligned} x_j &\geq 0 \qquad (j = 1, 2, \ldots, n) \\ \lambda &\geq 0 \\ W &\leq \bar{W}. \end{aligned} \tag{7}$$

If we eliminate the c_{ij}, the y_i and the w_j between the three relationships (1), (2) and (4), which express the static nature of the economy, we get:

$$\sum_{j=1}^{n} a_{ij}x_j + \lambda\alpha_i N = x_i \qquad i = 1, 2, \ldots, n \tag{8}$$

$$\sum_{j=1}^{n} v_j x_j = W. \tag{9}$$

To express this system of $(n + 1)$ equations we shall use matrix symbols:

production column vector: $x = (x_i)$
column vector of consumption coefficients: $\alpha = (\alpha_i)$
column vector of employment coefficients: $v = (v_i)$
line vector transposed from the previous vector column v'
matrix of technical coefficients: $A = (a_{ij})$.

(8) and (9) become:

$$Ax + \lambda\alpha N = x \tag{8a}$$

$$v'x = W. \tag{9a}$$

Finally, for any given level of labour W, the state of a static economy is known if one knows the $(n + 1)$ variables (x_i) and λ. For this state to be feasible these $(n + 1)$ variables must verify the $(n + 1)$ equations (8) and (9), although clearly this does not guarantee that this system will yield a positive solution. This question will be dealt with in Section 2.6. Before this, however, the concept of the price system will be introduced, and, in conjunction with hypotheses on the behaviour of markets and economic agents, states of equilibrium will be defined.

2.5 A state of equilibrium: definition

Price system, profit, budget surplus, excess demand

In real economies every commodity is associated with a positive number (which may be zero), which is *its price*. As we saw above (1.5), prices, according to the modern conception of value, are not an intrinsic characteristic of commodities, but are merely a convenient means of measuring the relationship by which one article is exchanged with another. Since we are here concerned with a non-money economy, prices will be expressed by means of arbitrary units of account, and to within a constant multiplier only.

The *value* of a given quantity of a commodity (expressed in appropriate units) is the price of each article multiplied by the number of articles.

The *price system* is arrived at by bringing together the prices of all commodities existing in the economy, and can be represented by a price vector, each commodity being indexed 1 to n:

$$p = \begin{vmatrix} p_1 \\ p_2 \\ \vdots \\ p_n. \end{vmatrix} \qquad \begin{matrix} i = 1, 2, \dots, n \\ p_i \geq 0 \end{matrix}$$

Such a system will, of course, include wages s, which is the price of labour.

Let us consider afresh the feasible states of an economy.

The *profit per unit* made by firm E_j is the sum by which the value of each unit of a commodity B_j exceeds the value of the commodities needed to produce it.

$$\pi_j = p_j - \sum_{i=1}^{n} a_{ij} p_i - s v_j.$$

When x_j articles are produced the profit is evidently the product of π_j and x_j.

Households' *budget surplus* is of course equal to total income earned, minus the amount spent on consumption, i.e.

$$b = sW - \sum_{i=1}^{n} p_i(\lambda\alpha_i)N$$

or, per person,

$$b = s(W/N) - p'\lambda\alpha$$

The *excess demand* for commodity B_j is equal to the difference between the quantities consumed (demanded) and the quantities produced (offered):

$$e_j = \sum_{i=1}^{n} a_{ij} x_j + \lambda\alpha_j N - x_j.$$

The maximum amount of labour that can be utilised during the period is known and is equal to $\bar{W}$. *The excess of demand for labour is therefore:*

$$e_T = \sum_{j=1}^{n} v_j x_j - \bar{W} = v'x - \bar{W} = W - \bar{W}.$$

Profit, budget surplus, excess of demand are of course algebraic quantities, whose absolute values, if negative, are usually called *loss*, *budget deficit*, *excess of supply over demand* and *unemployment*.

Assumptions about the behaviour of economic agents

Those economic agents that are producers, $E_1, E_2, \ldots, E_n$, increase or decrease their production according to whether their profit is positive or negative at any given moment in time t:

$$\pi_j(t) > 0 \Rightarrow x_j(t) \text{ increasing: } \dot{x}_j(t) > 0^1$$

$$\pi_j(t) < 0 \Rightarrow x_j(t) \text{ decreasing: } \dot{x}_j(t) < 0.$$

Households will tend to balance their budgets: if their incomes exceed the value of their consumption, then they will improve their standard of living (saving does not take place in this static economy). Conversely, the standard of living will fall when income drops below the value of their consumption.

$$b(t) > 0 \Rightarrow \lambda(t) \text{ increasing: } \dot{\lambda}(t) > 0$$

$$b(t) < 0 \Rightarrow \lambda(t) \text{ decreasing: } \dot{\lambda}(t) < 0.$$

Assumptions about the functioning of markets

If the demand for a commodity exceeds the supply, its price will tend to increase. If there is an excess of supply, its price, conversely, will come down.

$$e_i(t) > 0 \Rightarrow p_i(t) \text{ increasing: } \dot{p}_i(t) > 0$$

$$e_i(t) < 0 \Rightarrow p_i(t) \text{ decreasing: } \dot{p}_i(t) < 0.$$

The labour market functions in the same way.[2]

$$e_T(t) > 0 \Rightarrow s(t) \text{ increasing: } \dot{s}(t) > 0$$

$$e_T(t) < 0 \Rightarrow s(t) \text{ decreasing: } \dot{s}(t) < 0.$$

It can be seen that the laws stated above are similar to each other: the symbol of a variable indicating 'deviation' will determine the variations in prices or quantities. These laws will naturally be assumed to be *homogeneous in time*, i.e., that for a given value of a variable indicating deviation there will be a first derivative of the price or quantity associated with this variable, the value of this derivative being independent of t. For reasons of continuity a zero value of the first derivative will be made to correspond to a zero value of the variable of deviation.

Using these laws as a point of departure, it is possible to produce a fairly complex system of differential equations (whose solutions, i.e., the functions of $x_j(t)$, $\lambda(t)$, $p_i(t)$ and $s(t)$ must remain positive or zero) which would enable us to describe the evolution of the economy existing in a given state at moment 0.

Definition of a state of equilibrium

By definition, a *state of equilibrium* is reached as from the moment t_0 if all these magnitudes (prices and quantities) remain constant.

There are two possible ways of looking at this problem.

1. It may be considered that no production or consumption takes place until equilibrium is attained – a hypothesis that bears little relation to reality; only stock exchanges function roughly in this way. Prices and quantities are merely 'announced' by agents.
2. Consumption and production may be considered as taking place from the very first instant of the period; such an approach necessitates an even more complex analytical approach than the first one.

It is not the intention to solve the problem thus raised. Suffice it to say that, if we know from the outset the prices and quantities that satisfy the equations:

$$e(o) = o \qquad Ax(o) + \lambda(o)\alpha N = x(o) \tag{10}$$

$$e_T(o) = o \qquad v'x(o) = \bar{W} \tag{11}$$

$$\pi(o) = o \qquad p'(o) = p'(o)A + s(o)v' \tag{12}$$

$$b(o) = o \qquad p'(o)\lambda(o)\alpha = s(o)(\bar{W}/N) \tag{13}$$

then, provided they are positive, the constant functions equal to these initial values yield a solution to the system of differential equations shown above.

A state of equilibrium is therefore:

1. from the point of view of real variables, a feasible state of a static economy;
2. a specification of price variables (commodities and labour) such that firms and individuals balance income and expenditure.

2.6 Marx and the concept of equilibrium

Although this concept is particularly vulnerable to criticism, it has been (at least, up to the present) virtually indispensable. It is of course easy to ridicule those miraculous states where general agreement is reached on price levels and on all the other variables, where the economy is fossilised by a harmonious equilibrium of all market forces. And, indeed, it has to be admitted that such a concept seems quite inadequate to provide an explanation of the frenzy of buying and selling, of production and consumption, that animates the whole of society. Unfortunately, the theory of disequilibrium has still to be worked out.

In this respect, neo-Marxists would be ill-advised to take the 'bourgeois' economists to task, for although Marx's writings predate those of the Lausanne school, they nevertheless share a great deal of common thinking on this point. It could, indeed, be argued that Marx's entire analysis is conceived in terms of equilibrium, even if the model on which he bases his arguments is rather more complex than the one described above. There are abundant quotations in Marx's work to support this point of view: for example, the passage in which the word 'equilibrium' occurs several times:

> The different spheres of production, it is true, constantly tend to an equilibrium; for, on the one hand, while each producer of a commodity is bound to produce a use-value to satisfy a particular social want, and while the extent of these wants differs quantitatively, there still exists an inner relation which settles their proportions into a regular system, and that system one of spontaneous growth; and on the other hand, the law of the value of commodities ultimately determines how much of its disposable working time society can expend on each particular class of commodity. But this constant tendency to equilibrium, of the various spheres of production, is exercised only in the shape of a reaction against the constant upsetting of this equilibrium. The *a priori* system on which the division of labour, within the workshop, is regularly carried out, becomes in the division of labour within society, an *a posteriori*, nature-imposed necessity, controlling the lawless caprice of the producers, and perceptible in the barometric fluctuations of the market-prices. [I, 336]

Marx does not consider that the law of supply and demand explains many economic phenomena, an attitude that could be interpreted as supporting our thesis, since he pays scant attention to analyses outside equilibrium:

> The change in the relations of supply and demand explains in regard to the price of labour, as of all other commodities, nothing except its changes, i.e., the oscillations of the market-price above or below a certain mean. If demand and supply balance, the oscillation of price ceases, all other conditions remaining the same. But then demand and supply cease to explain anything. The price of labour at the moment when demand and supply are in equilibrium is its natural price, determined indepen-

dently of the relation of demand and supply. And how this price is determined is just the question! [I, 503–4]

Indeed, the Labour Theory of Value itself only comes into play, says Marx, when supply and demand are in equilibrium:

> If this commodity has been produced in excess of the temporary demand of society for it, so much of the social labour has been wasted .... The commodities must then be sold below their market-value, and a portion of them may even become unsaleable. The opposite takes place, if the quantity of social labour employed in the production of a certain kind of commodity is too small to meet the demand for them. But if the quantity of social labour spent in the production of a certain article corresponds to the social need for it, to that scale of production and for that same demand, then the article is sold at its market-value. The exchange, or sale, of commodities at their value is the rational way, the natural law of their equilibrium. It must be the point of departure for the explanation of deviations from it, not vice-versa, making the deviation the basis on which the law is explained. [III, 145]

Such quotations are quite sufficient to show that it would be pointless to criticise further the concept of equilibrium, especially if one adopts the Marxist point of view. However, our description of convergence towards equilibrium conceals a large number of surprising obscurities.

1. The rules for the functioning of markets are expressed in terms that are far too impersonal. Who, in our description, possesses the power to modify the price system? To attribute such a power to one or other of the economic agents would be tantamount to violating the thesis of atomicity, whereby economic agents consider prices as imposed on them from outside. And to confer this power, as Walras does, on some mythical 'auctioneer', who 'shouts out' prices and modifies them till equilibrium is reached, is to run away from the problem. It must be conceded that, before a single price for a product is arrived at, individual bargains are struck at variable prices in fragmented markets, and that the process of price uniformisation takes place after (or, at the earliest, at the same time as) the process of convergence towards a state of equilibrium properly so called.

Nor has Marx provided any convincing solution to this problem. The most that can be said for him is that he may have had the glimmer of a solution when distinguishing between 'individual values or production prices' and 'market values or production prices'. The former refers to the prices at which individual firms within a given sector offer their goods, bearing in mind their own particular conditions of production, while the latter refers to equilibrium prices (III, 137 *et seq.*). Thus, on the labour market, labour mobility is the mechanism that ensures uniformisation of salaries:

> If, e.g., in consequence of favourable circumstances, accumulation in a particular sphere of production becomes especially active, and profits in it, being greater than the average profits, attract additional capital, of course, the demand for labour rises and wages also rise. The higher wages draw a greater part of the working population into the more favoured sphere, until it is glutted with labour-power, and wages at length fall again to their average level, or below it, if the pressure is too great. Then, not only does the immigration of labourers into the branch of industry in question cease; it gives place to their emigration. [I, 598]

2. However, preserving the hypothesis of atomicity by resorting to rather dubious argument will not do. It can only be accepted if one denies the existence of all those phenomena coming under the heading of imperfect competition – coalitions, the provision of insufficient information, oligopolistic markets, etc. Marx is certainly aware of the importance of these exceptions to the rules of the behaviour of economic agents and markets. Such exceptions are often only lightly touched upon by him, and neglected in the working out of his theories. For example, the 'cunning ruses', which capitalists resort to in their dealings with one another, cancel each other out. 'The sum of the values in circulation can clearly not be augmented by any change in their distribution. ... the capitalist class, as a whole, cannot over-reach themselves' (I, 160).

Similarly, the movement towards the equalisation of wages can encounter all sorts of local difficulties. 'The study of such frictions, while quite important for any special work on wages, may be dispensed with as accidental and inessential in a general analysis of capitalist production' (III, 108).

The first exception, and a very important one, to this leaning Marx has in favour of an analysis conceived in terms of perfect competition, is his description of the working of the labour market, which for him becomes a veritable battleground between the capitalist and working classes. As this question lies at the very heart of the Marxian theory of profit, it will be examined in greater detail in the second part of this study. Marx also takes a second liberty with the hypothesis of the capitalist's passivity, favoured by the neoclassical economists, for he maintains that the entrepreneur possesses the initiative in the matter of technical progress. Since this is a question of great importance in dynamic analysis, it will be considered in Part III.

Before that, a study of the properties of the static model which will lead us to a partial validation of the Theory has to be undertaken.

3 A First Validation of the Theory

3.1 A state of equilibrium: existence and uniqueness

If we rewrite the equations defining equilibrium (equations (10), (11), (12) and (13)) without specifying that we are considering values at moment 0,

$$Ax + \lambda\alpha N = x \tag{10}$$

$$v'x = \bar{W} \tag{11}$$

$$p' = p'A + sv' \tag{12}$$

$$p'\lambda\alpha = s(\bar{W}/N) \tag{13}$$

we can simply add up the unknowns and equations and make sure they are equal in number

(10) ≡ n equations
(11) ≡ 1 equation
(12) ≡ n equations
(13) ≡ 1 equation
Total: $(2n + 2)$ equations

$x \equiv n$ variables
$\lambda \equiv 1$ variable
$p \equiv n$ variables
$s \equiv 1$ variable
Total: $(2n + 2)$ variables

However it is quite clear that equation (13) is the result of the preceding ones, for (12) gives

$$p'(I - A) = sv'$$

(where I is the identity matrix), but

$$\lambda\alpha N = (I - A)x.$$

Therefore

$$p'(\lambda \alpha N) = p'(I - A)x = sv'x = s\bar{W}.$$

On the other hand, it can be seen that prices and wage rates are only defined to within a constant multiplier, which reduces by one the number of independent variables. Finally, the system allows as many equations as there are unknowns, viz., $(2n + 1)$. Of course, this in no way constitutes a proof of the existence of a state of equilibrium. To do this, and at the same time show that there can only be one state of equilibrium, two further hypotheses regarding the techniques of production have to be made:

first, it will be assumed that the system of production is capable of satisfying any final consumption demand, provided that sufficient labour is available, and
second, it will be assumed that no commodity is obtainable without the direct or indirect consumption of labour.

These two – quite natural – assumptions can be expressed formally as follows.

First, if the net output vector, i.e., the excess of production of firms over their consumption, is called y, then:

$$y = x - Ax \geq 0$$

which produces $x \geq 0$ [1]

A matrix verifying such a relation for every value of $y \geq 0$ will be called *productive.*[2]

Such a definition yields three theorems whose detailed proofs can be found in the work quoted in n. 2.

Theorem 1 If A is productive, then $(I - A)$, where I is the unity matrix, is regular.
Theorem 2 If A is productive, then a net output vector y $(y \geq 0)$ necessitates a production vector x $(x \geq 0)$. This production vector is unique.
Theorem 3 For a matrix A of technical coefficients to be productive, it is necessary and sufficient that $(I - A)$ allow an inverse with non-negative elements.

The element z_{ij} of matrix $(I - A)^{-1}$, which is positive or zero, has a simple economic meaning: it is equal to the amount of commodity B_i that has to be produced in order to obtain a net output of commodity B_j. Vector x can be calculated for a given vector y by means of the formula: $x = (I - A)^{-1}y$. If therefore all coordinates of y are zero except for the jth, which is considered as being equal to unity, the corresponding vector x can only be the jth column vector of matrix $(I - A)^{-1}$. Its ith coordinate is z_{ij} and fully has the meaning indicated.

To calculate the amount of labour necessary to obtain one unit of commodity B_j, it is sufficient to add up the number of induced products multiplied by the corresponding labour coefficients, i.e.

$$u_j = \sum_{i=1}^{n} v_i z_{ij}.$$

The coordinate of line vector $u' = v'\ (I - A)$ is made up of n similar quantities.

This line vector u' increases the vector v' $(u' \geq v')$ for it can be written as the total of the vector series that has positive terms. (Convergent as soon as A is productive (according to [3], 265, theorem 5).)

$$u' = v' + v'A = v'A^2 + \cdots + v'A^n + \cdots.$$

The successive terms of the series may be interpreted as being the amounts of labour necessary at each stage in the production process.

Our second hypothesis on production techniques, viz., that nothing is produced without expenditure of labour, is represented analytically by the strict positivity of the line vector $u' = v'(I - A)^{-1}$. It will be noted that $v'(I - A)^{-1}$ is automatically positive since v' and $(I - A)^{-1}$ have non-negative elements (theorem 3). Only strict positivity is required for this hypothesis. To sum up, there is *an absence of free production.*

We are now is a position to state the theorem of the existence and unicity of the state of equilibrium.

Theorem 4 In a static economy for which the matrix A of technical coefficients is positive, and in which there is an absence of free production, there can be one and only one state of equilibrium, i.e.

a production vector	$x \geq 0$
an index of the standard of living	$\lambda \geq 0$
a price vector	$p \geq 0$
a wage rate	$s \geq 0$

which verifies equations (10), (11) and (12) (equation (13) being, as already shown, redundant).

Demonstration According to theorem 2, equation (10) gives a positive solution for x for any positive value of λ (α and N are obviously ≥ 0)

$$x = (I - A)^{-1}(\lambda \alpha N).$$

If we carry this value into (11) we get

$$v'(I - A)^{-1}(\lambda \alpha N) = \bar{W}.$$

Bearing in mind the absence of free production, and the fact that $\alpha \geq 0$ is different from the vector zero, the value of λ may be fixed: ($\lambda > 0$).

$$\lambda = \frac{\bar{W}}{v'(I - A)^{-1}\alpha N}. \tag{14}$$

With regard to prices, equation (12) produces:

$$p' = sv'(I - A)^{-1}. \tag{15}$$

Following the hypothesis of the absence of free production, the price vector p is > 0 if s is also > 0.

As already stated, the price system and wage rates are determined to within a constant multiplier. Subject to this reservation, and still following theorem (2), the state of equilibrium is unique.

3.2 Optimality of the equilibrium state

The 'productive' character of matrix A is shown geometrically by the fact that the linear transformation $x \to y = (I - A)x$ applies the positive orthant R^n_+ upon itself;[3] or again, that the image obtained by the transformation of the positive orthant R^n_+ of the space of the x's contains the positive orthant R^n_+ of the space of the y's (see Figure 3.1). We may attempt to define within this space-image all the net realisable output vectors, i.e., those that can be attained bearing in mind the amount of labour available $\bar{W}$. This set is a section of R^n (a part of R^n limited by hyperplanes).

$$Y = \{y \in R^n / y \geq 0;\ y = (I - A)x;\ x \geq 0;\ v'x \leq \bar{W}\}$$

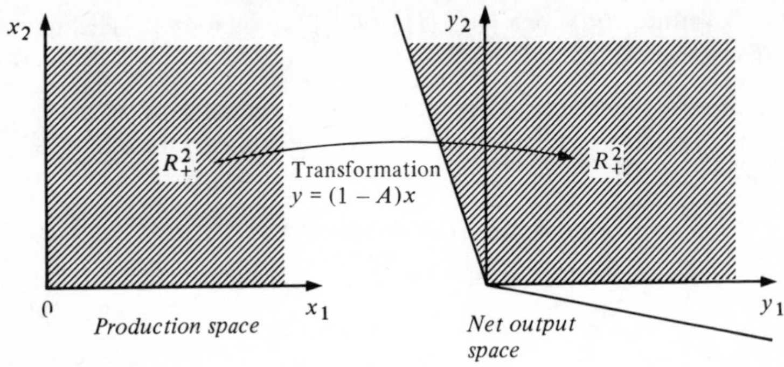

FIGURE 3.1

Now, since A is productive, $(I - A)x \geq 0$ produces $x \geq 0$. Hence

$$Y = \{y \in R^n/y \geq 0;\ v'(I - A)^{-1}y \leq \bar{W}\}$$

Y is therefore the point of intersection of the positive orthant R^n_+ and of the half-space limited by the hyperplane of the equation:

$$v'(I - A)^{-1}y = \bar{W}.$$

All the coordinates of the normal to this hyperplane are strictly positive according to our hypothesis of the absence of free production (Figure 3.2). The result is that, in order to remain on this hyperplane, any increase in one of the components of the net output must entail the reduction of at least one other. The portion of the hyperplane contained in the positive orthant R^n_+ is called the 'efficiency frontier'. Since consumer habits imply that the net output vectors desired by consumers are colinear with vector α ($\alpha \geq 0$), the equilibrium consumption vector is situated on the efficiency frontier:

$$y = \lambda\alpha N = \frac{\alpha N \bar{W}}{v'(I - A)^{-1}\alpha N}$$

$$v'(I - A)^{-1}y = \frac{v'(I - A)^{-1}\alpha N \bar{W}}{v'(I - A)^{-1}\alpha N} = \bar{W}.$$

In the language of modern theories about general equilibrium, the state thus attained is one of 'optimal production', i.e., one where production gives rise to no waste.

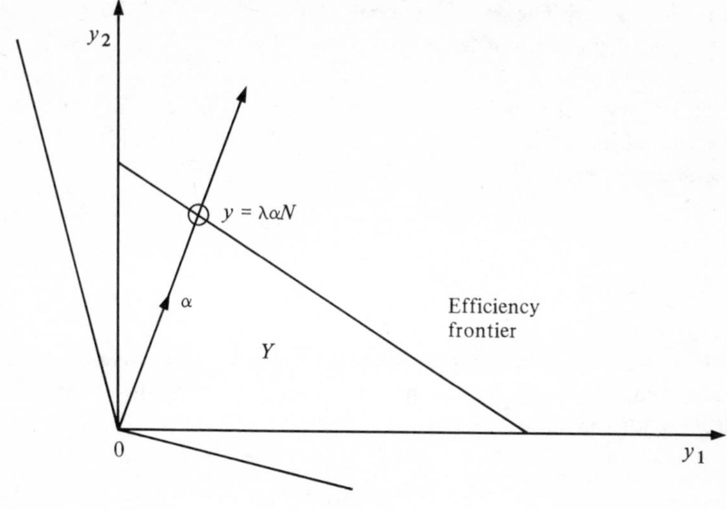

FIGURE 3.2

Similarly, it can be shown that from the point of view of consumers this state is also optimal: given the technology and the quantity of labour available, their standard of living is the highest that can be achieved. A state of the economy characterised by

$$0 \leq \lambda \leq \frac{\bar{W}}{v'(I-A)^{-1}\alpha N}$$

and

$$x = (I-A)^{-1}(\lambda\alpha N)$$

is feasible with a level of employment less than, or equal to, $\bar{W}$. The state of equilibrium is therefore that for which the standard of living is at its highest; for beyond

$$\lambda = \bar{W}/v'(I-A)^{-1}\alpha N,$$

the inequality $v'x \leq \bar{W}$ is no longer satisfied and the corresponding state of the economy is no longer feasible. Hence:

Theorem 5 Provided that the hypotheses of theorem 4 are observed, a state of equilibrium is optimal both from the point of view of consumption and production.

3.3 The Labour Theory of Value as a property of the state of equilibrium

The Theory will now be seen to be simply an algebraic property of the model. It is wholly contained within the equation (12) defining the states of equilibrium

$$p' = p'A + sv' \tag{12}$$

which was transformed into

$$p' = sv'(I - A)^{-1}$$

If, as we are assuming, the wage rate s is strictly positive, then we know that the prices vector must be strictly positive also. Commodity B_1 for example is worth:

$$p_1 = s \sum_{i=1}^{n} v_i z_{i1} = su_1.$$

The quantity u_1 has already been interpreted as being the amount of labour necessary, directly or indirectly, to produce one unit of the article B_1. A similar equation can be written for the price of article B_2:

$$p_2 = s \sum_{i=1}^{n} v_i z_{i2} = su_2.$$

The exchange relation r_{12} as between articles B_1 and B_2, which is equal to the price ratio p_1/p_2 is of course equal to the ratio between the quantities of labour employed directly or indirectly to produce one unit of each of these two articles:

$$r_{12} = \frac{p_1}{p_2} = \frac{u_1}{u_2}.$$

Marx would say that the exchange relation between these two commodities is equal to the ratio of their respective 'values', or that 'the commodities are being sold at their value'.

Is it, however, to the theorem enunciated above, that Marx is referring when he talks about the Theory? In his formulations of it, he uses the expression 'labour-time', rather than 'amount of labour'. And in fact, in a static economy these two terms coincide: the unit of a quantity of labour is the use of a unit of human capital (e.g., a man) for *that* length of time. Provided that we assume that individuals do not hire out their labour-power for a length of time less than the period, the quantities of labour thus measured can be added together, so that one can talk either of the work of thirty individuals in a day or a year, or of thirty days or years of labour. In a dynamic context the situation is no longer the same, *a priori*. Marx, however, continues to add together quantities of labour expended at different times, either in the past or the present. As far as he is concerned the value of an article is equal to the total amount of time needed to produce it, regardless of whether the time was spent today or yesterday, by X or Y, directly or indirectly. For Marx, therefore, the Theory has a wider meaning than that conferred upon it by our static model, a point that will be examined in Chapter 5 below.

3.4 The price of labour[4]

Within our model, how are wages determined? Does the Theory still hold in determining them? If the main hypotheses of our model are accepted, these questions have no meaning when put in those terms. For, after all, the wage rate is just one price among others, its magnitude is arbitrary. What counts is the relationship by which labour and commodities are exchanged. Thus p_1/s is the exchange ratio between commodity B_1 and labour ($(n+1)$th commodity), or $r_{1,n+1}$. The Theory simply tells us that one unit of commodity B_1 can be obtained in exchange for u_1 units of labour. It provides a measure of purchasing power of labour in terms of each other commodity.

At the level of the whole economy, the whole mass of labour is exchanged against total final output, as shown by the equation

$$p'\lambda\alpha N = s\bar{W}. \tag{13}$$

However, we shall find that Marx, following in the footsteps of the classical economists, understands this equation in quite a different way:

> We must now examine more closely this peculiar commodity, labour-power. Like all others it has a value. How is that value determined? The value of labour-power is determined, as in the case of every other commodity, by the labour-time necessary for the production, and consequently also the reproduction, of this special article .... Given the individual, the production of labour-power consists of his reproduction

> of himself or his maintenance. For his maintenance he requires a given quantity of the means of subsistence. Therefore the labour-time necessary requisite for the production of labour-power reduces itself to that necessary for the production of those means of subsistence; in other words the value of labour-power is the value of the means of subsistence necessary for the maintenance of the labourer. [I, 167]

So that, in Marx's view, the prices vector in equation (13) ought to be replaced by a formula expressing it in terms of quantities of labour:

$$p' = sv'(I - A)^{-1} \tag{15}$$

which gives

$$sv'(I - A)^{-1}\lambda\alpha N = s\bar{W}.$$

But in such an equation, the wage rate, the very element to be explained, seems to slip through our fingers! For we now have:

$$v'(I - A)^{-1}\lambda\alpha N = \bar{W}$$

which was the equation (14), enabling us to calculate the standard of living attained at the state of equilibrium:

$$\lambda = \frac{\bar{W}}{v'(I - A)^{-1}\alpha N}. \tag{14}$$

The denominator of this expression, $v'(I - A)^{-1}\alpha N$, is equal to the quantity of labour that yields a standard of living of unity, since $\lambda = 1$. At the point of equilibrium, λ is equal to the number of times this quantity is contained in $\bar{W}$.

This attempt to give an absolute value to labour has therefore failed ignominously, and Marx could even be accused of having created a vicious circle, explaining wages in terms of wages, of having made a completely pleonastic use of the Theory, were it not for the fact that he himself mercilessly condemned this sophism as this quotation shows:

> Nothing remains but to determine the necessary price of labour, by the necessary subsistence of the labourer. But these articles of food are commodities, which have a price. The price of labour is therefore determined by the price of the necessary means of existence, and the price of the means of existence, like that of all other commodities, is determined primarily by the price of labour. Therefore the price of labour, determined by the price of the means of existence, is determined by the price of labour. The price of labour is determined by itself. In other words, we do not know by what the price of labour is determined. [III, 687]

It would of course have been astonishing if such brilliant men as Marx, Ricardo, Malthus, etc., had in fact produced such a childish theory. Our misunderstanding arises from the fact that, to interpret classical theory correctly, we have to write the model of general equilibrium in a manner completely different from what we are used to today, making a demo-economic model of it – a model in which population variables play an active part and interfere with the purely economic variables of production and consumption. The following is a simplified version, which has the advantage of highlighting the main features of the classical system, and shows the differences between it, the Marxist, and the neoclassical systems.

3.5 The demo-economic model of the classical economists

The first version of our new model will be incomplete, but it has the advantage of being derived from the initial model, with only minor variations: equations (10), (11), (12), and (13) remain valid; all that is needed is to add further equations which will express the fact that the cost of subsistence (i.e., of standard of living) does not change, (16), and the fact that the active population $\bar{W}$ is a constant fraction of the total population N, (17).

$$Ax + \lambda\alpha N = x \tag{10}$$

$$v'x = \bar{W} \tag{11}$$

$$p' = p'A + sv' \tag{12}$$

$$p'\lambda\alpha N = s\bar{W} \tag{13}$$

$$\lambda = \lambda^* \tag{16}$$

$$\bar{W} = aN. \tag{17}$$

The reduced form of this system is contained in four equations:

$$Ax + \lambda^*\alpha N = x \tag{18}$$

$$v'x = aN \tag{19}$$

$$p' = p'A + sv' \qquad \text{(identical to (12))} \tag{20}$$

$$p'\lambda^*\alpha = sa. \tag{21}$$

It should be noted that, whereas in the previous model λ was a variable and N was given, the converse now applies.

By combining equations (18) and (19) in a single-matrix form, quantities at equilibrium can be determined to within a constant multiplier.

$$\begin{bmatrix} I - A & -\lambda^*\alpha \\ -v' & a \end{bmatrix} \begin{bmatrix} x \\ N \end{bmatrix} = 0. \qquad (22)$$

The linear system represented here is homogeneous. If it admits of a non-identically zero solution (x_0, N_0), then it admits any proportional solution (kx_0, kN_0). For this to be so it is necessary and sufficient that matrix M of the system be of a rank at most equal to n, thus that its determinant be zero. It can be shown,[5] according to the hypothesis, that $(I - A)$ is invertible, that the determinant of M becomes zero, if and only if the structural characteristics verify:

$$v'(I - A)^{-1}\lambda^*\alpha = a. \qquad (23)$$

This equation is none other than equation (14), corrected to take account of (16) and (17), which had been considered earlier as being unable to explain 'the price of labour' ('value of labour-power', in Marx's phrase). In its new form it shows quite clearly the meaning that Marx wanted to give to this expression. The quantity $v'(I - A)^{-1}\lambda^*\alpha$ is to be taken as the quantity of labour necessary for the 'production' of a member of the population, i.e., of a workers $(0 < a < 1)$. Equation (23) simply asserts that this new member of the labour force only replaced his equivalent.

From the point of view of prices, equation (20) expressed as (15) is still sufficient to validate the Theory. If (21) is added, a presentation symmetrical to that of matrix equation (22) can be given. System (22a) permits a non-identically zero solution if, as for system (22), the determinant of M is zero:

$$\begin{bmatrix} p' & s' \end{bmatrix} \begin{bmatrix} I - A & -\lambda^*\alpha \\ -v' & a \end{bmatrix} = 0. \qquad (22a)$$

Now that the solutions for the equilibrium equations have been worked out, a few remarks will help the reader to understand the model, and even go beyond it.

1. The households sector functions just like any ordinary production sector, in so far as the volume of output, here the population (i.e., the quantity of labour available), is directly related to the volume of inputs, i.e., the means of subsistence consumed by the workers. However, there the similarity ends: the maintenance of the standard of living at level λ^*, just sufficient for labour to reproduce itself exactly, is not the result of technical decisions within the firm, but of a demographic mechanism of internal compensation. It is assumed that, if the worker's resources exceed his needs, they will be absorbed by increased procreation and decreased mortality;[6] and vice-versa. This is the type of adjustment brought out by Ricardo in the following passage:

> If the shoes and clothing of the labourer, could, by improvements in machinery, be produced by one fourth of the labour now necessary to their production, they would probably fall 75 per cent; but so far is it from being true, that the labourer would thereby be enabled permanently to consume four coats, or four pairs of shoes, instead of one, that his wages would in no long time be adjusted by the effects of competition, and the stimulus to population, to the new value of the necessaries on which they were expended. [[16], 16]

Later he says 'The natural price of labour is that price which is necessary to enable the labourer, one with another, to subsist and to perpetuate their race, without either increase or diminution' ([16], 93). As for Malthus, he emphasises the role played by available (non-human) resources, and by 'real demand', in determining the standard of living of the worker, although he by no means minimises the importance of demographic factors:

> If the funds were to remain fixed the comforts of the lower classes of society would depend upon their habits, or the amount of those necessaries and conveniences, without which they would not consent to keep up their families to the required point. [[10], 224]

In this connection, Say accepts unreservedly the doctrine of his British friends and popularises it on the continent: 'the only way of increasing the population is by stimulating production. To encourage people to marry and have children is to encourage poverty. The problem is not having children, but bringing them up' (*Catéchisme d'économie politique*, Chapter XXIII, quoted in [18], 338).

Thus the most typical representatives of classical economic thinking are all more or less agreed on the role and character of the demographic adjustments occurring in the process of movement towards equilibrium. This insistence on combining economic and demographic variables implies that their analysis is concerned with *long-term equilibrium*, to be attained in the economic and demographic spheres in ten or twenty years' time, or even longer – depending on the size of the initial disequilibrium – and with no modification of existing structures.

2. As has been shown, there are a number of positions of equilibrium that can satisfy equation (22). The 'scale' of the economy remains undetermined, as a result of which each of these positions of equilibrium, taken separately, is unstable. A small gap either way between resources and the need of the workers can encourage an indefinite expansion, or contraction, of this scale. For example, an increase in the number of mouths to feed will in the long term result in a corresponding increase in the number of workers. It will thus be realised that the existence initially of an excess of resources over needs may be sustained or even increased. Figure 3.3 gives a possible interpretation of this phenomenon.

3. Finally, it may be wondered why it is that the equality (22) is verified, when all its elements are *a priori* structural parameters given independently of one another.

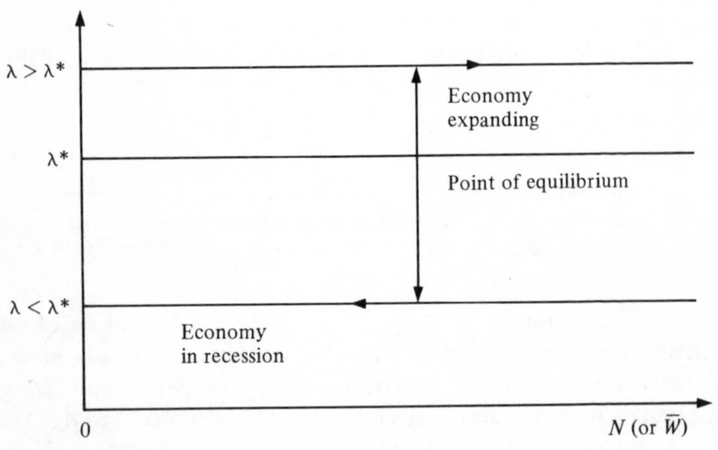

FIGURE 3.3

The classical economists avoid this dilemma by assuming that the improvements in living standards caused by corresponding growth in the labour force gradually decline.[7] Our model, if it is given in a more elaborate form, can take account of such a situation, provided that (given constant productivity) production techniques adopted so far are modified. It would be sufficient to assume, for example, that labour productivity applied to natural resources existing in fixed quantities diminishes when its volume increases.

As can be seen from Figure 3.4, the equilibrium and scale of the economy are in this case completely determined. The population N becomes *stabilised* at a figure such that the standard of living that it is capable of reaching by its labour coincides with that which allows it to reproduce itself exactly.

If the population should increase, the living standards of each of its members falls, causing in turn a reduction in numbers; and vice-versa. It may be said symmetrically: if the standard of living of the population should for any reason happen to rise, its tendency to procreate (or a lower mortality rate) will increase the number of mouths to feed, so that the standard of living will fall back to a previous level. And conversely. The state of equilibrium thus reached will therefore be a stable one.

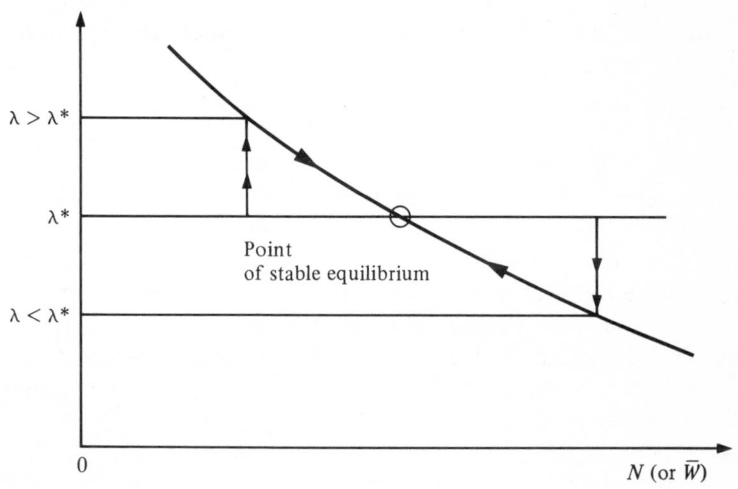

FIGURE 3.4

Finally the equality (23) is realised at the point of equilibrium not through some marvellous pre-established harmony, but quite simply because the technical coefficients, now considered as varying with the scale of production, adjust to the values desired.

3.6 Marx, neither classical nor neoclassical

In the last analysis what divides classical and neoclassical economists is the crucial problem of the 'price of labour', i.e., of how our equation

$$v'(I - A)^{-1}\lambda\alpha N = \bar{W}$$

is to be interpreted.

The classical economists believe that the standard of living hovers around a given level because of stabilising demographic factors. In the long term this standard of living at equilibrium is structurally linked to the other parameters of the economy by equation (23):

$$v'(I - A)^{-1}\lambda^*\alpha = a. \tag{23}$$

The neoclassical economists believe, on the other hand, that if we know what the population is and what proportion of it is at work, the standard of living reached can be calculated. This calculation is valid in the short term, and is unaffected by actual behaviour concerning fertility.

$$\lambda = \frac{\bar{W}}{v'(I - A)^{-1}\alpha N}. \tag{14}$$

We already know that Marx refuses this second, neoclassical, interpretation, since he does not abandon his efforts to explain the cost of labour by the cost of its production. But he just as firmly rejects the classical model, which attaches a great deal of importance to long-term demographic adjustments. Anticipating a little on Part II of our study, we may say here and now that Marx proposes a third interpretation of equation (23), which owes something to both theories. He considered (as did the neoclassical thinkers) that this third interpretation gives a short-term equilibrium, but like the classical economists he considers the index of the standard of living to be a permanent structural and exogenous factor. From there he naturally goes on to admit that a disequilibrium between the two members of equation (22) may appear and continue indefinitely. The inequality,

$$v'(I - A)^{-1}\lambda^*\alpha < a$$

means that the labour force reproduces more than its equivalent, and this surplus labour is appropriated by the idle fraction of society, which uses it to produce consumer goods intended to satisfy its own needs, or to increase the scale of production. As we shall see in Part II, it is just this division of society into two opposing classes, one of which exploits the other, that prevents any change, and in particular any improvement, in the standard of living of the working class.

It may be useful to conclude this section by making clear by means of quotations from Marx himself the important points on which he differed from classical economic thinking.

1. Marx asserts that the standard of living at equilibrium is not a fact of nature, but the resultant of historical evolution:

> His natural wants, such as food, clothing, fuel and housing, vary according to the climatic and other physical conditions of his country. On the other hand, the number and extent of his so-called necessary wants, as also the modes of satisfying them, are themselves the product of historical development, and depend therefore to a great extent on the degree of civilisation of a country, more particularly on the conditions under which, and consequently on the habits and degree of comfort in which, the class of free labourers has been formed. In contradistinction therefore to the case of other commodities, there enters into the determination of the value of labour-power a historical and moral element. Nevertheless, in a given country, at a given period, the average quantity of the means of subsistence necessary for the labourer is practically known. [I, 168]

This hypothesis on the variability of the equilibrium standard of living λ^* occurs in the writings of the classical economists, but only as a purely verbal concession to realism. If their demo-economic model is to be fully preserved in all its rigour,[8] they must be credited with the rather arbitrary hypothesis by which the evolution of λ^* is infinitely slower than that affecting the structure and size of the population. If our view is accepted that Marx's analysis of equilibrium is usually made over a short period of time, his statements contain no contradiction, since what varies over the long term may very well remain constant over the short term.

2. Marx is particularly hostile to the defenders of *The Population Principle*, especially to Malthus, their principal representative. In fact the whole thrust of Chapter XXV, Book I of *Das Kapital*, 'The General Law of Capitalist Accumulation' is directed at proving that over-population comes about not through the libidinous temperament of the working classes, but through the excesses provoked by the accumulation of capital. Marx's ideas on demography are far less simplistic than those of Malthus. 'An abstract law of population exists for plants and animals only', he writes (I, 592). Elsewhere he even notes a negative correlation between standard of living and birth rate: 'In a system of capitalist production it is poverty which creates births' (III, 170). He also has an intuitive feeling that fluctuations in economic activity take place over a much shorter time span than those that affect the absolute size of the population:

> Yet this is the dogma of the economists. According to them, wages rise in consequence of accumulation of capital. The higher wages stimulate the working population to more rapid multiplication, and this goes until the labour-market becomes too full, and therefore capital, relative to the supply of labour, becomes insufficient. Wages fall, and now we have the reverse of the medal. The working population is little by little decimated as the result of the fall in wages, so that capital is again in excess relatively to them; or, as others explain it, falling wages and the corresponding increase in the exploitation of the labourer again accelerates accumulation, whilst, at the same time, the lower wages hold the increase of the working class in check. Then comes again the time when supply of labour is less than the demand, wages rise, and so on. A beautiful mode of motion this for developed capitalist production. Before, in consequence of the rise in wages, any positive increase of the population really fit for work would occur, the time would have passed again and again, during which the industrial campaign must have been carried through, the battle fought and won. [I, 597]

3. Finally, the unchanging level of the workers' standard of living is not caused by saturation of their needs, bearing in mind their desire to procreate. Marx is aware of the distinction between potential demand and present demand:

> It would seem then that there is on the side of demand a definite magnitude of social wants which require for their satisfaction a definite quantity of articles on the market. But the quantity demanded by these wants is very elastic and changing. Its fixedness is but apparent. If the means of subsistence were cheaper, or money-wages higher, the labourers would buy more of them, and a greater 'social demand' would be manifested for this kind of commodities, leaving aside the question of paupers, whose

'demand' is even below the narrowest limits of their physical wants. [III, 146]

This short account of the Marxian theory of profit and exploitation shows what distinguished Marx's conception of economic equilibrium from those of the classical and neoclassical economists. These themes will be considered at length in Part II, after completion of the study of the validity of the Theory, in the next two chapters.

4 Limitation of the Field of Validity of the Theory: A Static Analysis

4.1 The problem posed

We have already seen that the Theory possessed a certain validity, since in Chapters 2 and 3 a model of general equilibrium was constructed by which it was borne out; it is now proposed, in this chapter and the next, to attempt to define exactly the extent to which the Theory is valid.

The field within which it functions is a theoretical, not an experimental or historical, one: and it is only a proposition in formal logic, not a statement of fact. It can of course be tested against real economic systems, but any confirmation by quantitative methods must occur at a later stage. It cannot be simply postulated (as Marx, out of respect for classical economic theory, is sometimes tempted to do); for, as we shall show later, such a postulate would be in flagrant contradiction with those implicit in the Theory of General Equilibrium and already accepted by Marx, albeit unwillingly.

Defining the area of validity of a theory is obviously a relative notion. It is not proposed to draw up a list of all the hypotheses that could be formulated upon the working of real economic systems and then to accept those, and only those, for which the Theory had proved valid. From the scientific point of view such a study would almost certainly have no meaning, for when different hypotheses are formulated relating to a single problem, they always contain common elements – postulates, definitions, or even basic terms which are not defined but are used in the definitions. We cannot explore all the possibilities that would be opened up by varying basic terms, definitions and postulates, for otherwise all theories, past, present and future, could be encompassed. Every theory contains a whole host of 'hidden', unformulated hypotheses, which seem to form part of concrete reality; and only the genius born with critical faculties acute enough to question one of them would be fortunate enough to create a new theory. This being so, all that can be done is to utilise existing theories as fully as possible by clarifying them and carrying them further; therefore limits will be assigned to the area of validity of the Theory within a theoretical field that is certainly very wide, but not limitless.

This field can only be that of the Theory of General Equilibrium, the only theory in our present state of knowledge capable of providing a coherent picture of the working of real economic systems. Opinions on whether it is a realistic theory may be divided, but it cannot be denied that it has become a point of reference and synthesis. Marx's economic theory belongs to that movement in the realm of ideas which, by continued questioning and modification, has led from Ricardo on to Walras. It is not – and this is the whole burden of our argument – just a possible alternative. To those who would object that Marx's Theory and the Theory of General Equilibrium are incompatible, we would answer that the onus is on them to define a new and completely different theoretical field in which the Theory could be tested. For ourselves, the task can be summarised thus: the model described in Chapters 2 and 3 was a very special application of the Theory of General Equilibrium, but since the Theory was found to be valid in this area of the theoretical field, we shall take it as the starting point for our subsequent study. In other words, using this model as a basis, we shall try to distinguish those hypotheses that are crucial for the establishing of the Theory from those that have no influence upon it whatsoever.

4.2 Enlarging the concept of equilibrium

We must now return to the concept of the state of equilibrium which in Chapter 2 was given an inadequate, traditional definition, laying emphasis on the equilibrium of market forces (equality as between supply and demand). The modern attitude is rather to stress that economic equilibrium is attained when each of the economic agents simultaneously achieves the consumption, production and investment targets suiting them best. According to this idea, which is complementary to the first one, the economic agents are also said to be in equilibrium, since they can have no reason for wanting to modify their economic behaviour.

The main lines of the Theory of General Equilibrium are well known. The economic universe is divided into two sectors: households, peopled by real individuals, and firms, which are the domain of more impersonal decision-making organisations. Both sectors are assumed to behave rationally in that they both aim for optimal targets within the constraints of their environment.

However, they have only an indirect knowledge of this environment, since it reveals itself to them through a price system, which has a twofold character: it imposes itself on the agents taken individually, and yet at the same time is merely the resultant of their collective actions. Social relationships are mediated by prices. This is what Marx calls 'the Semblance of Competition' (Vol. III, Chapter I), and on this point he would have agreed with any reasonably competent neoclassical economic theorist. His diatribe on the 'fetishism of commodities' (cf. I, 76–88) is therefore directed only at those who have not grasped this fundamental aspect of the theory of the formation of prices.

As for the other postulates of the Theory of General Equilibrium, it has already been shown (see Section 2.6 above) that Marx accepted them for the most part. Taking the theory in its neoclassical form, i.e., rejecting the demo-economic models of long-term equilibrium dear to Malthus and Ricardo, we see that the sector of consumption is kept quite distinct from that of production. The cycle of technical innovation is irreversible: consumable goods are produced, but the level of consumption has no effect upon the number of consumers, at least not in the very short time span we have chosen for our analysis – which, as we have seen, in no way distorts Marx's thought (see Section 3.6). The many interpretations given in that same paragraph of the phrase 'price of labour' are of only secondary importance compared with the question of the validity of the Theory, which is what concerns us at present. The point at issue then was the duration of the time period and whether or not demographic considerations should be taken into account; whereas the Theory is concerned with the values assumed by the factors of exchange when in equilibrium: whether this equilibrium is long- or short-term is quite unimportant.[1]

The splitting of the economy into two self-contained spheres is not explicitly admitted in *Das Kapital*, for Marx was still too marked by classical economic thinking. (See, however, Sections 6.1 and 6.3 below for some revealing asides.) As for the neoclassical economists, such a split was merely the consequence of the twofold origin of value: scarcity and utility. The first of these terms embraced techniques of production and the resources (including human resources) to which these techniques were applied, while the second term reflected the tastes and basic needs of the consumer. This description was general enough to take in several types of distribution of purchasing power, whether or not based upon the private ownership of the factors of production.

4.3 Determining the point of equilibrium in a static economy

So as to deal with the problems in progressive order of difficulty, this investigation into the theoretical field will be carried out in two stages: a fairly elementary static analysis will be followed in Chapter 5 by a dynamic analysis of greater complexity. As already indicated, a static economy is one that has neither past nor future, and which at the beginning of the period under analysis possesses no reserves except its own labour force and natural resources (land, water, minerals, etc.), known as non-reproducible, since their quantity cannot be altered. All other goods, known as reproducible goods, are produced and consumed during the period, since this society existing outside time does not wish to build up any reserves. If so desired, this concept of the static economy can be extended by assuming that some reproducible goods are also available at the beginning of the period.

If the details are omitted, the state of equilibrium of such an economy is determined in the following way. Having noted a certain system of prices, firms, i.e., 'the sphere of production', react by proposing to produce a certain quantity of each commodity. Given the same prices system,[2] 'the sphere of consumption' establishes a certain demand for each commodity. If the prices system is appropriate, production and consumption programmes will be compatible with each other and with the stocks of commodities held initially.

In formal terms, in any prices system (p, s), where p indicates the vector of reproducible and s the vector of non-reproducible goods, the production sector reacts by *proposing* to produce q_0 goods (the net output vector), *requiring* at the same time, however, that w_d non-reproducible goods be utilised for this purpose. The net offer by the production sector can thus be expressed by the pair $(q_0, -w_d)$. Similarly, any prices system (p, s) will create a demand for reproducible goods that can be expressed as q_d. Such an equation is based on the hypothesis that the consumer does not desire any non-reproducible goods nor can he change the quantity of such goods available. This means (a) that he does not value the possession of land for itself, and (b) that his labour supply is absolutely inelastic. If $(\bar{q}, \bar{w})$ represents the vector of reproducible and non-reproducible goods available, then the conditions defining prices at the state of equilibrium can only be:

$$q_0 + \bar{q} \geq q_d$$

$$\bar{w} \geq w_d.$$

It can be seen from the first inequality that some of the components of the vector q_0 may have negative or zero values. A net 'negative' supply of a reproducible commodity is in reality a net 'demand' originating in the production sector and satisfied by the initial supply of that commodity.

One cannot be certain of being able to calculate the values of q_0, w_d and q_d for every price system (p, s) whose elements are positive or zero. In some cases supply and demand may not be defined; for example, they may not grow indefinitely. The prices vector (p, s) will take its values from a sub-group P of the positive orthant ($p \geq 0$, $s \geq 0$) for the overall supply function, and from a sub-group P' for the overall demand function. Furthermore, for a single prices vector (p, s), there could be not one, but a whole series of, overall net supply vectors expressed Φ_0, and of demand vectors expressed Φ_d. In such cases it is more accurate to talk of a correspondence between supply and demand, rather than of the one being a function of the other (see Debreu [2], 47, 71). These reservations show quite clearly that there may be one or several prices vectors in equilibrium, or even none at all.

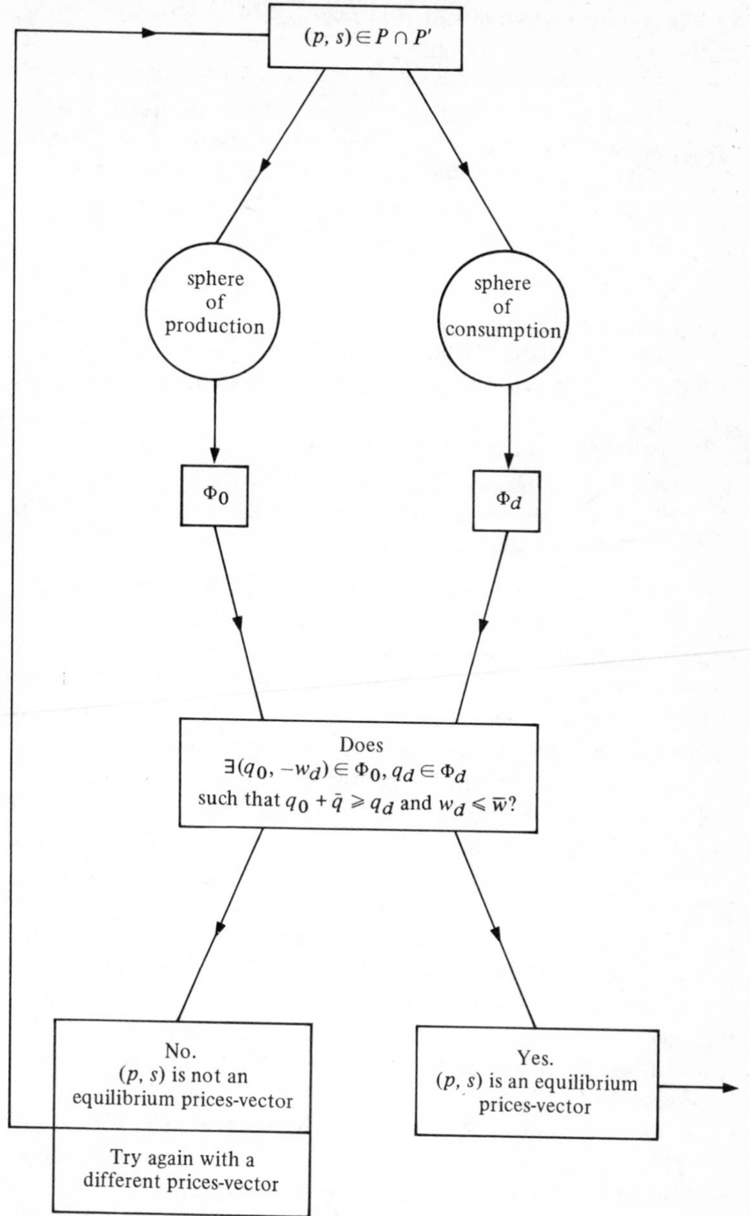
$(p, s) \in P \cap P'$
sphere of production
sphere of consumption
Φ_0
Φ_d
Does $\exists (q_0, -w_d) \in \Phi_0, q_d \in \Phi_d$ such that $q_0 + \bar{q} \geqslant q_d$ and $w_d \leqslant \bar{w}$?
No. (p, s) is not an equilibrium prices-vector
Try again with a different prices-vector
Yes. (p, s) is an equilibrium prices-vector

FIGURE 4.1

4.4 Formal expression of sufficient and necessary conditions of validity

As previously stated, the Theory is a property of equilibrium, or more precisely a relationship existing, at the state of equilibrium between the prices of different commodities and the amount of labour utilised in producing them. In the last analysis, these prices and amounts depend on four groups of elements:

1. techniques of production, which react upon the overall nett supply pattern of the production sector;
2. consumption habits, which, if combined with the principles of hedonicity, determine the overall demand pattern of the domestic consumer;
3. the production factors available initially, whether reproducible or not;
4. finally, those factors governing the distribution of purchasing power between different consumers.

Each point in the theoretical field to be considered is made up of specifications of these four groups of structural elements. At each point it ought to be possible to say whether or not the Theory is verified. A hypothesis regarding the structural elements is basically only a part of the theoretical field. However, the different parts of the field do not necessarily constitute a 'natural' hypothesis, i.e., one that could be given a simple economic interpretation. Despite the high degree of subjectivity in defining them, only such 'natural' hypotheses will be considered from now on, so as to avoid having to consider situations where the Theory might be validated purely accidentally. Throughout this study it will also be assumed that the structural elements we are considering are in a state of equilibrium. It will be necessary to verify *a posteriori* that the hypotheses for which the Theory is validated are compatible with those by which the existence of a state of equilibrium has been demonstrated elsewhere (e.g., by reference to Debreu [2], 90 for private property economics).

There are two ways of preparing a map of the area of validity of the Theory: from the inside, by showing clearly those areas of the theoretical field where the Theory is patently verified, in which case there are *sufficient conditions* for its validity; or from the outside, by enumerating the characteristics of those hypotheses that must be verified for the Theory to be valid. These are the *necessary conditions*. The area of the validity of the Theory will be exactly traced out if we discover those conditions that are at the same time necessary and sufficient. They can be expressed in the following general form:

Sufficient condition If the structural elements σ belong to class ϕ' of structural elements, then the Theory is verified; i.e., at equilibrium:

1. it is possible to calculate the amount u_j of labour indirectly and directly necessary to obtain one unit of any non-reproducible commodity B_j;
2. for any pair (i, j) the prices of these goods verify the equation:

$$\frac{p_i}{p_j} = \frac{u_i}{u_j} \quad (p_j \neq 0,\ u_j \neq 0)$$

3. $p_j = 0$ if, and only if, $u_j = 0$.

Necessary condition If the structural elements σ are such that the Theory is verified (see above), then they must necessarily belong to a class ϕ'' of structural elements.

These two formal expressions explicitly give the Theory a more restricted content than what was assumed in Section 1.6 above, for example. On their own admission Ricardo and Marx see the Theory as applying to reproducible goods only (see the quotations made in Section 1.1). If it were extended to those goods that are not the result of any labour, their price vector would necessarily be nil (at least until such time as available supplies were exhausted; in which case, $s_j = 0$ since $u_j = 0$; if we go further than that do we have to say u_j, and therefore $s_j = +\infty$? For Marx it was the first equation that was valid). It would appear that no natural hypothesis regarding the structural elements determining general equilibrium can be formulated, which would imply that the price of non-reproducible factors other than labour could be zero (see below Section 4.8). If this is understood, and if ϕ is the area of validity of the Theory, then it is clear that:

$$\phi' \subset \phi \subset \phi''.$$

4.5 Sufficient conditions for validity

Initially the search for sufficient conditions can be facilitated by varying only the first of the four groups of structural elements mentioned earlier, viz., techniques of production. Later it will be seen that, by formulating restrictive hypotheses on consumption habits, on amounts of non-reproducible commodities available and on the factors of distribution of purchasing power, certain hypotheses regarding techniques of production can be abandoned.

It will be shown that in all cases where techniques of production are made to observe four conditions derived from those forming the basis found in the model given in Chapters 2 and 3, the validity of the Theory is upheld. These four conditions are as follows.

H_1 Productivity is constant compared to the scale of production.

H_2 Labour is the only non-reproducible commodity necessary for the production of reproducible goods. Such a condition would allow us to stop taking account of non-reproducible commodities other than labour, whatever their cost. Unless otherwise stated, s will in the rest of the text represent that element of the vector s that is concerned with labour, i.e., wages.

H_3 Each reproducible commodity is produced by one, and only one, firm.

H_4 In any overall price system P where wages s are not zero, each firm can select at least one profitable 'technical process', such that its net supply of the commodity it produces is not necessarily zero.

In Chapters 2 and 3 each firm E_j ($j = 1, 2, \ldots, n$) was characterised by a single vector a_j of technical coefficients and a single employment coefficient v_j. This pair (a_j, v_j) formed a non-negative vector $\hat{a}_j$, of $(n + 1)$ dimensions. Now, however, there is a whole set of such vectors $A_j \subset R_+^{n+1}$. A_j has a finite or infinite number of elements, according to the number of 'technical processes'. The elements making up vector $\hat{a}_j$ are the quantities of each commodity necessary to produce one unit of B_j. For a certain level of production x_j the quantity of inputs must be x_j times greater, according to our hypothesis of constant productivity.

If these conditions are fulfilled, the only consideration governing the course of action of E_j is the question of the profit per unit, which is equal to

$$\pi_j = p_j - \sum_{i=1}^{n} p_i a_{ij} - sv_j$$

for a prices system (p, s).

If $\pi_j < 0$, $x_j = 0$ then its equilibrium production is nil.
If $\pi_j = 0$, $x_j \geq 0$ then its production may take on any positive, or zero value. We have a supply correspondence not a supply function.
If $\pi_j > 0$, $x_j = +\infty$ it can be said here that the supply correspondence is not defined. This third eventuality can in any case be excluded since it is one of our conditions that (p, s) should form part of P.

These rules governing the firm's strategy merely reflect its desire to maximise its total profit $\pi_j x_j$. According to condition H_4, it may select at least one technical process that is only just profitable, i.e., by which the profit per unit is zero. Using this process it will produce – or not, according to the requirements of the general equilibrium – some of the commodity B_j $(x_j \geq 0)$. The prices of all reproducible commodities n are therefore linked to wages by n linear equations similar to those that characterised the model explained in Chapters 2 and 3 (equation (12)). If we formulate adequate hypotheses on the sets A_j, we can calculate the amount of labour u_j that goes into each article, and the Theory is verified (equation (15)).

$$p' = p'A + sv' \tag{12}$$

$$p' = sv'(I - A)^{-1} = su' \tag{15}$$

The Theory is here seen to be a property of the equilibrium of the productive system, quite independent of the reactions produced on the form and existence of this equilibrium by the production factors available and the characteristics peculiar to the sphere of consumption. There is a striking similarity here between this problem and that of deciding the point of equilibrium between prices and quantities on any given market. This equilibrium depends on both the supply and demand curves. It may, however, be assumed initially that the supply curve has characteristics independent of the form of the demand curve. What is roughly true of a partial market is wholly true of the overall supply and demand function (or correspondence) when the whole economy is being considered. So that the meaning of the Theory is stood upon its head; what for Marx was the cause now becomes the effect, and vice-versa. Now we have to say: given a system of prices, i.e., of exchange relations, the technical processes adopted will be such that the labour expended directly or indirectly in the production of each commodity will be proportional to its cost. It is not technology that determines prices, but the reverse! Of course such a conclusion is not to be taken seriously: Walras, the first theoretician of interdependence, has shown that the relation between prices and technology is one of simultaneity, not one of direct cause and effect. Taking the opposite view to Marx, we go beyond thesis and anti-thesis in a perfectly orthodox dialectic movement. Unfortunately for Marx, the synthesis is provided by the neoclassicists!

Marx was in fact less dogmatic than this, and certainly had an intuitive feeling that the Theory could be extended to cover situations where a variety of technical processes compete with each other in the production of each commodity. This is an attractive interpretation of his expression, 'The labour-time socially necessary is that required to produce an article under the normal conditions of production, and with the average degree of skill and intensity prevalent at the time' (I, 47). And he goes on to describe how the replacement by power-looms of manual looms, i.e., the passing from one technical process to another, modifies the value of textile products.

> The introduction of power-looms into England probably reduced by one-half the labour required to weave a given quantity of yarn into cloth. The hand-loom weavers, as a matter of fact, continued to require the same time as before; but for all that, the product of one hour of their labour represented after the change only half an hour's social labour, and consequently fell to one-half of its former value. [I, 47]

The technical process used is the only one, out of a host of other potential mechanisms, that competition maintains, since the others are not profitable within a system of prices at equilibrium.

4.6 Other sets of sufficient conditions

The above set of sufficient conditions is clearly not the only one possible. If we set limits to the area of variation of the structural elements other than techniques of production, we can construct others.

Thus, if one considers an economy where the initial stocks of reproducible goods are nil ($\bar{q} = 0$) – and such was the definition given to the term 'static economy' in Chapter 2 – we now see that it is no longer necessary to suppose that all firms are willing to undertake production for any system of prices (hypothesis H_4 in Section 4.5). If we take firm E_j, which is in deficit when the prices vector is in equilibrium, then firms' 'net' overall supply of commodity B_j is certainly negative; so that domestic demand is added to what is in reality demand from firms. But if there are no initial stocks of this commodity, it is impossible to meet the demand from these two categories of economic agent. Therefore the prices vector under consideration is not the equilibrium prices vector, unless overall demand – the demand from individual units – is nil for the same prices vector. In this case commodity B_j is completely eliminated from the agents' economic horizon; it is not produced, or consumed, or exchanged. Its price is not determined and is of no consequence.

The prices of all other reproducible commodities, whose number is at the most equal to n, fit into a linear system having the same structure as equation (12):

$$p' = p'A + sv' \tag{12}$$

but with perhaps a smaller number of dimensions. When that point is reached there is no difficulty in establishing the Theory.

We can thus see the Theory's validity has been established for a set of conditions that is neither more nor less restrictive than the previous set, for hypothesis H_4 has been replaced by H_5: the initial stock of reproducible commodities is nil ($\bar{q} = 0$).

It is also possible to have a new set of hypotheses respecting the Theory if hypothesis H_2 is replaced by the less restrictive hypothesis H_6: for any system of prices, the goods required by households are such that the only element needed directly and indirectly in their production is the non-reproducible factor, labour. However, this hypothesis seems less 'natural' than the one it replaces and will not be considered further.

4.7 An illustration

The model put forward in Chapters 2 and 3 fits exactly into the framework of hypotheses H_1, H_2, H_3, H_5 formulated above. It constitutes the special case where the sets A_j are reduced to a single vector $\hat{a}_j = (a_j, v_j)$, possessing $(n + 1)$ dimensions. P is the total sum of vectors (p, s) such that

$$p' \leq p'A + sv'$$
$$p' \geq 0$$
$$s \geq 0.$$

This set is not empty, for bearing in mind the properties of A and v', the inequalities

$$p' \leq sv'(I - A)^{-1}$$
$$p \geq 0 \qquad s \geq 0$$

have at least one solution, i.e., the one contained in equation (12). For the demand correspondence to be defined, the set P' of prices vectors must be the entire positive orthant $(p \geq 0, s \geq 0)$, except for points such that we have

$$p'\alpha N = 0$$

(in such cases λ will tend towards infinity).

Since the domestic consumer seeks to maximise his standard of living λ, for all the prices vectors of P', we have:

$$p'\lambda\alpha N = s\bar{W}.$$

However there is nothing to prove that the equilibrium determined by solving equations (10), (11), (12) and (13), which were based upon the traditional conditions of equality of supply and demand of commodities and equality of labour and resources, is the only one that would be compatible with the more modern formulation presented in Section 4.3. In other words, the uniqueness of the state of equilibrium established by theorem 4 is once more open to question. For, given this more general framework, prices and quantity variables have only to verify the inequalities at equilibrium:

$$x \geq Ax + \lambda\alpha N \tag{10a}$$
$$v'x \leq \bar{W} \tag{11a}$$
$$p' \leq p'A + sv' \tag{12a}$$
$$p'\lambda\alpha N = s\bar{W} \tag{13a}$$

and also the relationship of 'correspondence' which reflects maximisation of profits:

$$p_j < \sum_{i=1}^{n} p_i a_{ij} + sv_j \Rightarrow x_j = 0$$

$$x_j > 0 \Rightarrow p_j = \sum_{i=1}^{n} p_i a_{ij} + sv_j.$$

If all these inequalities are combined, it is clear that at the point of equilibrium,

$$p'Ax + sv' = p'x = p'Ax + p'\lambda\alpha N.$$

From this double equation it can be seen that, for all goods where supply exceeds demand, the price is nil.

$$x_j > \sum_{i=1}^{n} a_{ij} x_i + \lambda\alpha_j N \Rightarrow p_j = 0$$

$$v'x < \bar{W} \Rightarrow s = 0.$$

And conversely, every factor having a strictly positive price is fully utilised:

$$p_j > 0 \Rightarrow x_j = \sum_{i=1}^{n} a_{ij} x_i + \lambda\alpha_j N$$

$$s > 0 \Rightarrow v'x = \bar{W}.$$

All these results will, of course, be familiar to the reader acquainted with linear models.

The problem is to demonstrate that when the economy has reached a stage of equilibrium the inequalities (10a) and (11a) are satisfied. Let us suppose for the moment that salaries are strictly positive ($s > 0$). The firms that are not functioning at equilibrium ($x_j = 0$) will be those producing goods demanded neither by other firms nor by households. With regard to such firms, the same arguments can be put forward as in Section 4.6. The prices of such goods remain quite arbitrary; one could choose the prices given by equation (15), i.e., proportional to the quantities of labour needed to produce them ($p_j = su_j$).

All other firms are working ($x_j > 0$), so their profit is zero:

$$p_j = \sum_{i=1}^{n} a_{ij} p_i + sv_j.$$

The prices of the goods they produce are now related to all other goods by equation (12) and not as before by the inequality (12a). Therefore they also take the form $p_j = su_j$, and so are strictly positive (u_j is strictly positive, by the hypothesis of the absence of free production); but, since we know that commodities having a price greater than zero are fully utilised, the inequalities (10a) are therefore satisfied at equality, both for undesired commodities – which are, of course, not produced – and for the others.

There remains the hypothesis of non-zero wages, which has to be justified. If $s = 0$, all prices $p_j = su_j$ are nil, as is the formula $p'\alpha N$. The prices vector being considered can no longer be the prices vector at equilibrium since it no longer belongs to the set P'. So s is strictly positive and all labour available is employed. The inequality (11a) has been replaced by the equation (11). The unicity of the state of equilibrium is fully established.

This model, used also in Chapters 2 and 3, provides us also with the possibility of testing a corollary resulting from the results achieved above: which is that the validity of the Theory, established by the set of hypotheses H_1, H_2, H_3, H_4, H_5, in no way depends upon the structure of domestic consumer demand. In our model we can for example:

1. distinguish r groups of consumers, each one characterised by its own consumption pattern α_l ($l = 1, 2, \ldots, r$), instead of assuming that consumers form a homogeneous whole as far as their consumer preferences are concerned. It is not necessary to carry out the calculations to have an idea that the structure of total consumption will be a 'barycentre' of the structures of the group, the structure of group l being weighted by the number of members of the population in that group (see Figure 4.2a).

$$\alpha = \sum_{l=1}^{r} \frac{N_l}{N} \cdot \alpha_l \qquad \text{with} \qquad \sum_{l=1}^{r} N_l = N.$$

The Theory thus remains valid;
2. allow a certain substitutability between goods in the utility function, which may then be written:

$$S = S(y_1, y_2, \ldots, y_n)$$

where S is increasing, continuous and derivable. The maximum for S on the compact Y (which is the set of net realisable output vec-

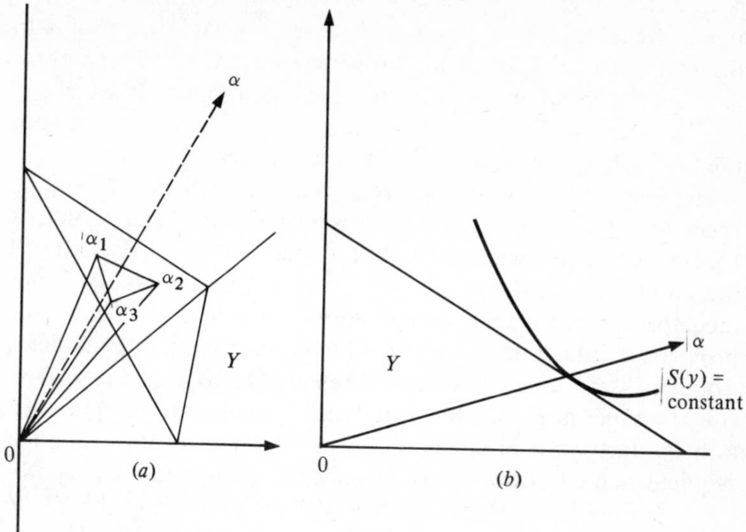

FIGURE 4.2

tors) exists, on the efficiency frontier of this field (cf. Section 3.2). We come back again to the central model in giving the symbol α to a colinear vector at the segment joining the origin to a point of Y where S is maximum (see Figure 4.2b).

4.8 The search for necessary conditions

In our opinion, it is not possible to produce a set of necessary conditions that can be easily interpreted, still less to formulate exactly (in 'natural' economic language) a set of conditions both sufficient and necessary.

We shall merely prove here that the Theory is not verified in large areas of the theoretical field lying outside those characterising the sufficient conditions posited above. For each of these areas it is simple to construct at least one, and in reality many, models of equilibrium where the Theory can be seen to be invalid.

Retaining the other three, let us abandon *the first* of the sufficient conditions of validity, i.e., the *hypothesis of constant productivity of the techniques of production.* It is known, for example, that at the point of equilibrium, even *diminishing* returns can yield profits to firms. In such cases, prices are broken down into labour and profit in a ratio that is not necessarily the same for all commodities, and so the Theory is no longer verified. As for *increasing returns*, they put the very concept of equilibrium in great danger.

However, in theory constant returns are the rule rather than the exception: we are of course discussing here productivity that is constant compared with the scale of production, i.e., yields where all the inputs vary in the same proportion. Such a hypothesis is not incompatible with diminishing returns from one of the inputs, provided that the others are present in given quantities. Thus yields from fertilisers or seeds decrease when applied to the same surface. But the same farm can be reproduced a thousand-fold, provided that the factors of production – in particular land possessing the required characteristics – exist in sufficient quantities. This hypothesis regarding constant yields tallies with the coming together of the traditional hypotheses of 'free entry into the branch' and the 'indefinite divisibility of factors'.

In actual fact it is *the second* of the sufficient conditions enunciated above that has to be treated with the greatest caution. Labour is not the only non-reproducible commodity indispensable to production. In addition to land, mentioned above, there are also: water, mineral deposits, natural forests, etc. If hypotheses H_1, H_3 and H_4 are maintained, the prices of reproducible goods will be joined together in a linear relationship similar to

$$\pi_j = p_j - \sum_{i=1}^{n} a_{ij} p_i - \sum_{k=1}^{m} s_k v_{kj} = 0, \qquad j = 1, 2, \ldots, m$$

where s_k $(k = 1, 2, \ldots, m)$ represents the prices of non-reproducible commodities (the cost of their utilisation during the time period), while the v_{kj} are the technical coefficients applicable to each type of input (the index 1 being reserved for labour); s_k and v_{kj} can be brought together in a vector s and a matrix $V(m \times n)$. With suitable hypotheses regarding the technical coefficients, we can say:

$$p' = s'V(I - A)^{-1}.$$

Prices are then seen to be the weighted average of the prices of non-reproducible goods necessary, directly and indirectly, for the production of each commodity. The Theory would be valid in such cases only if the prices of all non-reproducible goods except labour were zero.

For Marx the problem does not exist. 'Land is not a product of labour, and therefore has no value' (III, 504): this statement is made here purely for the sake of definition. The word 'value' has undergone the change of meaning already noted in Section 1.2 above. If 'value' is defined as the quantity of labour necessary, directly or indirectly, to produce an article, it is obvious that a product possesses 'value' only in so far as labour has been used to produce it. Given this, it is child's play for Marx to demonstrate that the existence of non-reproducible commodities other than labour does not invalidate the Theory. Here again it is difficult to avoid the impression that he is using the Theory as a postulate, and we know that he does so in his study of the capitalist mode of production, because he considers that it can logically be proved to be valid for any other type of society. In the language of Section 4.5, we can say that Marx claims that the Theory holds good even if hypothesis H_2 is abandoned – provided that it is not a capitalist regime that is being discussed, i.e., provided that hypothesis H_7 can be verified: the factors governing the distribution of purchasing power are not those pertaining to an economy where the non-reproducible factors of production are in private hands. Here it is the fourth group of structural elements that is being restricted.

Regarding the particular problem of the cost of utilisation of land, Marx is quite categorical:

> If we imagine that the capitalistic form of society is abolished and society is organised as a conscious and systematic association then those 10 quarters represent a quantity of independent labour, which is equal to that contained in 240 shillings [whereas they are sold for 600 shillings, i.e., 250% too dear]. In that case society would not buy this product of the soil at two and half times the labour time contained in it. The basis of a class of landowners would thus be destroyed. [III, 525]

Unfortunately, what Marx considered so natural is now recognised by all as false. The decentralised running of economies encourages the use of indicative prices for all commodities, including land, unless it be far in excess of requirements.

This has nothing to do with how land came to be owned and is equally valid for a collectivist society. The Theory would therefore be the norm for 'the Society of the Future' only if such a society gave greater importance to respecting it than it did to improving material standard by more effective utilisation of resources. To abandon belief in the Theory in no way imperils the norm, which is quite independent of it: 'To each according to his labour'. Extolling the working class and sanctifying labour do not excuse fallacious argument and an inefficient use of natural resources.

Let us pass on to the *third* of the sufficient conditions considered in Section 4.6: each commodity is produced by one firm, and only one. In fact, two quite separate hypotheses underlie this condition.

1. No two firms produce the same commodity. This is not a very severe restriction, since the firms producing the same commodity could be amalgamated. In mathematical terms this is equivalent to replacing the sets of vectors $A_j^1, A_j^2, \ldots, A_j^l$, which are the vectors of the technical coefficients of the different firms, by the set:

$$A_j = \left\{ \hat{a}_j / \hat{a}_j = \sum_l \lambda_l \hat{a}_j^l;\ \hat{a}_j^l \in A_j^l; \quad \sum_l \lambda_l = 1;\ \lambda_l \geq 0 \right\}$$

2. No firm produces more than one commodity. In other words, there can be no 'linked production', for if this condition is not observed, calculating the amounts of labour necessary to the production of each commodity becomes a very hazardous undertaking; the problem of apportioning common expenditure among the different commodities produced by a firm is met with every day in analytical accounting, and it is well known that no satisfactory theoretical solution has yet been found.

To illustrate our point, let us take an economy in which the same operation transforms one unit of labour into one unit of commodity B_1 and two units of commodity B_2. This economy possesses only these two commodities and this one technique. Thus, to produce one unit of commodity B_1, one unit of labour is required, and to produce one unit of commodity B_2, half a unit of labour is required. Mathematically:

$$u_1 = 1$$

$$u_2 = 0.5.$$

If we observe the structural characteristics:

$$S(y_1, y_2) = y_1 + y_2$$

$$\bar{W} = 10$$

the equilibrium equations are resolved thus:

$$x_1 = y_1 = 10$$

$$x_2 = y_2 = 20$$

$$p_1 = \frac{s}{3}$$

$$p_2 = \frac{s}{3}$$

the Theory being no longer verified:

$$\frac{p_1}{p_2} = 1 \neq \frac{u_1}{u_2} = 2.$$

Marx does not seem to have been concerned by this restriction on the area of validity of the Theory because the concepts of 'sphere' or 'branch' were so natural to him (III, 180). It was a purely unformulated hypothesis, such as is frequently seen in economic texts.

Finally we have the *fourth* sufficient condition, H_5, that there are no stocks of reproducible commodities in the economy at the beginning of the period being considered (hypothesis H_4 being too 'artificial' to be considered). It should be noted that, if stocks of certain reproducible commodities are reintroduced, the Theory is in danger of being invalidated, since they may no longer be produced and yet may continue to be demanded by both the domestic consumer and other firms: their price, probably positive, would be a factor in the calculation of other prices, as are non-reproducible commodities. It is only when a succession of periods is envisaged that all the prices of reproducible commodities in stock can be linked to those factors that contribute to their past production. The existence of such stocks is not therefore an obstacle *a priori* to the validity of the Theory, and Marx never thought that it could be. The question can only be solved by the use of models capable of describing the evolution of the economy over a series of periods. The presentation of such models and the study of the difficult questions that they raise will be found in the introduction to the following chapter.

5 Limitation of the Field of Validity of the Theory: A Dynamic Analysis

5.1 Labour Theory of Value and theories of profit

For Marx, the *surplus-value* of a productive operation is the amount by which the value of the output exceeds that of the reproducible inputs and labour utilised during this operation.

> And secondly he [the capitalist] desires to produce a commodity whose value shall be greater than the sum of the values of the commodities used in its production, that is, of the means of production and the labour-power that he purchased with his good money in the open market. His aim is to produce, not only a use-value, but a commodity also; not only use-value, but value; not only value, but at the same time surplus-value. [I, 181]

If we give to the word 'value' in this passage the meaning, not of the amount of labour contained, but of exchange-value, surplus-value is seen to be the sum of two factors:

1. the cost of using non-reproducible factors (land and other natural resources), of which the capitalist is considered to be the owner, and which therefore cost him nothing;
2. pure profit (in considering static economies, the existence of initial stocks of reproducible commodities is not generally taken into account).

The concept of surplus-value has a legitimate place in a study of the area of validity of the Theory, and it is no coincidence that Marx made so much use of it. It has already been observed that, on those occasions when the Theory was not verified, a surplus-value had been noted in firms' activities. There is nothing mysterious about this, for equations like:

$$p_j = \sum_{i=1}^{n} a_{ij}p_i + s_1 v_{1j} + \pi_j \qquad j = 1, 2, \ldots, n$$

can only take on the form of equation (12) ($p' = s_1 v_1(I - A)^{-1}$) if the quantities π_j are identically nil (the index 1 which is given to the symbols s and v relates to labour). There is only one exception to this rule: the Theory remains valid, in spite of the existence of a surplus-value, if the surplus-value is exactly proportional to wages paid ($\pi_j = hs_1 v_{1j}$). Although he realised that such a situation could hardly ever arise, Marx, anxious to safeguard the validity of the Theory, deliberately based himself on this type of imaginary economy (see Section 7.3). Therefore, apart from this special case, if the Theory is to be disproved a theory of surplus-value has to be propounded.

Non-reproducible commodities (except labour) used in the production process exist only in limited quantities, and it is beyond dispute that this fact alone is sufficient to account quite satisfactorily for a part of the total surplus-value received by the owners. Marx's hostility to such a conception seems definitively rejected by contemporary economists, so that a demonstration of the fallacy of the Marxian theory of ground rent seems pointless (but see Section 10.5). It is therefore necessary, if we are to continue this study of *Das Kapital* without sacrificing our convictions, to pass over the existence of natural factors of production, other than labour, or to assume that they exist in unlimited quantities (which comes to the same thing). In this context it is only the appearance of a pure profit[1] that can disprove the validity of the Theory, and vice-versa.

Among the theories of pure profit that can be used to attack the Theory – and that Marx himself tries hard to repulse – may be numbered the following.

5.2 Static theories of profit

Theories of pure profit may be divided into two categories, according to whether or not they bring into play the existence of a time lag between expenditure and income to explain the creation of a profit.

Under the heading of '*static theories*' we find the popular conception according to which profit comes from the exchange of goods, within the 'sphere of circulation'. According to this theory, all forms of trade create profit. Marx has no difficulty whatsoever in demonstrating the absurdity of such a belief (I, 159). 'A sale is a purchase', says Marx, following Dr Quesnay (I, 110). 'The creation of surplus-value can consequently be explained neither on the assumption that commodities are sold above their value, nor that they are bought below their value' (I, 159).

A second static theory is the one that conceives profit as being the payment the capitalist received for carrying out the tasks of supervision and control. Marx does not dispute that such functions need to be carried out if the firm is to flourish, but points out that their payment absorbs far less than all the profits. And he takes good care to support his assertions with hard facts:

> From the public accounts of the co-operative factories in England it is manifest that the profit, after the deduction of the wages of the superintendent, which form a part of the invested capital, the same as the wages of the other labourers, was higher than the average profit .... What interests us here is that the average profit ... presents itself actually and palpably as a magnitude which is wholly separated from the wages of superintendence. [III, 309]

And he further develops the argument in that polemical style in which he excelled: when questioned about the origin of profits:

> Our friend [the capitalist], up to this time so purse-proud, suddenly assumes the modest demeanour of his own workman and exclaims: 'Have I myself not worked? Have I not performed the labour of superintendence and of overlooking the spinner? And does not this labour too, create value?' His overlooker and his manager try to hide their smiles. [I, 187]

Attempts have been made to salvage this theory of profit by trying to separate from the tasks of direction and supervision (which the capitalist can quite safely entrust to a salaried employee) a specific function which he alone would be capable of carrying out. And pure profit, which is what remains once the salaries of the managers had been paid, would recompense this rare quality of 'entrepreneurial flair'. Marx could hardly do otherwise than attack with the utmost vigour such an 'apologetic' theory (III, 309).

> The industrial capitalist is a labourer, but a labouring capitalist, and exploiter of the labour of others. The wages which he claims and pockets for this labour amount exactly to the appropriate quantity of another's labour and depend directly upon the rate of exploitation of this labour, so far as he takes the trouble to assume the necessary burdens of exploitation. They do not depend upon the degree of his exertions in carrying on this exploitation. [III, 308]

What causes discrepancies in the amount of their profits is the difference in attitude of individual capitalists in the running of their firm, insofar as they personally assume control.

> And this fact leads the capitalist to the conviction that his profits are due, not to the exploitation of labour, but at least, in part, to other circumstances independent of that exploitation, particularly to his individual activity. [III, 105]

Marx cannot, indeed, be criticised for having too severely attacked such a questionable theory, both from the purely economic point of view and from the point of view of social morality. As this so-called factor of 'enterprise' can be neither isolated nor quantified, it would seem to have been dreamed up in pure self-defence. Its only merit, but this is also its weakness, is that it makes research into those deep-rooted causes of the origin of profit unnecessary.

5.3 Dynamic theories of profit

Dynamic theories of profit, which take into account the dimensions of time, take the form of theories of interest, or at least evolve against a general background of theories of interest. The fact that loans of money carry a rate of interest conditions, and is at the same time conditioned by, the fact that money invested in a productive process has a rate of profit added to it. This reciprocal dependence of the interest rate and the profit rate arises from the fact that those who possess money can choose from the whole gamut of investment possibilities open to them.

A unit of money, for example 1 franc, can be used either to buy a bond bearing interest at the rate of i or for investment in a production process involving the transformation of a single input X into a single output Y. At the point of equilibrium these two choices ought to give the same result, i.e., ought, at the end of the time period, to provide the investor with the same number of francs.

Figure 5.1 shows the financial or physical changes that a franc can undergo. Thus one unit of input X is transformed into m units of output Y. One unit of money produces $(1 + i)$ units of claim (a unit of claim is the promise that a unit of money will be paid at the end of the period). By the sale of a unit of Y, p_y units of money are obtained, etc.

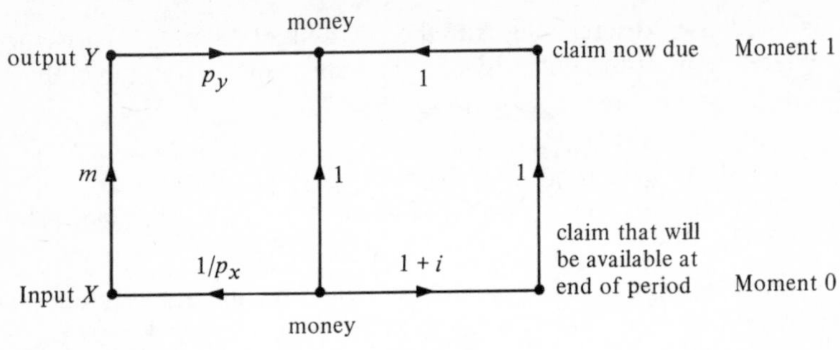

FIGURE 5.1

The symbols used on the diagram will be clear to the reader:

m: quantity of output produced per unit of input (this coefficient is independent of the scale of production, when productivity is constant);

p_x: price in francs of the input;

p_y: price in francs of the output;

i: rate of interest.

If it is to be immaterial for the holders of capital to invest their money in bonds or in a business enterprise, the transformation coefficients must be the same in both cases:

$$\frac{1}{p_x} \cdot m \cdot p_y = (1 + i) \cdot 1 \cdot 1$$

which can also be written

$$\frac{P}{p_x \cdot X} = \frac{p_y \cdot Y - p_x \cdot X}{p_x \cdot X} = i$$

where P is the total profit, and X and Y are the inputs and outputs utilised.

The profit on each franc invested, or *profit rate*, is equal to the interest rate. Marx maintains that profit is only 'the maximum limit of interest' (III, 284), in other words that the rate of interest is at most equal to the rate of profit. He gives the name 'company profit' to that part of the profit remaining after interest charges (including those on the capital provided by the firm's head and his associates). Incapable of discerning the permanent objective factors that determine this division (between interest and profit), Marx is reduced to falling back on the very law of supply and demand that he had so savagely attacked in other contexts:

> In the division into interest and profits of enterprise the average profit itself forms the limits for both of them. It furnishes the given magnitude of value, which they may divide among themselves and which is the only one that they can so divide. The definite proportion of this division is here accidental, that is determined exclusively by conditions of competition. Whereas in other cases the balancing of supply and demand implies the cessation of the deviation of market prices from their regulating average prices, that is the cessation of the influence of competition, it is here the only determinant. But why? Because the same factor in production, the capital, has to divide its share of the surplus-value between two owners of the same factor in production ['the industrial capitalist' and 'the financial capitalist']. [III, 685]

The lack of intellectual rigour of this argument must be blamed on the weakness characteristic of the whole of *Das Kapital* in its analysis of the phenomenon called credit. We shall not digress on this theme, but shall insist on the equality of the rate of interest and rate of profit shown above. The commodity called money is here reduced to the rank of a mere means of exchange in which prices and promissory notes are expressed.

Modern theories of dynamic equilibrium, which are not monetary either, pass over profit by the process of 'discounting'. The equality existing between interest and profit can also be noted:

$$-p_x X + \frac{1}{1+i} p_y Y = 0$$

so that the present value of the profit arising from a manufacturing operation is nil. Not without reason, Marx would have considered such a presentation of the facts rather mystifying, for there is quite clearly a pure profit – the difference between what has been received and what has been paid out – even if these different sums have been recorded at different times. The theoretician may have the satisfaction of noting that the profit (provided that 'future prices' (p_x, p_y) replace current prices[2] (p_x, p_y) for commodities at moment 0 and $(p_x/1+i)$, $(p_y/1+i)$ for those at moment 1), is nil, as is inevitable where yields are constant. In actual fact the enigma of profit remains, only the posing of the problem changes. It still has to be explained why, so long as the futures price of the output available at the end of a period is lower than its current price, firms will not try to increase their output indefinitely (or financial capitalists lend ever increasing sums of money) in order to accumulate the greatest possible amount of profit (or interest). In a word, it still has to be explained why a strictly positive rate of interest is possible at the point of equilibrium.[3]

Nowadays it is considered that the coexistence of three main factors creates a positive rate of interest: 'a preference for liquidity', 'the marginal efficiency of capital' and 'the preference for the present'.

Since the first of these factors is concerned with monetary analysis, it will not be considered here. However, it should be pointed out that an 'integrated' presentation of the theory of interest is possible, in which money is treated no differently from other forms of wealth (cf. Keynes [6], Chapter XVII). So the argument regarding 'marginal efficiency of capital' and 'preference for the present', which condition the strict positivity of the rate of interest, can easily be extended to an economy with money.

5.4 Interest, as the rent paid for material capital

The need to make a dynamic analysis arises not only because such an analysis permits a more accurate description of economic reality, but also because of the logical contradictions contained in any static analysis. For example, in the static model considered in Chapter 2, the transformation processes take place within the period under consideration, but exactly how is not made clear.

The firm, so it is said, obtains the necessary inputs in the market, and combines them so as to obtain the desired output, the mutual compatibility of the plans of the various firms and of households being succinctly reflected in the bald statement that the sum of intermediate or final consumption is at the most equal to all the production of the period. But this is to forget that one group's input is another group's output, and that, without previously constituted stocks of reproducible goods, production is impossible (except in the highly improbable case of activities being ordered in such a way that the inputs of the firm of rank k would be the outputs of a firm inferior in rank to k, the firm of rank l utilising labour only). Marx has written: 'But the flow of the process of production and reproduction requires that a certain mass of commodities (means of production) should always be in the market, should therefore form a supply' (II, 140). We saw, however, at the end of Chapter 4, that the existence of initial stocks of reproducible goods, which as we can now see are necessary, greatly imperilled the validity of the Theory, although not inevitably condemning it to failure.

To bring out the consequences arising from this further complication, we shall assume that the 'time of production' (II, 124) in all firms, i.e., the time needed to transform inputs into outputs, is the same as the period of analysis. (It will be seen in Sections 6.6 and 6.7 that Marx makes similar hypotheses.) This being so, all the inputs are available from the very first moment, whether they can be reproducible goods or labour. Reproducible goods can, of course, be reproduced, but these new factors of production will become available only at the end of the period, to be utilised during later periods.

Let us therefore suppose that several inputs contribute to the production of the same output in varying proportions and in the dynamic conditions we have just described. Figure 5.1 now has added to it many arcs representing the alternative uses to which a unit of money may be put in a productive activity that has reached equilibrium (see Figure 5.2).

At equilibrium, the profit earned by the last dollar invested is quite independent of the type of input purchased by it. The 'marginal rate of profit' (or the 'marginal efficiency of capital', as Keynes

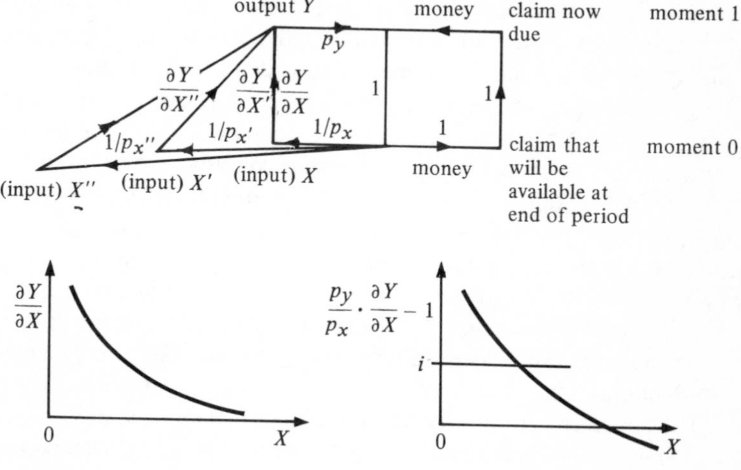

FIGURE 5.2

says ([6], 150) to describe an analogous situation), which is the value common to these different relationships, is, as was the average profit rate, equal to the rate of interest.

$$\frac{p_y\,\Delta Y - p_x\,\Delta X}{p_x \cdot \Delta X} = \frac{p_y}{p_x} \cdot \frac{\partial Y}{\partial X} - 1 = \frac{1}{p_x} \cdot \frac{\partial P}{\partial X} = i$$

Similarly:

$$\frac{1}{p'_x}\,\frac{\partial P}{\partial X'} = \frac{1}{p''_x} \cdot \frac{\partial P}{\partial X''} = \cdots = i.$$

When the impact of each type of input is increased, its 'marginal efficiency' diminishes. This is so as soon as the marginal productivity of each input is a decreasing function of its volume, the price structure being assumed to be invariable.

For a given rate of interest and price system, the firm works out its requirements for each type of input with the aid of curves similar to those shown in Figure 5.2. As in a static system, it will probably be necessary to modify this rate of interest and price system later so that compatibility between the plans of the various economic agents and with the economy's resources – in other words, equilibrium – may be realised. It can thus be seen that at equilibrium a strictly positive rate of interest may be needed to prevent overall demand in certain inputs exceeding supply at the beginning of the period.

A strictly positive rate of interest is therefore characteristic of a certain scarcity of 'material capital' (meaning, here, all reproducible goods that are factors of production). There is an intuitive feeling that, provided the domestic consumer will make the corresponding savings, firms will tend to increase the scale of their production so long as the slightest profit can be made, so that over a number of periods firms will accumulate material capital until the marginal efficiency of each is nil. At that point the economy reaches a state of immobility, optimal in one sense, and characterised by a *nil rate of equilibrium interest*. When such a situation is reached it may be conjectured that the system of current prices will conform to the Labour Theory of Value, provided, of course, that the hypotheses H_1, H_2 and H_3 discussed in Chapter 4 continue to prove valid.

Certain non-Marxist economists have not hesitated to put forward similar arguments calling into question the bourgeois dogma of the absolute necessity of interest and forecasting the disappearance of the capitalist class by the elimination of its source of income. The most illustrious of these, Lord Keynes, saw in the accumulation of capital to such a point that its marginal efficiency would be nil the means of achieving a peaceful social revolution ([6], Chapter XVI). Marx for his part remains imprisoned in socialist dogma, refusing to wait for some hypothetical Golden Age that will produce a nil rate of interest but postulating it like some eternal truth transcending observed fact: the value of the inputs is totally reflected in the price of the outputs, there being no enhancement of their value because, for example, they exist only in limited quantities at the commencement of the production process, or because this process takes place over a period of time.

Profits, and therefore interest rates, would be nil '*as of right*'.

> Since past labour always disguises itself as capital, i.e., since the passive of the labour of *A*, *B*, *C*, etc., takes the form of the active of the non-labourer *X*, bourgeois and political economists are full of praises of the services of dead and gone labour, which according to the Scottish genius MacCulloch ought to receive a special remuneration in the shape of interest, profit, etc. [I, 569]

Engels also allows himself this comment:

> Political economy teaches us that there exists what may be called a store of accumulated labour, which economists call capital; and that this capital, on account of the resources it has built up, multiplies many times over the productivity of present-day labour; for which it demands payment, which we call profit, or gain. [III, 219; Engels's article on *Das Kapital*, March 1868]

It is quite clear therefore that, just like the Labour Theory of Value, the theory of a nil rate of interest (which is its corollary) has begged the question. For Marx, profits and interest gained in real, live economies are not the product of objective circumstances, like the productivity of material capital, or the existence of the time factor in the production process; but of the 'exploitation' of labour by capital. 'Capital is dead labour, that, vampire-like, only lives by sucking living labour and lives the more, the more it sucks' (I, 224). Such is Marx's answer to the problem of profit, and we shall have occasion to consider this theory of exploitation in greater detail in Part II, which is almost wholly devoted to this question.

5.5 Interest as the reward for abstinence

Others have traced the origins of interest to the time lags inevitably arising in the process of consumption. According to such theories man is willing to forgo the consumption of a certain quantity of a commodity only if he can be sure of being able to consume a greater quantity of that commodity at a later date. In neoclassical authors this psychological trait is called 'preference for the present'. At equilibrium the relative increase in consumption, expressed in terms of value, is equal to the rate of interest, and this is true for all commodities and all consumers. This equality can be easily seen from Figure 5.3. $S(X_0, X_1)$ is the degree of satisfaction experienced by the individual who is going to consume quantities X_0 and X_1 of commodity X at moment 0 and moment 1. S'_0 and S'_1 are the two partial derivatives of function S. They should, at equilibrium, verify:

$$1 \cdot \frac{1}{p_x} \cdot S'_0 \cdot 1/S'_1 \cdot p_x = 1 + i$$

which gives

$$\frac{S'_0 - S'_1}{S'_1} = i.$$

At equilibrium the strictly positive i is a function of that found in the expression $(S'_0 - S'_1)/S'_1$, i.e., of the situation of the various marginal utilities relative to unity. An examination of the individual's 'indifference map' along (X_0, X_1) makes it clear that the rate at which future consumption is substituted for present consumption is sometimes greater, sometimes less than 1.[4] The latter, corresponding to a 'preference for the future', will most probably arise when the economy's resources, and therefore consumption, seem set upon a rapid contraction. It is worth repeating that, if in such an economy certain commodities could be stocked at no expense, the rate of interest would fall to zero, but could not be negative (see Figure 5.4). One can see therefore that in expanding, stagnant and even slightly depressed economies, 'a preference for the present' cannot

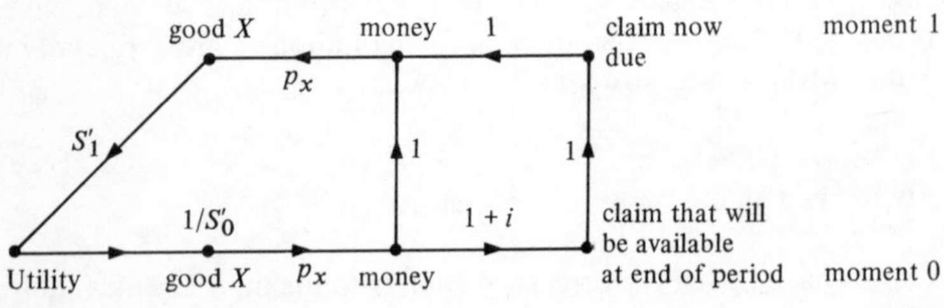

FIGURE 5.3

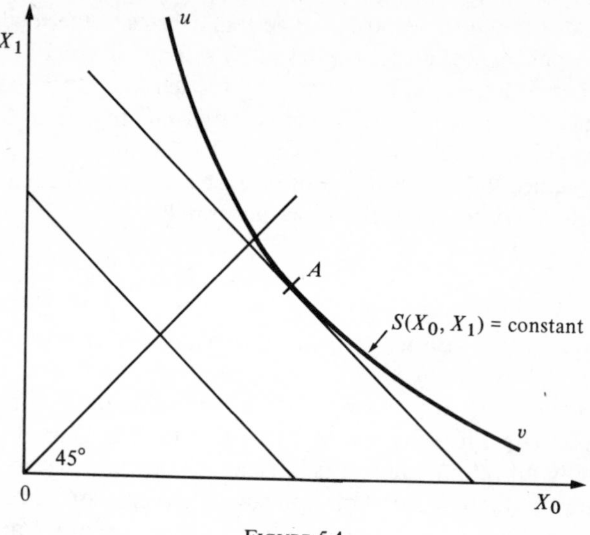

FIGURE 5.4

be reconciled with a zero rate of interest – nor, therefore, with a zero rate of marginal efficiency of capital.

Against this theory of interest as the reward for 'abstinence' Marx unleashes his most ferocious jibes (I, 559, 610; III, 86). And it is child's play for him to ridicule this theory by showing that behind the *homo economicus*, having a perfectly legitimate preference for the present, there lies the prosperous capitalist whose consumption is no doubt near saturation point. Like Keynes, Marx considers that there are factors in the savings behaviour of the consumer other than the rate of interest – factors like the ethic of moderation, or its opposite, the desire to show off, the passion for wealth, etc. (I, 564). Marx notes that the development of credit has of course encouraged and facilitated saving (III, 196) but has not forced the capitalist into an austere way of life.

> What the speculating wholesale merchant risks is social property, not his own. Equally stale becomes the phrase concerning the origin of capital from saving, for what he demands is precisely that others shall save for him. The other phrase of the abstention is given the lie by his luxury, which now becomes a means of credit by itself. [III, 352–3]

Marx seems here to be confusing two types of analysis, that of the economist and that of the novelist. While the latter, usually with a moral aim in mind, tries to depict certain aspects of the social life of an age through the vicissitudes of his fictitious characters, the former aims at creating the bases of a scientific, objective understanding of economic phenomena. That *homo economicus* lacks the psychological richness of the heroes of Balzac and Zola should not be the subject of astonishment or disgust, but rather the reason why one should try to paint him more accurately.

5.6 What can be learned from the modern theory of growth?

Since the essentially intuitive and heuristic approach used so far has probably failed to convince Marxists that their dogma of an automatically nil rate of interest is fallacious, mathematical techniques will now be used, in an effort to provide a demonstration.

The modern theory of growth (as given, for example, in Stoleru [19], Chapters XVII and XVIII) can provide us with an appropriate framework for discussion. Since it gives a highly aggregated model of the domestic consumption sector, it also has the advantage of being better adapted to the problems of a planned economy than a free enterprise economy. It gives the planning department of a hypothetical socialist society information about the rate of interest to be used by the productive apparatus of the country in its investment calculations. It shows in particular that, contrary to what Marx imagined, the rate of interest falls to zero only in very rare and special circumstances.

In addition, independently of the highly aggregated form of Stoleru's growth models, there is a striking similarity between the hypotheses subtending them and those that in a static economy confirm the Theory:

- H_1 The rate of productivity is constant.
- H_2 There are no non-reproducible commodities apart from labour. Accumulated capital (which is made up of the same commodities as output) and labour are thus the only two factors of production.
- H_3 The output, consisting of a single commodity, is produced by one firm and only one.

Following neoclassical theory, population evolves exogenously, growing in this case at constant rates. However, the methods used to make the above static model dynamic – methods also used by Marx – are slightly different from those normally utilised in modern theories of growth:

1. The rate of interest applies only to 'dead labour', and not to the whole of 'the capital advanced'.[5]
2. Material capital may be used over several periods of analysis.

These special hypotheses are in no way responsible for the phenomenon we call interest. Whether they are adopted or not, the lessons to be learned from the theory remain unchanged.

The theory's main lines, but without mathematical demonstration, are given below.

Definition 1 The term 'growth programme' (GP) is a given specification of variables such as capital, production, population, consumption, investment, etc., which is compatible with the structural data for all periods, from the present to the most distant future.

Definition 2 The term 'growth regime' (GR) is applied to a specification of the same variables for all periods, going from those in the past to those in the most distant future.

To any GR we may put in correspondence a GP for the period going from the present to the most distant future.

Definition 3 A balanced growth programme (BGP), or balanced growth regime (BGR) is one where all the elements characterising it grow at the same rate.

Proposition 1 The growth rate characteristic of a BGR is equal to the growth rate of the population.

Proposition 2 In a BGR the magnitudes of each period are in a constant ratio; the rate of saving, consumption per head, the quantity of capital equipment per head, etc., will therefore remain invariable.

Proposition 3 A BGR is wholly characterised by the volume of capital per head.

Definition 4 A BGR is maximal (MBGR) if consumption per head is the greatest that can be achieved in a BGR.

Proposition 4 The MBGR is sustained[6] by an interest rate equal to the rate of growth in production, hence in population.

Proposition 5 The MBGR is such that all revenues from capital are saved.

Definition 5 A GP is said to be optimal (OGP) if it maximises the function of collective utility. This will be taken as being the weighted total of individual consumption utilised relative to present and future periods.[7]

Proposition 6 An OGP is sustained by a series of interest rates equal to the rates of growth of the population as increased by the rate of depreciation of the future and net of the rate of growth of current marginal utility of individual consumption.

Proposition 7 In an OBGP, individual consumption is invariable, and the rate of interest is constant and equal to the sum of the rates of growth of the population and of the rate of depreciation of the future.

Proposition 8 An OBGP can be derived from an MBGR only if the rate of depreciation of the future is zero. The rate of interest will then be equal to the rate of growth of the population.[8]

Definition 6 A stationary programme (SP) or regime (SR) is a BGP (or BGR) for which the rate of growth of the population, and therefore of all variables, is zero.

Proposition 9 An optimal SP is characterised by a rate of interest that is equal to the rate of depreciation of the future.

Proposition 10 An SR that is maximal and the OBGP that derives from it are characterised by a zero rate of interest.

Proposition 11 Every OGP converges towards an OBGP.

These two latter propositions, together with proposition 8, constitute a strict proof of the axioms tentatively suggested in the course of Sections 5.4 and 5.5. The *capitalistic optimum*, optimum in the sense that individual consumption is the greatest possible, will in the long term tend to be established simultaneously with the Labour Theory of Value, if two conditions are present:

1. that consumers show no 'impatience';
2. that the population remains unchanged.

It is therefore clearly established that time, 'in itself', does not create interest, but only in so far as it is the basis of structural modification (real when related to demographic growth, psychological only in considering the preference for the present). If we have a 'homogeneous' temporal continuum, consisting of identical moments, a nil rate of interest will eventually be realised.

Does this mean that Marxists can boast that such eminent representatives of neoclassical economic thought[9] as Allais, Phelps and Solow have come over to their side? In actual fact, modern theorists of growth subject the validity of the Theory – which Marxists consider universally valid – to such a series of restrictive conditions that there is practically nothing of it left. In dynamics the Theory is valid if:

1. productivity is assumed to be constant compared with the scale of production;
2. non-reproducible factors other than labour are ignored;
3. linked products are eliminated;
4. only a stationary regime with a stable population is considered;
5. it is granted that the consumer does not depreciate the future.

These are, obviously, sufficient conditions, but they are also probably the only ones that are at the same time necessary and 'natural'.

Thanks to his excellent intuition, which sometimes made him forget dogma, Marx clearly felt that a zero rate of interest is not suitable for all circumstances. The rate of interest, which of course he does not name as such, but by some alternative description, has as its task the leading of the economy, and especially a socialist economy, towards the best possible balanced growth regime. It therefore plays a crucial role in fixing the rate of collective capital equipment per head that could sustain such a rate of growth.

> On the basis of socialised production the scale must be ascertained on which those operations – which withdraw labour-power and means of production for a long time without supplying any product as a useful effect in the interim – can be carried on without injuring branches of production which not only withdraw labour-power and means of production continually, or several times a year, but also supply means of subsistence and of production. Under socialised as well as capitalist production, the labourers in branches of business with shorter working periods will as before withdraw products only for a short time without giving any products in return; while branches of a business with long working periods continually withdraw products for a longer time before they return anything. This circumstance, then, arises from the material character of the particular labour-process, not from its social form. [II, 362]

Or again:

> If we conceive society as being not capitalistic but communistic, the question then comes down to the need of society to calculate beforehand how much labour, means of production, and means of subsistence it can invest, without detriment, in such lines of business as for instance the building of railways, which do not furnish any means of production or subsistence, nor produce any useful effect for a long time, a year or more, while they extract labour, means of production and means of subsistence from the total annual production. [II, 318–19]

5.7 Temporary equilibria

The neoclassical economists, too, have also described how the rate of interest is determined, but they have done so after looking at the facts, not in the abstract, in a private enterprise economy, and not in a socialist one, in a situation where initial stocks have purely arbitrary values, and not in regimes of balanced growth, where the economic agents anticipate quite independently what prices will be in the future. The economy then passes from one state of *temporary equilibrium* to another, at the mercy of the shocks and structural changes that it suffers because of the discrepancies between the forecasts of the economic agents and reality, and also because of the fact that these forecasts differ so considerably (see Hicks [5], 104).

In this unplanned world, the rate of interest does not obey simple rules; equilibrium prices are created by the confrontation between present and future factors, these prices being questioned at every period. 'Value' is entirely turned towards the future. In an unstable system the past does not matter. In every situation it is zero, but it is legitimate to speak of the past if it is merely a prefiguration of the future, as is the case with regimes of balanced growth.

Marx also perceived that the working of regimes of balanced growth or static regimes could be disturbed by any fortuitous events, in which case the Theory could no longer work freely. He noted further that value was determined by the conditions of the moment, and not by what had been spent in the past. He writes for example:

> If the time socially necessary for the production of any commodity alters – and a given weight of cotton represents, after a bad harvest, more labour than after a good one – all previously existing commodities of the same class are affected, because they are, as it were, only indivi-

duals of the species, and their value at any one time is measured by the labour socially necessary for their production under the then existing social conditions. [I, 203]

Or again:

> A commodity represents, say, 6 working-hours. If an invention is made by which it can be produced in 3 hours, the value, even of the commodity already produced, falls by half. It represents now 3 hours of social labour, instead of the 6 formerly necessary. It is the quantity of labour required for its production, not the realised form of that labour, by which the amount of value of a commodity is determined. [I, 502–3]

More concisely: 'There are, in the first place, constant improvements which lower relatively the use-value, and therefore the exchange-value of existing machinery, factory equipment, etc.' (III, 85).

We have already seen (see Section 4.8) that generally the validity of the Theory is undermined if initial stocks of goods exist, as Marx envisages here. And it is only in very particular cases of stationary regimes that the Theory invariably determines exchange relationships. Therefore, although the above quotations show him in too dogmatic a light, they do show that on at least one point Marx is at one with modern theories of value: he recognises the primacy of the future over the past in the formation of prices. Marx's use of the phrase 'socially necessary labour' conceals this, but this is what it must mean, otherwise it would be meaningless.

There is therefore only an apparent contradiction between the above quotations and propositions such as the following.

> In determining the value of the yarn, or the labour-time required for its production, all the special processes carried on at different times, and in different places, which were necessary, first to produce the cotton and the wasted portion of the spindle, may together be looked on as different and successive phases of one and the same process. The whole of the labour in the yarn is past labour; and it is a matter of no importance that the operations necessary for the production of its constituent elements were carried out at times which, referred to the present, are more remote than the final operation of spinning. If a definite quantity of labour, say thirty days, is requisite to build a house, the total amount of labour incorporated in it is not altered by the fact that the work of the last day is done twenty-nine days later than that of the first. [I, 182–3]

In that example Marx takes a stationary point of view, whereas previously he had envisaged 'changes in value' (I, 203), i.e., disturbances in the stationary system. It is therefore clear that formulae such as the one to be found at the beginning of *Das Kapital* are not to be taken literally: 'How then is the magnitude of this value to be measured? Plainly, by the quantity of the value-creating substance, the labour, contained in the article' (I, 46). If the amount of labour contained in the commodity coincides with 'the quantity of labour required for its production' (I, 502), it is because Marx has deliberately taken up a stationary viewpoint, one in which past and future coincided. It will be seen that Marx does this frequently, at least each time that he describes the 'process of reproduction of social capital', i.e., the development of the economy taken as a whole.

Part II

THE MARXIAN THEORY OF PROFIT AND EXPLOITATION

Introduction

The denial of the existence of profit, which is the basis of the Labour Theory of Value, is in turn denied by the real economic world. This much is clear from the first part of this study, and Marx himself was perfectly aware of the fact.

However, in Marx's view the negation of a negation is not an *affirmation*, and profit exists despite the Theory, not against it. Put in ordinary language, profit appears in capitalist societies, but not for any of the reasons put forward by the bourgeois economists – for such reasons would have endangered the validity of the Theory. Marx's main thesis is that profit arises from the division of society into two antagonistic classes, and is quite simply the result of the exploitation of one class by the other.

To bring out this specific character of the origin of profit, we shall try to justify Marx's thesis by constructing a model according to which, in the view of the classical economists, profit should in fact disappear. This model, descriptive first of all (Chapter 7), will then take up the mechanism and behaviour that make the creation of profit possible (Chapter 8). Prior to that, the principal hypotheses regarding such mechanisms will have been indicated, remaining as faithful to the text of *Das Kapital* as possible (Chapter 6). In Chapter 9, static analysis will be replaced by a study of stationary regimes – what *Das Kapital* calls 'simple reproduction'. Finally, Chapter 10 will show how the theory of the conversion of values into production prices, a real stumbling block for Marxist economists, tries to reconcile the dogma of the Theory of Labour Value with the harsh reality of profit.

6 The Main Hypotheses

6.1 The division of society into classes

It will by now have become clear to the reader that the model used in Chapters 2 and 3 is only a simplified form of the neoclassical model of general equilibrium, but suitably modified it will provide a perfectly acceptable basis for an interpretation of *Das Kapital*, and as such will provide a forum where the disagreements between Marxists and neoclassicists may be discussed. The model cannot, of course, fit the whole of the work, but it will at least have the merit of respecting the main hypotheses formulated by Marx on the working and structure of the economy.

Of these the most important is undoubtedly that which divides society into two mutually antagonistic classes: capitalists and workers. To represent this, the population can simply be divided into two groups, N_1, (representing the workers), and N_2 (for the capitalists).

$$N = N_1 + N_2.$$

What distinguishes these two categories is that the latter possess, and the former do not possess, the means of production. 'The basis of the capitalist system is the complete separation of the producer from the means of production' (I, 669). This separation is not peculiar to the capitalist mode of production:

> Wherever a part of society possesses the monopoly of the means of production, the labourer, free or not free, must add to the working-time necessary for his own maintenance an extra working-time in order to produce the means of subsistence for the owners of the means of production, whether this proprietor be the Athenian noble, Etruscan theocrat, *civis Romanus*, Norman baron, American slave-owner, Wallachian boyard, modern landlord or capitalist. [I, 226]

What singles out the capitalist mode of production is the existence of a wage-earning class, i.e., of workers who are free,

> Free in the double sense, that as a free man he can dispose of his own labour-power as his own commodity, and that on the other hand he has

> no other commodity for sale, is short of everything necessary for the realisation of his labour-power. [I, 166]

The worker is neither a serf nor a slave:

> He must constantly look upon his labour-power as his own property, and this he can only do by placing it at the disposal of the buyer temporarily, for a definite period of time. By this means alone can he avoid renouncing his rights of ownership over it. [I, 165]

The worker therefore works for the capitalist, purchasing with his salary those consumer goods that he finds necessary. But in that case, what about the capitalist, what does he do? He consumes, of course, and in that respect he is the equal of the worker. Selling his labour

> promotes the individual consumption of the labourer, the transformation of the means of subsistence into his flesh and blood. True, the capitalist must also be there, must also live and consume, to be able to perform the function of a capitalist. To this end, he has, indeed, to consume only as much as the labourer .... [II, 60]

Let us suppose the consumption patterns of the two classes to be different – no very severe restriction, since they may also be the same:

α_1 for the workers

α_2 for the capitalists

The vectors α_1 and α_2 each have n coordinates positive or zero, but not all zero. The total of their respective consumption will be

$\lambda_1 \alpha_1 N_1$ for the workers

$\lambda_2 \alpha_2 N_2$ for the capitalists

(where λ_1, λ_2 indicate the level of the standard of living of the two groups). Marx asserts that consumption is not the final aim of the capitalist. Just as he often tends to consider the workers as dependent objects rather than as free agents, their consumption being limited to what is necessary for their reproduction (cf. Sections 3.6 and 8.2), so capitalists are similarly transformed into objects: 'As capitalist, he is only capital personified. His soul is the soul of capital' (I, 224). Or: 'For capitalism is abolished root and branch by the bare assumption that it is personal consumption and not enrichment that works as the compelling motive' (II, 123). To turn such assertions into a theory is a delicate task; what we shall do here is consider that Marx would accept the dichotomy posited by neoclassical economists between firms and consumers. The behaviour of the capitalist as consumer would have little or no effect upon his behaviour as the owner of the means of production, as entrepreneur whose sole function is to make the maximum use of the capital he possesses, in neoclassical terms, to maximise the profits of the firm in which he has placed this capital.

If the capitalist consumes, is he therefore only a parasite? This question has already been answered in Section 5.2 when we examined the theory that put forward profit as the reward for 'qualities of enterprise'. Within the capitalist's total activity within the firm, Marx carefully distinguishes between that element which the complex processes of production make indispensable, and therefore deserving of a salary. 'A single violin player is his own conductor; an orchestra requires a separate one' (I, 313), and that element which is only necessary because of the latent hostility between employer and worker: 'the antagonistic nature of capital and labour ... and the domination of the one by the other' (III, 310).

If he so wishes, the capitalist can off-load these two functions on to paid staff – foremen, managers, etc. – but it is only the first of these tasks, which would have to be carried out even in a collectivist economy, that is worthy of being called work. When he carries that task out himself, the capitalist belongs to the working class in respect of that fraction of his time which he devotes to it. And the salary he earns as a manager legitimately provides him with a certain quantity of consumer goods which are therefore to be considered as a part of the consumption of the working class. The capitalist of theory is what is left of the capitalist once his managerial role (if any) has been taken away.

When all comes to all, Marx cares little about the tasks on which the capitalist spends his time. What he *does* see is that he obtains a pure profit (after his managerial salary has been deducted[1]) which he uses for his private consumption. But only in part, because a further aspect of the behaviour of the capitalist is that he saves a proportion of this pure profit, in order to increase the amount of capital he holds already. The causes and consequences of this practice will be discussed later, in the final chapters devoted to the dynamics of the economy. It is only mentioned here so that it may be contrasted with the attitude that Marx attributed to the worker in the matter of savings. Of course, given the abject poverty in which the capitalist is deemed to keep the workers, even to speak of the working class's savings is an insult; but, Marx, quite incidentally, mentions that, when it *does* occur, this type of saving is of a quite different type from that of the capitalist. For the worker, saving is quite simply deferred consumption; for the capitalist it is a method of self-financing. 'If the labourer saves a part of his wages – we necessarily discard here all credit relations – he converts part of his wages into a hoard' (II, 121); and he writes further: 'What the labourer may save up in money is not capital' (II, 312). Such a distinction seems quite artificial today, but it had to be made by Marx because his division into two classes is partly based on it. Marx is compelled to admit that, when he acts as manager, the capitalist belongs to the working class, and he would have got into inextricable difficulties if he had had to admit also that the worker was a financial capitalist who had savings that bore interest!

Be that as it may, we will accept this simple division of society into two parts each having clearly distinguished economic characteristics. Their specific features, labour and capital, will now be examined.

6.2 Labour

Marx makes a subtle distinction between 'labour' and 'labour-power', a distinction we have not made in previous discussions of the question (cf. Section 3.4 on the price of labour). 'By labour-power or capacity for labour is to be understood the aggregate of those mental and physical capabilities existing in a human being, which he exercises whenever he produces a use-value of any description' (I, 164). And he continues:

> Labour-power can appear on the market as a commodity if, and only if, and so far as, its possessor, the individual whose labour-power it is, offers it for sale, or sells it, as a commodity. In order that he may be able to do this, he must have it at his disposal, must be the untrammelled owner of his capacity for labour, i.e., of his person. [I, 165]

And again: 'Labour-power in use is labour itself' (I, 173). From these three quotations it can be seen that by labour-power Marx means 'personal capital' in Walras's sense of the word (cf. [20], lecture 23, 267), and by labour the free use of this capital over a given period, as in this quotation: 'labour power ... which is as different from its function, labour, as a machine is from the work it performs' (I, 504).

It has already been noted that what distinguishes the slave from the free worker is that the former's 'personal capital' belongs to someone else, whereas the worker only hires out his personal capital, remaining its owner at all times. Labour-power has no observable price, since slave markets have ceased to exist in a capitalist economy. Only the term 'value of labour' has meaning in our society, since 'the value of labour-power' can only be calculated *a posteriori* by the use of the same formula as that which relates the price of a consumer durable to the price of the services that it produces. But Marx's point of view is just the opposite:

> Labour is the substance, and the immanent measure of value, but has itself no value. In the expression '*value of labour*', the idea of value is not only completely obliterated, but actually reversed. It is an expression as imaginary as the value of the earth. [I, 503]
>
> The value of labour-power thus determines the value of labour. [I, 505]

Marx's conception, quite irrational within the framework of neoclassical theory, can be justified only if the word 'value' is considered to be a synonym of 'quantity of work socially necessary', and if one assumes that the worker's consumption is kept to an absolute minimum, either by 'exploitation' (Marx) or by demographic pressure (the classical economists). And it is this justification that is to be found in the 'demo-economic' formulation of Chapter 2's model, which was proposed in Section 3.5, when the period of analysis was made co-extensive with the length of a human life.

Another distinction that Marx gravely makes is the one between 'abstract labour' and 'concrete labour'. Such a distinction could be made in almost any field, between 'abstract potatoes' and 'concrete potatoes'. The latter are highly individual, each one different from the other by its size, weight, owner, provenance, etc. The former are an abstraction, a set of 'thoughts' about potatoes of all times and all places, occurring within another abstraction, an economic model. It is of course quite fair to make use of such an abstraction, since 'concrete' potatoes are indistinguishable in reality, as a means of exchange. One may, of course, need to separate these abstract potatoes into 'new potatoes' or 'old potatoes', 'French potatoes' or 'German potatoes', 'potatoes available immediately' and 'potatoes available in twelve months' time'. Similarly for the term 'labour', which supposes a minimum of interchangeability therefore between men at work. The fact that this situation is more or less true in a given economy which is situated at a specific point in space and time may suggest to those who would like to make a formal model that labour should be divided into as many sub-categories as may seem necessary, but the pure theory of competitive capitalism – and this is something that it shares with socialism, seen as a theory of the organisation of a collectivist economy – really only needs the sub-division of labour, into a very small number of sub-categories given the institutions that it presupposes.

Having made this distinction clear, we can now study three of the coordinates that for Marx are characteristic of each type of social work: *productivity*, *intensity*, *duration* (I, 486).

The first of these three terms is used in its modern sense:

> The efficacity of any special productive ability during a given time depends on its productiveness. Useful labour becomes, therefore, a more or less abundant source of products, in proportion to the rise and fall of its productiveness. [I, 53]

In the model presented in Chapters 2 and 3, *productivity* in each firm E_j is indicated by a coefficient of employment, v_j, (i.e., the quantity of labour necessary to produce one unit of the commodity B_j) which is inversely proportional to it.

By duration is meant the number of hours per day spent at work. Marx considers that in theory the capitalist hires out the worker's services twenty-four hours a day, allowing him a period of rest – the shortest possible – only so that the worker's labour-power may once again become productive.

> To appropriate labour during all the 24 hours of the day is, therefore, the inherent tendency of capitalist production. But as it is physically impossible to exploit the same labour-power constantly during the night as well as during the day .... [I, 245]

Measuring a quantity of work by the time taken, the method suggested in Section 3.3, presupposes that duration, in Marx's sense, is constant within the framework of the model studies.

This measurement of the amount of labour by the labour-time taken further supposes that the degree of *intensity* in the accomplishment of the task is also given.

> In addition to a measure of its extension, i.e., duration, labour now acquires a measure of its intensity or of the degree of its condensation or

> density. The denser hour of the ten-hour working day contains more labour, i.e., expended labour-power, than the more porous hour of the twelve-hour working-day. [I, 386-7]

The same thing applies in any other field: the service provided by a car is different when driven at 60 mph from that provided when driven at 30 mph. This 'intensity' factor is therefore a very important one, and Marx has made a detailed study of consequences arising when it varies. However, applied to labour it is difficult to quantify, and so, as in the case of duration, theoretical models quite rightly consider it to be constant.

6.3 Means of subsistence and luxury goods

If the working class provides labour, what does it consume? Marx divides consumer goods into two:

> a) Articles of consumption, which enter into the consumption of the working class, and, to the extent that they are necessities of life – even if frequently different in quality from those of the labourers – also form a part of the consumption of the capitalist class. For our purposes we may call this entire subdivision consumer *necessities*, regardless of whether such a product as tobacco is really a consumer necessity from the physiological point of view. It suffices that it is habitually such.
> b) Articles of luxury, which enter into the consumption of only the capitalist class. [II, 407]

Such a classification, which Marx almost certainly inherited from Ricardo, hardly seems very valid, since it is based upon the very imprecise criterion of 'habit of consumption'. It may be useful in resolving certain special questions, such as the effect upon salaries and profits of differential variations in productivity as between branches (cf. Section 8.4), but since the increase in the standard of living has brought about a certain uniformity in consumer habits, the dichotomy Marx makes in the field of consumption has become rather arbitrary, and of only secondary interest. It will therefore not be taken account of in our study, thus avoiding the complication to our model that would have resulted.

To conclude this section on Marx's conception of consumption, it need only be pointed out that on this point he is at one with the neoclassical economists; he differentiates between:

1. productive consumption, i.e., the using-up of certain commodities to produce others;
2. individual consumption, i.e., the using-up of goods by individuals for the satisfaction of their own personal needs (cf. I, 179).

He refuses to include the worker's individual consumption in the productive consumption – yet another indication of his reluctance to accept the hypotheses of the demo-economic model of the classics (cf. I, 540, where he argues against Ricardo on this point).

6.4 Capital

We come now to the capitalist and his salient characteristic, 'capital'; for, says Marx, 'the description "capitalist" applies to a man only in so far as he makes his money function as capital'. To define a capitalist we therefore have first to define capital, more precisely the money – capital cycle.

Let us take the sum of money M, used to purchase a number of different inputs c which enter the production process and come out as outputs c'. These are sold for a certain amount of money M', usually greater than the original M. This series of transformations can be represented by Figure 6.1. We have here the definition of the term 'capital' which gives its title to Marx's work: 'Money that circulates in the latter manner is thereby transformed into, becomes

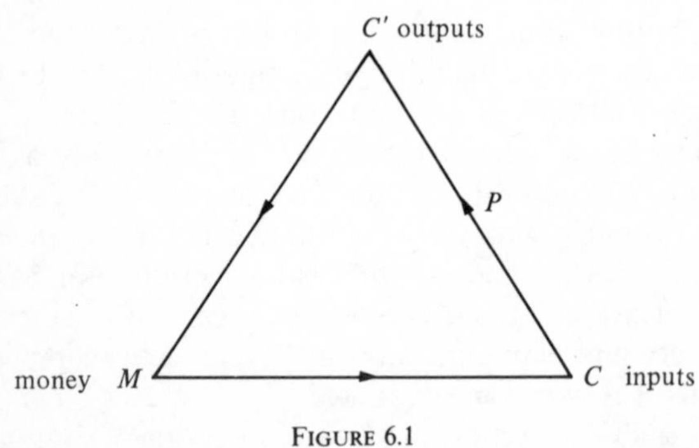

FIGURE 6.1

capital, and is already potentially capital' (I, 146). Thus the word *capital* is not given the same meaning as in modern economic literature, where it conveys fundamentally the idea of an accumulation of raw materials, semi-finished products, factories, buildings and infrastructure occurring as factors of production complementary to the labour factor – what was termed 'material capital' in Chapter 5. Does capital then have a purely monetary definition for Marx? By no means, for although defined as money-capital initially, it undergoes the metamorphosis which transforms it successively into commodity-capital, productive capital, commodity-capital yet again, and finally money-capital when the cycle is completed. Capital is therefore to be seen as the substance appearing in the balance sheets of the entrepreneur.

Since monetary considerations form no part of this work, the definition of the capitalist, based essentially on the notion of the possession of the means of production (postulated at the beginning of this chapter), fits in with the more general definition proposed by Marx.

It is for the same reason that only the physical transformation of c into c' will concern us here. The duration of the transformation period is the 'time of production' (II, 124). The time taken to complete Mc and $c'M$ is called 'the time of circulation' (II, 124), the total of the two periods being called the 'time of turnover of capital' (II, 156). Since we take no account of the monetarist element, we will neglect the circulation time, so that for us the time of turnover coincides with the time of production. Marx's theory allows this, since

> The more the metamorphoses of circulation are only ideal, i.e., the more the time of circulation is equal to zero, the more does capital function, the more does its productivity and the self-expansion of its value increase. [II, 128]

In considering periods of production characteristic of each activity, Marx makes a significant attempt to break with the traditional division of time into homogeneous units – a practice prevalent in present-day microeconomic theory, and one that explains why microeconomic theory is so often inadequate to describe the real world. It is incorrect to say that discontinuous time is an approximation of continuous time and that one passes from the former to the latter by a continuous reduction of the base period. For this base period cannot be shorter than the time needed by the economy to reach a state of equilibrium. However, this attempt of Marx's to think economic time differently leads us nowhere because what was easy to do for an individual firm proves impossible for a whole economy. The fact that Marx makes a clear distinction between the two types of analysis is proved by the fact that he devoted Section I and II of Book II ('The Metamorphoses of Capital and Their Circuits'; 'The Turnover of Capital') to the first type and Section III of Book II ('The Reproduction And Circulation Of The Aggregate Social Capital') to the second. In the aggregation process differences in length and phase of periodic movements that give life to the different parts of the social capital will be neglected, and throughout this Section III of Book II the formula for the cycle of capital posited for individual capital – $M—c—c'—M'$ – will be applied to capital in general (II, 396), which means that all individual capitals will have the same period of production, and that this period of production will coincide with the period of analysis. Furthermore, the input made at the beginning of the period – Marx chooses a period of a year – are the products of the labour of the previous year, from which have been deducted all individual consumption. The outputs created by these inputs will reappear at the beginning of the following year, as inputs and money for consumption.

6.5 Fixed and circulating capital

This picture of a steady succession of inputs and outputs is manifestly contradicted by the existence of goods that, on account of their special role in the production process and their own physical characteristics, are not destroyed in that process. They are the durable material capital as described in standard neoclassical works. First, these goods can be stocked, they are not perishable, at least not in the period under analysis. Second, they participate in the production process beyond the limits of the period. These two criteria make it possible to divide the factors of production into what Ricardo already called fixed capital and circulating capital: 'According as capital is rapidly perishable and requires to be frequently reproduced, or is of slow consumption, it is classed under the heads of circulating or fixed capital.' And he added this note: 'A division not essential, and in which the line of demarcation cannot be accurately drawn' (II, 227). The vagueness of the dividing line – which Ricardo had already pointed out – is the result of the arbitrary length of time conferred upon the period of analysis.

It is for this very reason that Marx refuses to admit these definitions of fixed and circulating capital (II, 200 *et seq.*). He begins by pointing out that his own criterion of classification is concerned with productive capital, i.e., for a set of commodities about to be combined productively:

> Hence it is only the productive capital which can be divided into fixed and circulating capital. But this antithesis does not apply to the other two modes of existence of industrial capital, that is to say, commodity-capital and money-capital. It exists only for productive capital and within its sphere. [II, 170]

As was only to be expected, this criterion breaks with the technique whereby time is sliced into periods of equal length, for Marx is very aware of the development of each process and of the rhythm that is peculiar to it.

> The turnover of the fixed component part of capital and therefore also the time of turnover necessary for it, comprises several turnovers of the circulating constituents of capital. In the time during which the fixed capital turns over once, the circulating capital turns over several times. One of the component parts of the value of the productive capital acquires the definiteness of form of fixed capital only in case the means of production in which it exists is not wholly worn out in the time required for the fabrication of the product and its expulsion from the process of production as a commodity. One part of its value must remain tied up in the form of the still preserved old use-form, while the other part is circulated by the finished product, and this circulation on the contrary simultaneously circulates the entire value of the fluent component parts of the capital. [II, 171]

Although very attractive, this conception of fixed capital must be abandoned as soon as one goes on to study 'the reproduction' and 'circulation of the whole of social capital', i.e., when one attempts to construct an overall economic model. For the cutting up of time into equal segments has once more to be resorted to, and with it the pretence that different productive operations require the same amount of time; therefore the Ricardian definition of fixed capital comes once more into its own.

At all events, whether the time of turnover of circulating capital varies, or is given a fixed 'conventional' time, a solution must be found for the thorny problem of depreciation, or, as Marxists would put it, the amount of value transferred to the product by the fixed capital elements in its production. Here, Marx does not go in for complications, proposing a straightforward linear law of depreciation:

> It is known by experience how long on the average a machine of a particular kind will last. Suppose its use-value in the labour-process to last only six days. Then, on the average, it loses each day one-sixth of its value to the daily product. The wear and tear of all instruments, their daily loss of use-value, and the corresponding quantity of value they part with to the product, are accordingly calculated upon this basis. [I, 197]

Such a principle applied to depreciation is of course quite arbitrary: first because the life of an item of capital equipment is not one of its intrinsic factors, like its weight or its volume; and second because nothing justifies such a mathematically regular loss of its value – unless it be the simplicity of the calculation. A rational depreciation principle can be devised only by reference to the value on the open market of second-hand machines of all ages. If V_t and V_{t+1} represent the two values of the same commodity at moment t and moment $(t + 1)$ (being only an expected value in the case of the latter), the value transmitted to the product will be $(V_t - V_{t+1})$. Furthermore, the owner of this machine will take the decision to put it on the rubbish-heap only when he calculates that the cumulative costs of keeping it working will be greater than the cost of a new machine fulfilling the same task. Marx goes a (very) little way towards accepting this line of argument when he talks of the 'moral depreciation' (obsolescence) of capital equipment (II, 173), and cannot really be criticised for neglecting this subject of 'replacement' which is only marginal to pure theory (cf. II, 172–84 and 457–74 for some valuable insights into this question). What the neoclassical economist *would* object most strongly to would be the omission of the interest element iV_t, which is also transmitted to the product by the fact that a productive capital, initial value V_t, tied up in the machine is immobilised. This omission by Marx is quite deliberate, and is clearly linked to his devotion to the Theory, even in a temporal economy.

6.6 Constant capital and variable capital

Since we are studying Marx's theories on the origins of profit and interest, the difference between fixed and circulating capital is not relevant here. Like Marx, the neoclassical economists reject 'the wholly erroneous explanation that profit is made by fixed capital staying in the process of production' (II, 203). It has been shown in the previous chapter that pure profit (or interest) can arise only from the time lags occurring between the different phases of the production and consumption processes. The quite fortuitous fact that capital equipment has a life-span longer than the period of analysis has nothing to do with the creation of profit, even if the growth models so plentiful in the present-day literature tend to give that erroneous impression. Since Marx's theory of profit is based on the exploitation of the worker's labour, he divides productive capital not into fixed and circulating capital, but between 'means of production, by the raw material, auxiliary material, and the instruments of labour' (I, 202). To these two fractions of productive capital Marx gives the names of 'variable capital' (= labour), and 'constant capital' (for other factors of production), for reasons that will be explained in Chapter 8. It is not that Marx denies the practical importance of the concept of fixed capital, or its strategic role in the theory of crises (II, 232); but he suspects that its sole function within a bourgeois economy is to keep the workers in ignorance of the division between constant capital and variable capital, and thus to hide from them the real origin of profit, which is quite simply the exploitation to which they are subjected by the capitalist class. To defeat such a criticism, we have to meet Marx on his own terms and assume that in the models that will be developed in the course of the following chapters there is no fixed capital, or, as Marx puts it, that 'the constant capital consumed' is equal to 'the value of constant capital employed' (II, 400). Marx often makes this hypothesis when the object of his study is not harmed.

> The magnitude of the actual product of this capital depends on the magnitude of the fixed part of the constant capital, and on the amount of it passing by wear and tear over to the product. But as this circumstance is immaterial so far as the rate of profit and the present analysis are concerned, we assume for the sake of simplicity that the constant capital is transferred everywhere uniformly and entirely to the annual product of the capitals named. [III, 118, and also II, 400 for a similar formulation].

6.7 Recapitulation

The Marxist theory of profit and exploitation does not have the arid form and intellectual rigour of a mathematical model, and in this chapter we have tried to prune it of some of its excesses, so that we may perceive its logical structure, This last section will present a summary of some of the concepts and hypotheses that make up the basis of the theory.

First, two opposing sets of domestic consumer are to be found within the economic system:

1. the capitalists, possessing the means of production and holding power with the business, and hence the receivers of a pure profit which they use partly to satisfy their own needs as consumers, partly to accumulate capital;
2. the workers, owning only their labour-power, which they hire out to the capitalist, in other words selling their labour, which is assumed to be constant in duration and intensity. Their productivity will be a function of the techniques used in each individual business.

In later pages, the distinction sometimes made by Marx between means of subsistence and luxury goods will be disregarded. Similarly, a complete absence of fixed capital will be assumed, i.e., of any means of production of duration longer than the period under analysis. Although such a hypothesis may seem unreal, it is in fact 'neutral' as far as the subject of this study is concerned: exploitation and the theory of profit. The reverse hypothesis would only lead to greater complexity in the calculation and to a greater heaviness in the exposition. On the other hand, the dynamic aspect of the economy will be represented by introducing time lags into the production process. Here again, it has been assumed that the periods of time separating inputs and outputs are equal in all firms, and that the process of production was begun at the same time – the beginning of the time period – and ends when the period ends.

7 Marxian Equilibria

7.1 Equations of definition

In Chapter 2 the states of equilibrium of an economy were defined in relation to (1) the behaviour of the two agents, firms and households and (2) the rules for the functioning of markets; and it was only later that the equations characterising such states were formulated (equations (10), (11), (12), (13)). In the present chapter we shall proceed in reverse order. First, we shall define a *Marxian state of equilibrium* as being a specification of the consumption and production variables, and of the prices vector satisfying a certain system of equations. Only when that has been done shall we consider the laws governing the behaviour of economic agents and the rules governing the working of the markets capable of maintaining the economy in such a state.

The model used will be basically the one presented in Chapter 2. Which means that the initial analysis will be static. Into this model, the first to enable us to validate the Labour Theory of Value, will be incorporated the hypotheses enumerated at the end of Chapter 6 (except, of course, those referring to the dynamic of production).

We shall first formulate equality of employment and resources of each commodity in this static economy, which has neither initial nor final stocks. Hence equation (24), similar to equation (10) except that domestic consumption has now become the sum of the two separate consumptions of the capitalist $\lambda_1 \alpha_1 N_1$ and the workers $\lambda_2 \alpha_2 N_2$:

$$x = Ax + \lambda_1 \alpha_1 N_1 + \lambda_2 \alpha_2 N_2. \qquad (24)$$

The mathematical symbols have here the same meaning as in Chapter 2. Equation (25) expresses the fact that the work force is fully employed:

$$v'x = \bar{W}. \qquad (25)$$

The equilibrium of the firm's operations is expressed by:

$$p' = p'A + sv'. \tag{26}$$

Lastly, the accounts of domestic consumers must also be in equilibrium:

$$p'(\lambda_1 \alpha_1 N_1 + \lambda_2 \alpha_2 N_2) = s\bar{W}. \tag{27}$$

It can easily be verified that this system (equations (24), (25), (26), (27)) contains the same number of scalar equations as the previous one (equations (10)–(13)), but the variable λ, the index of the standard of living, has become split into two λ_1, λ_2, representing the standards of living of the two classes. If this system is to give a single solution it may be surmised that a further equation will be necessary.

Before that, however, let us try to characterise the whole series of possible equilibria. The simplest is obviously the extreme case in which the existence of the capitalist class is denied, so that this class consumes nothing, giving:

$$\lambda_1 = \lambda_1^0 = \frac{\bar{W}}{v'(I-A)^{-1}\alpha_1 N_1} \quad \text{and} \quad \lambda_2 = 0.$$

The equilibrium thus obtained is identical to that described in Chapters 2 and 3. Equation (27) becomes:

$$p'(\lambda_1^0 \alpha_1 N_1) = s\bar{W}$$

All the income derived from labour is distributed to the workers, with the capitalist receiving nothing and therefore consuming nothing. According to theorem 4, this state of equilibrium exists and is unique, which implies that the hypotheses regarding A and v are satisfied, viz. that A is productive and $v'(I-A)^{-1}$ is strictly positive.

A second case is obtained for:

$$\lambda_1 = 0 \quad \text{and} \quad \lambda_2 = \lambda_2^0 = \frac{\bar{W}}{v'(I-A)^{-1}\alpha_2 N_2}$$

where the capitalists appropriate and consume all the '*social product*', by which is meant here the net output vector (cf. Section 3.1). The value of their consumption $p'(\lambda_2 \alpha_2 N_2)$ is equal to $s\bar{W}$, the income derived from labour, which they appropriate in its entirety:

$$p'(\lambda_2^0 \alpha_2 N_2) = s\bar{W}$$

Between these two extremes all intermediate positions are possible, where $k(0 \leq k \leq 1)$, a part of the total revenues $s\bar{W}$, goes to the workers and the rest $(1-k)$ goes to the capitalist. If k is given, the indetermination of the system disappears. Indeed the values λ_1, λ_2, x, p, s shown below satisfy the equations (24), (25), (26), (27), and so characterise one of the possible states of equilibrium.

$$\lambda_1 = \frac{k\bar{W}}{v'(I-A)^{-1}\alpha_1 N_1} \tag{28}$$

$$\lambda_2 = \frac{(1-k)\bar{W}}{v'(1-A)^{-1}\alpha_2 N_2} \tag{28a}$$

$$x = (I-A)^{-1}(\lambda_1 \alpha_1 N_1 + \lambda_2 \alpha_2 N_2) \tag{29}$$

$$p' = sv'(I-A)^{-1}. \tag{30}$$

Quite clearly, (24) is satisfied, bearing in mind (29), and (25) is verified if (28) and (29) are combined; (30) is identical to (26). In addition, the conditions necessary for the budgetary equilibrium of the two classes are arrived at separately:

$$p'(\lambda_1 \alpha_1 N_1) = ks\bar{W} \qquad \text{and} \qquad p'(\lambda_2 \alpha_2 N_2) = (1-k)s\bar{W}.$$

The solution given to the system of equations (24), (25), (26) and (27) by the values of λ_1, λ_2, x, p and s, taken from (28), (28a), (29), (30), will be called the *Marxian state of equilibrium*. Here again, as in the case of a one-class model, we are dealing with a realisable state of a static economy where the available work-force is fully employed, and also with a specification of the price variables (prices of commodities and salaries), such that firms and consumers balance their income and expenditure. However – and this is what differentiates it from the neoclassical state of equilibrium – a group of non-workers, namely the capitalists, appropriate some of the social product.

For each value of k there is a corresponding equilibrium, and one only, on account of the hypothesis of absence of free production and the fact that α_1 and α_2 are positive and different from the nil vector, λ_1^0, λ_2^0 are strictly positive, and λ_1 and λ_2 cannot both be nil at the same time, for

$$\lambda_1 = k\lambda_1^0 \qquad \lambda_2 = (1-k)\lambda_2^0$$

(which is another way of writing (28) and (28a)). The vector x given by (29) is therefore positive, for A is productive and theorem 2

(Section 3.1) comes into play; vector p is strictly positive. The fact that x only has one value is also affirmed by the same theorem 2. Finally, the following proposition about the Marxian states of equilibrium may be enunciated:

Theorem 6 Provided the general hypotheses formulated in the enunciation of theorem 4 are observed, for every number $k (0 \leq k \leq 1)$ representing *the distribution of the social product* between the two classes, there will correspond one, and only one, Marxian state of equilibrium.

The neoclassical state of equilibrium shown in Chapter 3 is a Marxian equilibrium when the parameter $k = 1$.

7.2 Efficiency

Within the n-dimensional space R^n let us consider the set Y of the realisable net output vectors. It has already been seen in Section 3.2 that Y is obtained from the intersection of the positive orthant R^n and the semi-space $v'(I - A)^{-1} y \leq \bar{W}$.

$$Y = \{y \in R^n / y \geq 0 \quad \text{and} \quad v'(I - A)^{-1} y \leq \bar{W}\}.$$

The efficiency frontier is obtained, being the point of intersection of the positive orthant and the equation hyperplane:

$$v'(I - A)^{-1} y = \bar{W}.$$

For a state of equilibrium given by the neoclassical model, the consumption vector of the domestic consumer is situated on the efficiency frontier, and for the same reason the Marxian states of equilibrium when $k = 1$ and $k = 0$ are also on the efficiency frontier. It will be shown that this is so for all values of k between 0 and 1.

By construction, the total consumption vector of the two classes $y = \lambda_1 \alpha_1 N_1 + \lambda_2 \alpha_2 N_2$ is non-negative, for in such a case neither λ_1 nor λ_2 is nil.

It also verifies the equation of the limit hyperplane:

$$v'(I - A)^{-1}(\lambda_1 \alpha_1 N_1 + \lambda_2 \alpha_2 N_2) = k\bar{W} + (1 - k)\bar{W} = \bar{W}.$$

Hence the theorem below:

Theorem 7 A Marxian state of equilibrium is efficient.

Since according to (28) and (28a) we have

$$\lambda_1 = k\lambda_1^0 \qquad \text{and} \qquad \lambda_2 = (1-k)\lambda_2^0$$

the total consumption of the two social classes is the weighted sum that each class would consume if it appropriated the whole of the social product, viz, $y_1^0 = \lambda_1^0 \alpha_1 N_1$ and $y_2^0 = \lambda_2^0 \alpha_2 N_2$ respectively:

$$y = ky_1 + (1-k)y_2 \qquad 0 \leq k \leq 1.$$

This means that when k varies between 0 and 1, y describes the segment (y_1, y_2) of R^n. Figure 7.1 gives visual representation of this result.

There are no references in *Das Kapital* to this type of result for the simple reason that the concept of efficiency is much later than 1867, and Marx is in any case attempting to demonstrate the inefficiency of a capitalist management of the economy.

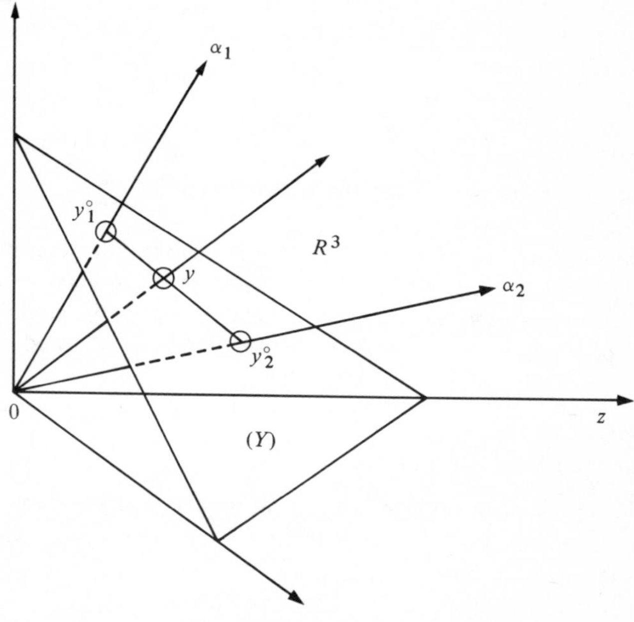

FIGURE 7.1

> In spite of its meanness, the capitalist mode of production is extremely wasteful of human material, just as through its method of distributing products via commerce and its manner of organising competition, it is extremely wasteful of other material means, thus losing for society what it has gained for the individual capitalist. [II, 116]

This attack misses its target because the characteristics shown above are realised at a state of equilibrium (and even then it is only a static equilibrium). What Marx *is* entitled to question is the capacity of the competition mechanism to attain such efficient states – quite a different problem, to which Marx doesn't even begin to provide a solution. The extract just quoted shows quite clearly that Marx fails to give the notion of waste any scientific precision. On this subject he is purely ideological, as can be further shown by this second extract defining waste, this time in relation to the absence of such waste in planned economies:

> Within capitalist production there is on the one side much waste of material, because nothing is undertaken according to a social plan, but everything depends on the infinitely different conditions, means, etc., with which the individual capitalist operates. This results in a great waste of the productive forces. [II, 176]

Today such naïve confidence in the virtues of planning could not fail to raise a smile.

7.3 Surplus-value in the firm and in the nation

So far nothing in our model differentiates the capitalists from the workers and we can invert the indices 1 and 2 applied to them without in any way changing the formal structure of the model. The first distinction Marx makes between them is to describe the revenue of each class in mutually exclusive terms:

1. *wages* for the workers;
2. *surplus-value* for the capitalists.

The term 'surplus-value' implies of course that the capitalist's income appears as an excess of the firm's receipts over its expenditure (cf. Section 5.1). However, in his desire to show that this '*subtraction*' is only apparent, Marx will assume right through the first two books of *Das Kapital* that the distribution of revenue within each firm is in the same proportion k as in the whole economy, so that the distribution of revenue seems to be the result of a *division*. The workers' salary is $\tilde{s} = ks$, the total salary bill is ksv_j in firm E_j when $x_j = 1$, and $ks\bar{W}$ for the whole nation. The *surplus-value per unit* (reduced here to a pure profit) is the surplus-value added to each unit produced $\pi_j = (1 - k)sv_j$ and the surplus-value realised in the whole of the economy amounts to $(1 - k)s\bar{W}$.

Marx utilises the concept of constant and variable capital to describe this method of redistribution: they are valid for firm E_j, still functioning at the level of the unit of production:

$$CC_j = \sum_{i=1}^{n} p_i a_{ij}$$

$$CV_j = \tilde{s}v_j = ksv_j$$

To the ratio of the surplus value to the variable capital (cf. I, 213), Marx applies the term '*rate of surplus value h*'.

$$h = \frac{\pi_j}{CV_j} = \frac{(1 - k)sv_j}{ksv_j} = \frac{1 - k}{k}. \qquad (31)$$

With the method of redistribution chosen, this rate is the same in all firms, being equal to the ratio of the surplus value to wages as calculated at the level of the economy as a whole.

Marx formulates the law thus:

> The masses of labour and of surplus-value produced by different capitals – the value of labour-power being given and its degree of exploitation being equal – vary directly as the amounts of the variable constituents of these capitals, i.e., as their constituents transformed into living labour-power [I, 290]

It is this rule of proportionality between surplus-value and salaries distributed that lies at the heart of the adjectives 'variable' and 'constant' used to describe the human and material components of capital. Marx writes:

> That part of capital, then, which is represented by the means of production, by the raw material, auxiliary material and the instruments of labour, does not, in the process of production, undergo any quantitative alteration of value. I therefore call it the constant part of capital, or, more shortly, *constant capital*. On the other hand, that part of capital, represented by labour-power, does, in the process of production, undergo an alteration of value. It both reproduces the equivalent of its own value, and also produces an excess, a surplus-value, which itself may vary, may

> be more or less according to circumstances. This part of capital is constantly being transformed from a constant into a variable magnitude. I therefore call it the variable part of capital, or, more shortly, variable capital. [I, 202]

As will be seen later (Chapter 10), the method of distribution expressed by equation (31) is not the one that takes place at the microeconomic level. It is quite clear – and Marx is perfectly aware of this – that profit is obtained by applying a uniform rate of profit to all sectors and to all capital utilised, whether constant or variable. However, he will refuse to accept this mode of creating surplus-value, primarily because only by so doing can he keep the Theory alive and make use of it for two-thirds of his book. This point has already been touched on (Sections 1.5 and 5.1), and will be referred to again (especially Section 7.5).

It may be wondered why Marx was led to prefer the rate of surplus-value h to the coefficient of distribution k of the social product, since these two *ratios* correspond for the formulae $h = (1 - k)/k$ and $k = h/(1 + h)$, and the second is the easier to interpret. His preference is based partly on basic economic reasons, which will be described in the next section (dealing with absolute and relative surplus-value), and partly on pedagogic reasons.

> The habit of representing surplus-value and value of labour-power as fractions of the value created – a habit that originates in the capitalist mode of production itself, and whose import will hereafter be disclosed – conceals the very transaction that characterises capital, namely the exchange of variable capital for living labour-power, and the consequent exclusion of the labourer from the product. Instead of the real fact, we have the false semblance of association, in which labourer and capitalist divide the product in proportion to the different elements which they respectively contribute towards its formation. [I, 499]

In a footnote Marx quotes contemporaries who attempt to pass over 'the antagonistic character' 'of the well-developed forms of capitalist production', and try 'to transform them into some form of free association'. Even today some still believe in what Marx calls 'conjuring tricks' (I, 499) capable of 'transforming' a system that makes the workers merely the instruments of the enterprise of which they are part

> into a fruitful and dignified association of those who within the same enterprise, would pool their contribution be it their labour, their technique, or their capital, and honestly and equitably share the risks and profits. [General de Gaulle's Strasbourg speech, 7 April 1947]

Since we are here dealing with pure economy, which is indifferent to either morals or metaphysics, we leave to their quarrels those who maintain that surplus value is the result of a 'division' of the social product, and those who, like Marx and his disciples, see it as an addition to variable capital, and also those 'practical capitalists' who see it as merely the *difference* between receipts and expenditure.

7.4 Relative and absolute surplus values

In his theory of surplus-value (Book I, Chapter X), Marx studies at great length the variations possible in the parameter, length of the working day. We must therefore return to the hypothesis we made on this subject at the end of Chapter 6, which is implicit in our present model.

Let g equal the length of the working day, and let the period of analysis consist of more than one calendar day. Let us further suppose that, in our formulation of the two-class static model in Section 7.1, $g = 1$, corresponding, for example, to a working day of eight hours. Of course, g can vary: if less than 1 it implies that the working day is one of less than eight hours; if greater than 1, then the reverse is true.

Other things being equal, the quantity of employment available is thus equal to $g\bar{W}$. In the solution of our model variations in the factor g will affect the magnitudes λ_1, λ_2, x in the same proportions. The prices system, which is defined only to within a constant multiplier, is unchanged. The new expression for the solution is obtained by 'injecting' into (28), (28a), (29) and (30) values that are 'g times greater' for the index of the standard of living:

$$\lambda_1 = gk\lambda_1^0 \tag{32}$$

$$\lambda_2 = g(1-k)\lambda_2^0 \tag{32a}$$

where, it will be remembered, $\lambda_1{}^0$ (alternately $\lambda_2{}^0$) is the value given to the index of the standard of living when the working class (or, alternately, capitalist class) appropriates the whole of the social product (cf. Section 7.1).

The rate of surplus-value does not change provided that k, the coefficient of distribution of the social product, does not change either. However, as soon as it is considered that the standard of living of the working class is a structural constant ($\lambda_1 = \lambda_1^*$), as Marx and the classical economists (though for different reasons) do regularly, this is no longer so; for the rate of surplus-value h according to (16), (31) and (32) is now written:

$$h = \frac{1-k}{k} = \frac{g}{kg} - 1 = \frac{g\lambda_1^0}{\lambda_1^*} - 1 \tag{33}$$

and is seen to be a growing function of g. Put simply, this means that, if the standard of living of the working class remains constant, then the rate of surplus-value – the rate of exploitation, as Marx would put it – increases with the length of the working day.

Equation (33) places a *lower limit* on this length, below which no surplus-value can be created ($h \leq 0$). This limit is such that the standard of living that the worker needs merely to reproduce himself is just realised by the distribution among the working class of all the social product: $g_{\min} = \lambda_1^*/\lambda_1^0$.

> If on the one hand the process be not carried beyond the point where the value paid by the capitalist for the labour power is placed by an exact equivalent, it is simply a process of producing value; if, on the other hand, it be continued beyond that point it becomes a process of creating surplus-value. [I, 190]

As for the *upper limit* to the length of the working day, this is determined by the following:

1. the fact that it cannot exceed twenty-four hours: 'The absolute limit of the working-day – this being by nature always less than 24 hours' (I, 289);
2. 'the physical bounds of labour-power .... During part of the day this force must rest, sleep; during another part the man has to satisfy other physical needs, to wash, feed and clothe himself' (I, 223);
3. 'Besides these purely physical limitations, the extent of the working-day encounters moral ones. The labourer needs times for satisfying his intellectual and social wants, the extent and number of which are conditioned by the general state of social advancement' (I, 223).

There exists therefore, regarding the length of the working day, the same kind of ambiguity that we saw affecting the determination of the level of subsistence, since a historical element creeps into the reckoning, viz. 'the general state of civilisation', which in reality takes away from the theory all possibility of precision.

As for the length of the working day, Marx hazards one or two conjectures regarding the process which tends to fix its 'normal' length (I, 281). In some parts of his work, he asserts that the capitalist will tend to prolong the working day as long as possible, even if his workers' health suffers, but that this tendency is countered by the efforts of 'society' or 'the State', who are aware of the necessity of maintaining intact the work-force, which is the source of surplus-value. However, only a few pages further on, and quite unconcerned about the contradiction, he states that the reduction of the length of the working day is due to the battle fought by the trades unions. Thus, in Volume I, p. 258 we read that

> Hence it is natural that the lengthening of the working-day, which capital, from the middle of the 14th, to the end of the 17th century, tries to impose by State-measures on adult-labourers, approximately coincides with the shortening of the working-day which in the second half of the 19th century has here and there been effected by the State, to prevent the coining of children's blood into capital.

Meaning that the State, after long being in favour of the lengthening of the working day, then realises the disastrous effects of going too far in this field and orders an 'about-turn', in the very interests of the capitalist class, of which the State is the expression.

Further on, we read: 'The creation of a normal working-day is, therefore, the product of a protracted civil war, more or less dissembled, between the capitalist class and the working class' (I, 283). Can these two passages be reconciled other than by admitting that the State is open to the political influence of the working class? But would not such an admission be a dangerous flirtation with social democracy?

To conclude this section on the possible variations of the length of the working day, we can say that the parameter g normally $= 1$; or to use Marxian terminology, '*absolute surplus-value*, produced by prolongation of the working-day', will not be considered, giving way to the notion of *relative surplus-value*, arising from a curtailment of the necessary labour-time (I, 299) (i.e., necessary for the production of the means of subsistence of the working class).

7.5 The theory upheld

As noted in Section 7.3, the relationship between the capitalist's selling price and the factors making up his cost price, now that he receives a surplus-value of π_j for each unit produced, can be written:

$$p_j = \sum_{i=1}^{n} p_i a_{ij} + \tilde{s}v_j + \pi_j. \tag{34}$$

This equation might cause us to wonder how the Theory is going to fare when confronted with the Marxian equilibria (cf. Section 5.1 for a discussion on the relationship between the Theory and theories of profit). And indeed the matrix form of equation (34) is written as:

$$p' = p'A + \tilde{s}v' + \pi'$$

(provided that by π' is meant the line-vector of surplus values per unit).

Hence the price vector

$$p' = \tilde{s}v'(1 - A)^{-1} + \pi'(I - A)^{-1}.$$

The price of commodity B_j would therefore consist of two elements, the first being the wages paid, the second the various surplus-values received at the various phases of the production process used to produce one unit of this commodity. Marx castigates 'the absurd formula that the three revenues, wages, profit and rent,[1] form the three component parts of the value of commodities' (II, 389). In his view,

> This separation of the production of value into a reproduction of advanced value and a production of new value (surplus-value) which does not replace any equivalent, does not alter in any way the substance of value itself or the nature of the production of value. The substance of value is and remains nothing but expended labour-power. [II, 389–90]

Marx is here reciting once more the principal article of his credo, the Labour Theory of Value. It so happens that, if, as he supposes, the same rate of surplus-value must be applied in all firms to the variable capital in order to calculate the absolute magnitude of the surplus value, the Theory remains valid, despite the appearance of a surplus-value, for in those circumstances we know that:

$$\tilde{s} = ks \qquad \pi_j = h\tilde{s}v_j = (1 - k)sv_j$$

and therefore:

$$p' = ksv'(I - A)^{-1} + (1 - k)sv'(I - A)^{-1} = sv'(I - A)^{-1}.$$

But this is in no sense a widening of the field of validity of the Theory. What has happened is that Marx has constructed a world to fit in with the Theory far different, as he well knows, from the real world.

This then, studied in detail, is the 'special case' of the validity of the Labour Theory mentioned in Section 5.1.

8 Materials for a Theory of Exploitation

8.1 The popular form of the Theory of Exploitation

In the previous chapter we dealt only with the 'anatomy' of the capitalist mode of production according to Marx, and not with its 'physiology': in other words, we limited ourselves to describing states of the economy, i.e., indicating which relationships verify the different variables characterising such states, in which a certain category of individuals, the capitalists, appropriate, without any labour, a certain fraction of the social product. However, we do not as yet know what mechanisms make this appropriation possible, or in what proportions the social product is divided.

We know that, after rejecting all rival theories, Marx answers this question, which is central to the origin of profit, by saying that it lies in the exploitation of labour. But this explanation is surely unsatisfactory, since the concept of exploitation of itself explains nothing, having at most the capacity to stir up the proletariat and fuel revolutionary energy. And yet this is the type of answer that Marx supplies in the early chapters of *Das Kapital*. The theory of profit has become a theory of exploitation, and takes on a popular but unsubstantial form (I, 500).

Starting from equation (34), which describes the financial equilibrium of the firm,

$$p_j = \sum_{i=1}^{n} p_j a_{ij} + \tilde{s} v_j + \pi_j \qquad (34)$$

since the Labour Theory of Value, as we saw in Section 7.5, remains fully valid, we can write:

$$p_j = s u_j$$

where u_j is the quantity of labour *directly* and *indirectly* necessary for the creation of one unit of commodity B_j. Since this expression of equality is valid for all values of j ($j = 1, 2, \cdots, n$), expenditures in means of production can be evaluated in quantities of labour, representing the amount of labour *indirectly* utilised to produce one unit of B_j. Thus:

$$\sum_{i=1}^{n} p_i a_{ij} = s \sum_{i=1}^{n} u_i a_{ij}.$$

As for $\tilde{s}v_j$, wages per unit produced, it is the monetary form of the goods consumed by those workers who are employed *directly* in firm E_j, functioning at the level of unity. These consumer goods have themselves meant the use of a certain amount of labour throughout the various sectors of the economy. Writing the equation for the budget of the working class, we get:

$$\tilde{s}v_j = p'(\lambda_1 \alpha_1 N_1)v_j \cdot \frac{1}{\bar{W}}.$$

Then, according to the Theory,

$$\tilde{s}v_j = s \cdot \lambda_1 \frac{N_1}{\bar{W}} \cdot v_j \cdot \left(\sum_{i=1}^{n} u_i \cdot \alpha_{i1} \right).$$

Finally equation (34) is written:

$$\pi_j = \left(p_j - \sum_{i=1}^{n} p_i a_{ij} \right) - \tilde{s}v_j$$

or again, as a function of the amount of labour,

$$\pi_j = s \left\{ \left(u_j - \sum_{i=1}^{n} u_i a_{ij} \right) - \lambda_1 \frac{N_1}{W} \cdot v_j \left(\sum_{i=1}^{n} u_i \alpha_{i1} \right) \right\}. \qquad (35)$$

Since the difference between su_j (direct and indirect labour) and

$$s \sum_{i=1}^{n} u_i a_{ij}$$

(indirect labour) obviously represents the amount of *direct* labour utilised in the enterprise being considered, we can write

$$\text{Surplus value} = s \left(\begin{array}{l} \text{Quantity of labour} \\ \text{expended directly} \\ \text{on the production} \\ \text{of a unit of } B_j \end{array} - \begin{array}{l} \text{Quantity of labour} \\ \text{necessary for the} \\ \text{satisfaction of the} \\ \text{needs of the workers} \\ \text{who produce this} \\ \text{unit } B_j \end{array} \right). \qquad (36)$$

Marx explains to the working classes that surplus-value is created because the right-hand half of this equation is positive; or, more concretely, that the capitalist class received a surplus-value because labour-power provides it with more labour than it needs to satisfy its own needs. The slogans that he uses to hammer home 'his truth' are models of their kind:

> The fact that half a day's labour is necessary to keep the labourer alive during 24 hours does not in any way prevent him from working a whole day. Therefore, the value of labour-power, and the value which the labour-power creates in the labour process, are two entirely different magnitudes; and this difference of the two magnitudes was what the capitalist had in view, when he was purchasing the labour-power. [I, 188]

Or again:

> That portion of the working-day, then, during which this reproduction takes place, I call necessary labour-time, and the labour expended during that time I call necessary labour .... During the second period of the labour-process, that in which his labour is no longer necessary, the workman, it is true, labours, expends labour-power; but his labour being no longer necessary labour, he creates no value for himself. He creates surplus-value, which for the capitalist has all the charms of a creation out of nothing. This portion of the working day I name surplus labour-time, and to the labour expended during that time I give the name surplus-labour. [I, 209]

The rate of surplus-value, or degree of exploitation of labour, then takes on its popular form:

$$h = \frac{\text{surplus labour}}{\text{necessary labour}}.$$

It should be noted that the expression 'day's labour' in this passage is only an image intended to strike the imagination, not the parameter 'length of a day's work'. The eight hours the worker spends at his machine cannot be split into the time necessary for the satisfaction of his own needs and that appropriated by the capitalist. The social division of labour makes these two periods indistinguishable. Nor is it possible, in a marginalist analysis, to designate the 'last labourer', whose productivity is the basis for fixing wages.

Within the logic of our model, exploitation provides no explanation of surplus-value. Equation (36) has to be read in reverse: it is because there is surplus-value that labour-power provides more labour than it consumes. Exploitation is the result of the existence of surplus-value. At the very most it is a suggestive interpretation of the existence of such a surplus-value.

8.2 Wages as the cost of subsistence

It may well be felt at this point that it is being presumptuous to accuse such a brilliant thinker as Marx of committing such a grave error of reasoning. Is there not another interpretation of the above passages that might give them a more positive meaning, and enable us to penetrate below the surface, to the very heart of Marx's thought?

The answer lies, as in the case of the price of labour (Section 3.4), in an alternative formulation of the two-class model of general equilibrium proposed in Chapter 7, bringing it very close to the classical demo-economic model discussed in Section 3.5. This new interpretation is obtained by supposing the workers' standard of living index λ_1 to be fixed, and the number of people composing this class, N_1, to be variable, as of course must be the quantity of work available, $\bar{W}$, which is proportional to it. To the equations (24), (25), (26), (27) must now be added

$$\lambda_1 = \lambda_1^* \tag{37}$$

$$\bar{W} = aN_1. \tag{38}$$

It has already been pointed out that Marx differs from the classical economists in the interpretation he gives to this model. However, its form permits a large number of propositions contained in *Das Kapital* to be interpreted coherently, especially the proposition relative to exploitation as the source of surplus-value, which on previous pages had seemed no more than an irritating tautology.

Marx is insistent in his assertions that the working classes' share of the social product is just enough to enable it to satisfy its most elementary physiological needs (although, of course, he is just as categorical in declaring that consumption is to some extent determined by history; such contradictions make it more difficult to understand his theory of profit, but do not destroy its logical basis). In support of his theory that salaries are based strictly upon the cost of subsistence – the cost of survival would be more accurate – we have extracts such as:

> Labour-power, however, only becomes reality by its exercise; it sets itself in action only by working. But thereby a definite quantity of human muscle, nerve, brain, etc., is wasted, and these require to be restored. This increased expenditure demands a larger income. If the owner of labour-power works today, tomorrow he must again be able to repeat the same process in the same conditions as regards health and strength. His means

> of subsistence must therefore be sufficient to sustain him in his normal state as a labouring individual. [I, 167–8]

The cost of subsistence must of course be interpreted in a wide sense; it will include the cost of the upkeep of the workers' children and the cost of apprenticeship, the cost of transforming 'simple work' into 'complex work'.

> The labour-power withdrawn from the labour market by wear and tear and death must be continually replaced by, at the very least, an equal amount of fresh labour-power. Hence the sum of the means of subsistence necessary for the production of labour-power must include the means necessary for the labourer's substitutes, i.e., his children. [I, 168]

Or again, 'The expenses of this education (excessively small in the case of ordinary labour-power), enter *pro tanto* into the total value spent in its production' (I, 168–9).

Let us reconsider equation (35), where the surplus-value per unit, π_j, is expressed as the difference between the amount of labour carried out by 'the worker' and 'the amount of labour necessary' (i.e., for him to reproduce himself):

$$\pi_j = s\left\{\left(u_j - \sum_{i=1}^{n} u_i a_{ij}\right) - \lambda_1 \frac{N_1}{\bar{W}} v_j \left(\sum_{i=1}^{n} u_i \alpha_{i1}\right)\right\}.$$

Since u_j = coordinate of rank j of $v'\ (I - A)^{-1}$, we get:

$$\pi_j = sv_j\left\{1 - v'(I - A)^{-1}\alpha_1 \lambda_1 \frac{N_1}{\bar{W}}\right\}$$

which, bearing in mind (37) and (38), can be written:

$$\pi_j = sv_j\left\{1 - v'(I - A)^{-1}\alpha_1 \lambda_1^* \cdot \frac{1}{a}\right\}. \tag{39}$$

We can now read (36), and therefore (39), from left to right: in firm E_j the surplus-value per unit produced is positive if (1) some labour is employed there, and (2) the amount of labour needed for the production of means of subsistence 'reproduces' more than its equivalent, i.e., if it allows the upkeep of a work-force capable of producing more work. Mathematically, these two conditions may be written

$$v_j > 0 \tag{40}$$

$$\frac{1}{a} v'(I - A)^{-1}\alpha_1 \lambda_1^* < 1. \tag{41}$$

The single-class demo-economic model examined in Section 3.5 is an extreme example of what we are discussing here. In that case, the inequality (41) is replaced by the equality (14a):

$$\frac{1}{a}v'(I-A)^{-1}\alpha_1\lambda_1^* = 1 \tag{14a}$$

and all surplus-value is eliminated, so that the Theory quite naturally comes into its own, and the capitalist class disappears for lack of its material basis.

The quantity

$$\frac{1}{a}v'(I-A)^{-1}\alpha_1\lambda_1^*$$

seems therefore to be an intrinsic structural fact for Marx, and the fact that it may be greater than, equal to or less than unity is an accident of history, 'a great stroke of good fortune for the buyer [of labour, i.e., the capitalist]' (III, 137) (at least, until the capitalists try to reduce the technical coefficients a_{ij} and employment coefficients v_j). One or two passages scattered throughout *Das Kapital* support this thesis. For example:

> The general conditions for existence of surplus-value and profit are: The direct producers must work beyond the time necessary for the reproduction of their own labour-power. They must perform surplus labour in general. This is the subjective condition. The objective condition is that they must be able to perform surplus-labour. The natural conditions must be such that a part of their available labour-time suffices for their reproduction and self-maintenance as producers, that the production of their necessary means of subsistence shall not consume their own labour-power. [III, 505]

Or again: 'Productivity in the agricultural field exceeding the workers' individual needs is the basis of all societies' (II, 115).

Marx even goes as far as to define very strictly what the level of subsistence, λ_1^*, is, quite apart from the mode of production. Surplus-value is then merely the form-value of goods produced over and above these strict needs. Marx says, for example:

> Let us assume that the labourers themselves are in possession of their respective means of production and exchange their commodities with one another .... In that case, two labourers, both working one day, would have in the commodities produced by them, first, an equivalent for their outlay .... In the second place, both of them would have created equal amounts of new value, namely the working day added by them to the means of production. This would comprise their wages plus the

surplus-value, the last representing surplus-labour exceeding their necessary wants, the product of which would belong to them [III, 136]

which may be thought rather a curious conception, since it re-creates surplus-value in a classless society. Neo-Marxists (cf. Baran [1]) prefer to use the term 'surplus', but the problem still remains of defining what these minimum needs are, when no class of exploiters exists to measure them empirically (cf. also I, 480).

If we look again at the inequality (41), considered as being verified, we see that this is really a rewriting of equality (28):

$$\lambda_1 = \frac{k\overline{W}}{v'(I - A)^{-1}\alpha_1 N_1} \tag{28}$$

and at the same time a means of calculating the coefficient of the distribution of the social product k and the rate of surplus-value $h = 1/(1 + k)$. However, the theory of wages as the cost of subsistence is in no sense a theory of surplus-value. We have to remember here that Marxian equilibria have so far only been given a formal definition, and all we have done in this section is to shift the problem without solving it. Earlier, the coefficient k was undetermined, and now it is the turn of λ_1^*; to say that it represents a minimal standard of living, a level of mere survival, is not enough to excuse us from making explicit the types of behaviour and the institutional rules that perpetuate such a situation, such a state of equilibrium.

8.3 Slavery and the wage-earning class

An extension of the demo-economic model of Section 3.5 provides us with one explanation of the phenomenon of surplus-value, valid however only for the old slave societies. In many passages of his book Marx seems in fact very close to adopting this conception. However, his own theory of exploitation, though not properly formulated, prevents him from proclaiming the identity of the slave with the worker.

In the single-class demo-economic model, a disequilibrium in households' budgets was offset by their fertility:

$$p'(\lambda^*\alpha) < as \Rightarrow \dot{N} > 0 \;\; \dot{\overline{W}} > 0$$

$$p'(\lambda^*\alpha) > as \Rightarrow \dot{N} < 0 \;\; \dot{\overline{W}} < 0.$$

In a two-class model, the sector of the working-class households is a productive sector like any other, and as such comes under the domination of the capitalists. It can be compared to a sector for the rearing of human cattle; the capitalists decide upon the required level of production in this sector, in other words on the number of workers necessary, and then rely on wage-rates and the laws of natural fertility. Slavery in olden times, or in the American colonies, reflects faithfully this type of social organisation.

The number of reproducible commodities has now been increased by one, since labour is now one of those commodities. Production and net output spaces have $(n+1)$ dimensions. A feasible state of the economy is defined by equations similar to (8) and (9):

$$x = Ax + \lambda_1^* \alpha_1 N_1 + y_2 \tag{42}$$

$$v'x = aN_1. \tag{43}$$

It should be noted that:

1. y_2 represents net output in the hands of the capitalist irrespective of its structure;
2. x and N_1 are now the $(n+1)$ components of the production vector;
3. these equations can be presented matricially in R^{n+1}:

$$\begin{array}{|c|c|}\hline A & \lambda_1^*\alpha_1 \\ \hline v' & 1-a \\ \hline\end{array} \cdot \begin{array}{|c|}\hline x \\ \hline N_1 \\ \hline\end{array} + \begin{array}{|c|}\hline y_2 \\ \hline 0 \\ \hline\end{array} = \begin{array}{|c|}\hline x \\ \hline N_1 \\ \hline\end{array}$$

In other words, in condensed form and by analogy with the formulation used in Section 3.1, $Ax + y = x$,

$$\mathbf{Z}\,X + Y = X. \tag{44}$$

However, the last coordinate of Y is zero, for, after all, the capitalists cannot be suspected of cannibalism. (44) can be inverted; i.e., the production vector allowing the demand y_2 of the capitalist class to be satisfied can be calculated. Thus:

$$N_1 = \frac{v'(I-A)^{-1}y_2}{a(1-k)} \tag{45}$$

$$x = (I-A)^{-1}y_2 + (I-A)^{-1}\lambda_1^*\alpha_1 N_1. \tag{46}$$

Bearing in mind the usual hypotheses about A and v (A is productive; there is absence of free production), remembering also that the structural constant k is less than unity, these equations enable us to state that any consumption demand $y_2 (y_2 \geq 0)$ made by the capitalist class can be realised by suitable production decisions in both the sector of material goods and the sector of the production of human beings (vector $x \geq 0$ and $N_1 > 0$).

The whole matrix **Z** is now productive (always assuming that the capitalists do not devour their workers). Would this slave society therefore be an earthly paradise? No obstacles can prevent its indefinite expansion; using only existing techniques, its most outrageous demands can be fulfilled. Consumption y_2 is free of all obstacles, and the model explodes. In this respect our construction already seems open to criticism; the economists of such a society will soon be reminded that non-reproducible factors such as land, space, water and minerals are necessary for production and that they are not inexhaustible.

The fact that the set of feasible states has no upper limit is reflected, as far as prices and incomes are concerned, in the fact that no price system can keep productive activities in equilibrium. Thus, if one chooses a price system (p, s) where income and expenditure of the n firms are equal, the producers of slaves will pocket a surplus-value and develop their industry out of all reason. For if p and s are linked by

$$p' = p'A + sv' \tag{26}$$

we know then that

$$p'(\lambda_1^* \alpha_1 N_1) = ksW \tag{31}$$

which gives

$$p'(\lambda_1^* \alpha) < as.$$

This theory of a mode of production based upon slavery is therefore imperfect, or at least incomplete. The economists of that period would no doubt have 'produced' a theory of ground rent, a sort of 'Land Theory of Value'. However, this theory does contain an element of truth, for it would have proved to those economists that an essential condition for the creation of a surplus-value, and therefore for its distribution among the slave-owners (for example, in proportion to the stocks of non-reproducible goods they held), is that the overall matrix **Z** should have a productive character, a character that can quite legitimately be identified with the exploitation of the slave class.

But Marx is not a contemporary of Spartacus, nor do the problems of colonisation interest him other than marginally. In any case a slave is not a wage-earner. Otherwise why would Marx have differentiated between them? Speaking of surplus labour, he writes:

> The essential difference between the various economic forms of society, between, for instance, a society based on slave-labour and one based on wage-labour, lies only in the mode in which this surplus-labour is in each case extracted from the actual producer, the labourer. [I, 209]

The difference between the two modes of production may seem minimal but it nevertheless exists. And it was summed up thus by an observer of the American Civil War,

> Peter of the North wants to break the head of the Paul of the South with all his might, because the Peter of the North hires his labour by the day, and the Paul of the South hires his by the life. [I, 244 n. See also the theoretical formulation Sections 6.1 and 6.2]

A further proof that Marx has no wish to develop a theory of slavery can be seen in his refusal to identify the workers' individual consumption with the 'productive consumption' of firms (cf. Section 6.3).

It is this slight difference, the temporary, not permanent, alienation of a man's labour, that prevents the creation of a surplus-value in the neoclassical model of equilibrium seen in Chapter 2. Capitalist behaviour and the workings of the labour market, together with those institutions that go with the existence of a paid working class, all prevent the economy from being stabilised in a Marxian state of equilibrium. Indeed, the existence of a pure profit in firm E_j encourages the capitalists to invest in this type of activity, increasing continuously the production of commodity B_j. The extra demand for labour thus created eventually exceeds the number still unemployed, an imbalance that tends to cause wages to rise, thereby eliminating profits. This reaction by the labour market is in reality the result of a series of individual actions by capitalists and workers, the former offering rates of pay higher than the current average, the latter hiring themselves out to the highest bidder, since they are 'free' and therefore 'mobile'. (See Section 2.6 for a detailed study of this point and of the passages in *Das Kapital* where Marx recognises the existence of such labour mobility.)

If therefore the salary system cannot be identified with slavery, the theory developed in this section is inadequate to its purpose of explaining the creation of surplus-value in a capitalist regime. Marx seems to be replying to this objection when he says that

> The Roman slave was held by fetters: the wage-labourer is bound to his owner by invisible threads. The appearance of independence is kept up by means of a constant change of employers and by the *fictio juris* of a contract. [I, 538]

Behind the apparently harmless restriction contained in the last part of this statement can be heard the authentic Marxian theory of exploitation. It alters the terms of the problem and takes us outside the theoretical field of general equilibrium to which our study had hitherto been confined. To bring in the idea of a coalition of agents – here the capitalist class – possessing a unity of decision radically complicates the model. Profit will therefore be created in a context where the neoclassical Theory of General Equilibrium expressly denied such a possibility.

8.4 The class struggle: an illustration

Just as in *Das Kapital* a theory of pure profit was sought, based on capitalist exploitation of the worker, so it is tempting to find in it a theory that sees wages as being the cost of the worker's subsistence. Such a theory gives an imperfect description of the slave society, and is quite inappropriate to explain the appearance of surplus-value in a capitalist regime. In fact, the message of *Das Kapital* is quite different. What has to be looked for, in its very depths, as it is well hidden, is a theory of 'the class struggle', a theory that would explain the mechanism of the distribution of the social product between salary and surplus value in terms of an overall confrontation of the two classes.

Obviously the phrases 'class struggle' and 'world-wide confrontation' explain nothing in themselves, being purely analogical and metaphorical; capitalists and workers do not fight it out gun in hand, either individually or in groups, to decide what level of wages should be paid. To describe these conflict situations the economist needs, not stirring accounts *à la* Homer or Victor Hugo, but appropriate theoretical instruments. Of course, the Theory of General Equilibrium already describes a situation where all the economic agents confront each other; but the fact that they exist in such great numbers leads to the introduction of a most important simplifying factor: exchange-values, hence the price system, evolve by a sort of anonymous competition, and appear to the combatants to be an inevitable fact of life. This was described in Section 2.6 as 'the hypothesis of atomicity'. If this hypothesis is now abandoned, we shall at the same time have to leave the comfortable world of General Equilibrium, and embark upon the uncharted seas of Games Theory.

We shall consider here a very rudimentary economy comprising two agents only, who consume and produce a single commodity. We shall show that one of the agents can squeeze surplus work out of the other if he is the only possessor of the means of production and subsistence. 'Since Robinson Crusoe's experiences are a favourite theme with political economists, let us take a look at him on his island' (I, 81). Man Friday has just arrived, and on that day Robinson has in his possession fourteen rabbits and a certain amount of poaching equipment (traps and various nets); as for Friday, he is bereft of everything. Robinson will come to his aid only if, in exchange for seven rabbits, which will enable him to subsist for a week, Man Friday will spend the week hunting, and hand over to Robinson the product of his hunting, viz. fourteen rabbits. During that first week, Robinson will also be able to live off the seven remaining rabbits as well as wandering idly around the lagoon. And a week later the two men will be in the very same situation as on the first day – a situation that will, in fact, be repeated week after week. The significance of our example will be clear: to grasp the essence of the capitalist mode of production, Robinson has only to be identified with the capitalist class, and Man Friday with the working class.

It is evident that, in the 'Robinsonian' economy that has just been described, the rate of surplus-value is 100 per cent; the surplus expressed in rabbits is seven, the salary distributed is also seven. Previous discussion may have shown that a strictly positive rate of surplus is possible, but has given no indication of the rate at which it should be fixed. The model systematising the 'games' situation in which our two protagonists are engaged will provide an answer to this questioning: wages will be fixed at the level of subsistence; and secondarily, it will show quite conclusively, to those not yet convinced, that Friday cannot avoid being exploited.

How is this 'game' played out?

Robinson and Friday come separately to decisions regarding the wage rate to be paid.

Friday refuses to work for a wage of less than $s_1 (0 \leq s_1 \leq 14)$.

Robinson is unwilling to go above a weekly wage of s_2 for this week or any other future week $(0 \leq s_2 \leq 14)$.

These two decisions, assumed to be irrevocable, are separately submitted to an arbiter. We now have two possibilities:

1. $s_2 < s_1$. The arbiter notes that no contract can be made. Friday is condemmed to die of hunger, since without means of subsistence or means of production he cannot produce on his own account. For 'ever since the first moment of his appearance on the world's stage, man has always been, and still must be, a consumer, both before and while he is producing' (I, 166). As for Robinson, he will have to work himself. He will succeed in trapping his fourteen rabbits a week, but at the cost of an effort presenting a clear 'disutility'.
2. $s_2 \geq s_1$. The arbiter fixes the wage midway between s_1 and s_2. Friday, in exchange for a salary $s = (s_1 + s_2)/2$, agrees to go hunting for Robinson. The enthusiasm he puts into this task, and therefore the number of rabbits trapped, will depend upon the salary paid, since his physical strength is physiologically linked to his level of consumption. Without doing any work, Robinson will get the rest.

These two hypotheses can be given a simple mathematical expression. $G_1(s_1, s_2)$ and $G_2(s_1, s_2)$ may be called the gains, or the level of satisfaction achieved by Friday and Robinson respectively, s_1 and s_2 being the decision made by each one.

For Friday:

$$s_2 < s_1 \qquad G_1(s_1, s_2) = -\infty \text{ (death, the supreme loss)}$$

$$s_2 \geq s_1 \qquad G_1(s_1, s_2) = \frac{s_1 + s_2}{2} - d_1 = s - d_1$$

where d_1 is the disutility felt by Friday and expressed in 'rabbit-equivalents'.

For Robinson:

$$s_2 < s_1 \qquad G_2(s_1, s_2) = 14 - d_2$$

where d_2 is the disutility felt by Robinson and expressed in rabbit-equivalents;

$$s_2 \geq s_1 \qquad G_2(s_1, s_2) = \Phi(s) - s$$

where $\Phi(s)$ is the relation between the number of rabbits trapped by Friday and the number he consumes (the consumption–productivity ratio). We can give a probable form to $\Phi(s)$ (see Figure 8.1). For all cases where $s \geq \bar{s}$, there is a maximum production of 14. Below that, it is proportional to s. The salary $\bar{s}$ corresponds to the cost of subsistence (an almost definitional equality here).

Let us call (s_1^0, s_2^0) the two decisions that will finally be adopted and G_1^0 and G_2^0 the gains associated with them. These decisions must be such as to:

1. lead to a value of $G_1 > -\infty$, otherwise Friday would prefer to die of hunger (decision announced: $s_1 = 14$);
2. lead to a value of $G_2 > 14 - d_2$, otherwise Robinson would decide to do his own trapping and leave Friday to his fate. To produce this result it would be sufficient to announce $s_2 = 0$;
3. lead to a maximisation of G_1 by (s_1^0, s_2^0) provided that $G_2 = G_2^0$, otherwise Friday would be able to improve his own situ-

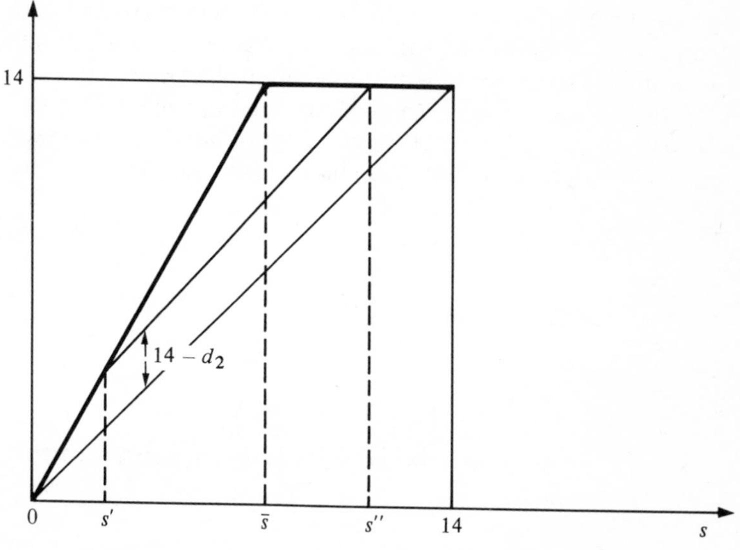

FIGURE 8.1

ation, without in fact harming Robinson, who would have no reason to react to such a modification.

4. lead to a maximisation of G_2 by (s_1, s_2), provided that $G_1 = G_1^0$, for reasons that are precisely symmetrical to the previous case.

These four conditions are based on those to be found in E. Malinvaud's study of bilateral monopoly [cf. [9], 124]. They fix limits on the plane (G_1, G_2) to the zone of results which each player will not try to prevent systematically (the 'kernel' of the game.) For such a range of results G_1^0 and G_2^0 are functionally bound by:

$$G_2^0 = \Phi(G_1^0 + d_1) - (G_1^0 + d_1).$$

With the specification adopted for the function Φ, the result is shown in Figure 8.2. The wages s' and s'' are such that the surplus-value paid by Robinson is precisely the same as if he were to work himself. (These wages have already been determined on the diagram as $s \to \Phi(s)$ (see Figure 8.1).

The kernel of the game is limited to the one segment BC, because of conditions (1), (2), (3) and (4).

We shall exclude the situation where the kernel is empty, which is the case if Robinson derives more from his own labours than from his exploiting Friday, however great this might be, i.e., if $14 - d_2 > 14 - \bar{s}$. The image of the kernel BC on the plane (s_1, s_2) is, in Figure 8.3, made up of the shaded part of the square whose sides are equal to 14 units. The choice of a solution within the kernel can result only from an explicit agreement between the two players. They can, for example, agree to revise their decisions if the arbiter tells them that the previous decisions have taken them outside the kernel.

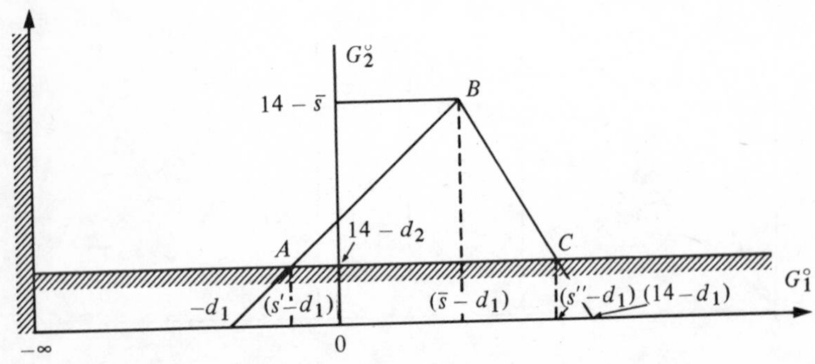

FIGURE 8.2

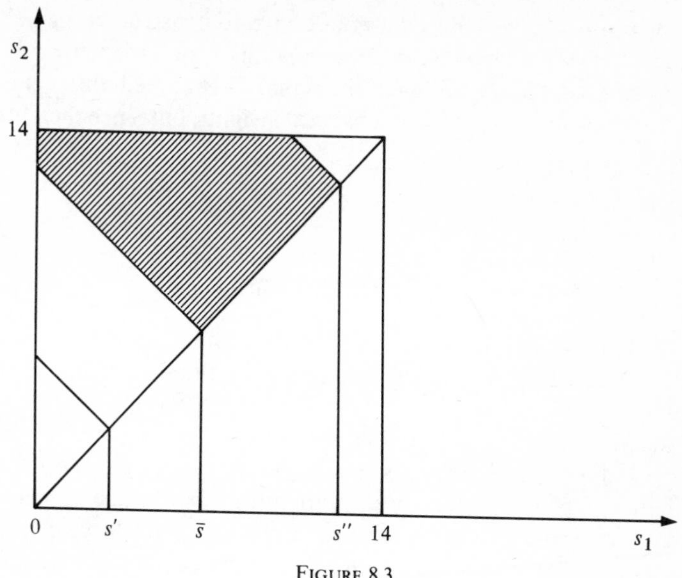

FIGURE 8.3

They could, of course, threaten to break this agreement, but such an eventuality would be unlikely, since it would mean death for Friday and an economic loss for Robinson.

Which solution will finally be adopted? Our model does not offer an unambiguous answer. Of all the points along the segment *BC*, *B* is the one that is the best for Robinson, but the worst for Friday, since his salary is then reduced to the bare cost of his subsistence.

It is likely that Robinson can impose his solution, since his threat to 'lock out' Friday is more credible than the latter's threat to go on strike (a strike that would become a suicide?). At all events such seemed to be Marx's point of view.

The above illustration is intended only to present an image of the problem, and makes no pretence even to approximate to the real world. It would first have to be demonstrated that individuals tend to come together in two perfectly homogeneous coalitions, according to what they have inherited, with the capitalists all on the one side and the 'free' workers all on the other. Other social cleavages are possible and indeed have been found in the past. During the Middle Ages in Europe, there was for example the corporation system, or at world-wide level the long-continued existence of nation-states. Even assuming that society was condemned to be divided into two groups, one would have to construct a 'game' in which the two sides behaved like capitalists and workers collectively, and not as individuals. Marx has illuminated this field of study with a few penetrating theoretical insights, but since then little has been done.

8.5 The class struggle: Marx's point of view

In real capitalist economies the truth is much more complex, probably coming about half-way between the model of general equilibrium shown in Chapters 2 and 3 (where competition cancels all surplus value), and the bipolarised world, where the capitalist class and the working class, each endowed with great internal cohesion, face each other in an unremitting battle, the capitalists being the inevitable victors because of their superior force of arms.

It is possible to find in *Das Kapital* many references indicating that it is upon the bipolarised model that Marx tries to maintain his Theory of Surplus Value.

For example, in his description of the law of supply and demand, the atomistic hypothesis receives short shrift at his hands:

> In a question of supply and demand, however, the supply means the sum of the sellers, or producers, of a certain kind of commodities and the demand the sum of the buyers, or consumers of the same kind of commodities .... These two bodies react on one another as units, as aggregate forces .... The side of competition which is momentarily the weaker, is also that in which the individual acts independently of the mass of his competitors, and often works against them, whereby the dependence of one upon the other is impressed upon them, while the stronger side always acts more or less unitedly against its antagonist. [III, 150]

Marx then goes on to give a very good definition of coalitions: 'The common interest is appreciated only so long as each gains more by it than without it' (III, 150). These general propositions apply both to capitalists and workers acting among themselves, and also to the capitalists acting against the workers.

> So long as everything goes well, competition effects a practical brotherhood of the capitalist class; ... so that each shares in the common loot in proportion to the magnitude of his share of investment. But as soon as it is no longer a question of sharing profits, but sharing losses, everyone tries to reduce his share to a minimum, and load as much as possible upon the shoulders of some other competitor. [III, 198]

In other words, except in bad times, 'the capitalists form a veritable freemason society arrayed against the whole working class, however much they may treat each other as false brothers in the competition among themselves' (III, 154).

Similarly, when they come together in trades unions, the workers cannot fail to be in a much stronger bargaining position than if they dealt with their employers on an individual basis, although even then they cannot prevent the capitalist class from squeezing a certain amount of surplus-value out of them. This is clearly shown in the confrontation between Robinson and Friday. Fundamentally, it is the coming together of the capitalists as a body that is the necessary condition for the creation of surplus-value, although the pooling by the workers of their slender reserves does enable them to hold out longer, in the case of an open conflict. If Friday had landed with a consignment of bananas, he could have held out against Robinson for a time. The capitalists realise this only too well, which is why they tried for so long to prevent the workers from coming together. What Marx condemns above all are the hypocritical reasons put forward to justify these 'barbarous laws' (I, 691). When the workers close ranks, 'Capital and its sycophants, Political Economy, cry out at the infringement of the "eternal" and so to say "sacred" law of supply and demand' (I, 599), and protest at 'this attempt against liberty and the declaration of the rights of man' (I, 692).

8.6 Profit and imperfect competition

We have already considered the two laws of economic behaviour (cf. Section 7.3), which when functioning together are sufficient to cancel out surplus values:

1. workers' mobility, which enables them immediately to leave their work for other, better paid, employment;
2. competition between firms, which leads them to increase their production indefinitely as long as it is profitable.

The *first theory* of surplus-value considered (cf. Section 8.3) denied *ad absurdum* the validity of the first of these laws; the worker is bound to his employer, almost like the slave bound to his master. If this were true, surplus work could of course be squeezed out of him. *The second, Marxian, theory* of surplus-value, which is built around the concept of the class struggle, presupposes the abandonment of the second of these laws. Competition between capitalists is to some extent 'suspended'. It is just as if there were a single centre of decision in each class, a 'collective' capitalist and a 'collective' worker, with the two classes confronting each other like two autonomous blocks. Our illustrative 'game' suggested (without proving it conclusively) that in such a situation the capitalist could demand from the worker a certain amount of surplus labour.

These two theories are only the extreme and dramatised forms of the 'imperfect competition' that would be obtained if the two hypotheses outlined above were partially abandoned. Competition between capitalists is neither total nor totally suspended, and workers' mobility, though neither perfect nor immediate, is not impossible either. The theory of General Equilibrium is a theory of 'perfect gases', but in Marx's version these gases have solidified! Is it not possible to find a middle term, a sort of theory of 'imperfect gases', which could account for the creation of a surplus value? There are hints of this in *Das Kapital*, when Marx points out the objective causes that limit *the competition of capital*, on the one hand, and the *mobility of labour*, on the other.

On the first point, Marx maintains that there is a minimum magnitude below which a certain sum of values, monetary or otherwise, cannot function as capital, i.e., cannot be injected into a productive operation. Leaving aside monetary and financial factors, this minimum size is linked to the indivisible nature of the means of production and also of labour. It is reduced by the value of the worker's subsistence, and must be such that it creates a surplus greater than the current consumption of the capitalists (we are dealing here with an individual entrepreneur – I, 291). These are really wholly theoretical lower limits, since in reality the figures are much larger than this; for 'With the development of the capitalist mode of production, there is an increase in the minimum amount of individual capital necessary to carry on a business under normal conditions' (I, 587).

The constraints imposed by this indivisibility impede not only the creation of new factories, but also any type of new investment.

> Whether or not *m*, the surplus-value turned into money, is immediately added to the capital-value in process and is thus enabled to enter the circuit together with capital *M* now having the magnitude *M'*, depends

> on circumstances which are independent of the mere existence of *m*. If *m* is to serve as money-capital in a second independent business, to be run side by side with the first, it is evident that it cannot be used for this purpose unless it is of the minimum size required of it. And if it is intended to be used for the expansion of the original business, the relations between the material factors of *P* and their value relations likewise demand a minimum magnitude for *m*. [II, 84]

It may be surmised that indivisibility is not an obstacle to the existence of a state of equilibrium identical with, or at least very close to, that described in the static neoclassical model. What will be most affected is the laws of convergence towards equilibrium. The return towards equilibrium, once it has been departed from, always takes place more slowly. Until it is sufficiently large, capital cannot be used in profitable activities; profits can be secreted in many different parts of the economy. In addition, technical progress, leading to the creation of large units of production, favours monopolistic behaviour, the coming together of the capitalist class in a homogeneous block, limiting competition and presenting a united front on the labour market.

From the workers' point of view, too, various frictions and types of inertia make them less quick to go from one sector of production to another in search of higher wages. For 'To effect a change in the state of being costs time and labour power' (II, 132). Marx is talking here about the costs involved in every buying–selling operation. When he sells his labour, the worker has to pay part of the costs of the transaction (cost of finding out about the new job, the cost of travelling). He will therefore be attracted only by a substantial difference between his present wages and the new wage promised him by another employer. The economy will eventually attain a state of equilibrium, but while it is doing so some firms will receive a regular flow of profit.

Such are the milder forms of the various theories of surplus-value, reached by moderating the more extreme character of the hypotheses that lie behind them. To show again that there exists a continuum between Marxian equilibria and the neoclassic equilibria, let us use an analogy from physics. If a liquid at rest is stirred, bubbles of air will be trapped within it, but they will escape if the liquid is left to settle. The time taken for the bubbles to come to the surface and burst will increase with the viscosity of the liquid; it will, for example, take longer in the case of oil than of water. The same is true of the economy; if we stir the economy, bubbles of profit are created, which will last longer, the thicker the liquid. But Marx sees a colloidal setting of the economy, within which the profit bubbles are eternally entrapped, whereas neoclassical theory is only sure of the fact that it is in the presence of a liquid that in a state of equilibrium contains no bubbles.

9 Simple Reproduction

9.1 From static equilibrium to a stationary regime

We saw in Section 5.2 that the concept of a static economy was an unreal one. Since it is possible to make the analysis of production dynamic, while at the same time remaining faithful to the spirit of *Das Kapital* (cf. Sections 6.4 and 6.5), the equations representing static equilibrium in the Marxian sense (24), (25), (26), (31), (32) can quite easily be reinterpreted as equations governing the working of a stationary regime.

Equation (24) expressed the idea that production and consumption (private and productive) were equal for each commodity, during the period of analysis:

$$Ax + \lambda_1 \alpha_1 N_1 + \lambda_2 \alpha_2 N_2 = x. \tag{24}$$

Since the vector x of the second half of the equation represents the stocks of each commodity existing at the beginning of the period, moment 0, it can be called x_0. From these stocks private consumption that will take place during the period, period 0, is deducted. It could be dated thus: $\lambda_{1,0} \alpha_1 N_{1,0}$ and $\lambda_{2,0} \alpha_2 N_{2,0}$. The volume of productive consumption, also deducted from initial stocks x_0, will depend on production decisions for the current period; this production will constitute stocks for the period that is to follow, period 1, and can be noted x_1. In the last analysis, equation (24) is obtained from

$$Ax_1 + \lambda_{1,0} \alpha_1 N_{1,0} + \lambda_{2,0} \alpha_2 N_{2,0} = x_0.$$

If we add the condition of *stationarity*, we get

$$x_1 = x_0 = x \qquad \lambda_{1,0} = \lambda_1 \qquad \lambda_{2,0} = \lambda_2$$
$$N_{1,0} = N_1 \qquad N_{2,0} = N_2.$$

This equation is valid for any later period t, enclosed by moments t and $(t + 1)$, since it can be derived from

$$Ax_{t+1} + \lambda_{1,t} \alpha_1 N_{1,t} + \lambda_{2,t} \alpha_2 N_{2,t} = x_t \tag{47}$$

by positing

$$
\begin{aligned}
x_{t+1} &= \cdots = x_0 \quad = x \\
\lambda_{1,t} &= \cdots = \lambda_{1,0} \;= \lambda_1 \\
\lambda_{2,t} &= \cdots = \lambda_{2,0} \;= \lambda_2 \\
N_{1,t} &= \cdots = N_{1,0} = N_1 \\
N_{2,t} &= \cdots = N_{2,0} = N_2.
\end{aligned}
$$

Similar reasoning applies to equation (25), which will come from

$$v'x_1 = \bar{W}_0 \tag{48}$$

simplified by

$$x_1 = x_0 = x \qquad \text{and} \qquad \bar{W}_0 = \bar{W}.$$

The question of how to interpret dynamically equations containing prices and revenues is a more difficult one, since the method of distribution of the social product adopted by Marx at the microeconomic level (application of a uniform rate to variable capital for the calculation of the surplus value) prevents us from attributing independent behaviour to the economic agents, especially to the capitalists. The full significance of the fact that capitalists derive their revenue from holding stocks x_t, will be examined in Chapter 10, in a model derived from our present one. For the moment we shall simply indicate by p_t the price system obtaining at moment t, and assume that the Theory functions in a dynamic situation for Marxian equilibria. Equations (26), (31) and (32) derive from the following equations:

$$p'_{t+1} = p'_t A + s_t v' \qquad \text{or: } p'_{t+1} = p'_t A + \tilde{s}_t v' + h\tilde{s}_t v' \tag{49}$$

$$p'_t \lambda_{1t} \alpha_1 N_{1t} = k s_t \bar{W}_t \qquad \text{or: } p'_t \lambda_{1t} \alpha_1 N_{1t} = \tilde{s}_t \bar{W}_t \tag{50}$$

$$p'_t \lambda_{2t} \alpha_2 N_{2t} = (1-k) s_t \bar{W}_t \qquad \text{or: } p'_t \lambda_{2t} \alpha_2 N_{2t} = h\tilde{s}_t \bar{W}_t \tag{51}$$

on which will have been imposed:

$$
\begin{aligned}
p_{t+1} &= p_t = \cdots = p \\
s_t &= \cdots = s
\end{aligned}
$$

and similar conditions of stationarity on $\tilde{s}_t$, $\lambda_{1,t}$, $\lambda_{2,t}$, $N_{1,t}$ and $N_{2,t}$.

It has thus been shown that the equation used for a description of a state of Marxian equilibrium can also serve to characterise a stationary system leading to the same distribution of the social product. However this provides no new information to explain the creation of surplus-value, which is as unrealisable in a dynamic interpretation as it was in our static model of Chapters 2 and 3. The time continuum in which this stationary regime evolves is 'objectively' homogeneous (the amount of employment, and production techniques, do not change in time) and also 'subjectively' homogeneous (the consumer attaches the same degree of importance to each moment, without any preference for the present). This being so, surplus-value, here profit or interest, cannot arise from the gap between inputs and outputs in the productive processes; and proposition 10 of Section 5.6 supports this affirmation.

However, such a conclusion in no way contradicts the fact that, given certain initial conditions (here: supplies of means of production and labour, x_0 and N_0), the growth programme that takes place can make certain activities profitable. It should be pointed out however that, according to neoclassical theories of growth, in a planned economy, and given 'homogeneous' economic time, such a programme would tend asymptotically towards a stationary régime and a nil rate of interest (cf. propositions 8, 10 and 11 of Section 5.6).

In Chapter 12 we shall examine what Marx, under the heading of the General Law of Capitalist Accumulation, has to say about private economies characterised by an imbalance between stocks of the means of production and labour.

9.2 Simple reproduction schemes in *Das Kapital*

Marx, too, recommends moving from a static analysis to a dynamic one, for 'Whatever the form of the process of production in a society, it must be a continuous process, must continue to go periodically through the same phases' (I, 531). When Marx makes this statement, his theory of surplus-value is already formulated (its main lines were given in Section 8.4 and 8.5), and he is anxious to test it out, and see whether, based as it is upon the 'exploitation' of one class by another and quite independent of physical time, it will stand up to a dynamic analysis. He will try to prove that it does, and that the succession of periods of time does not eliminate the creation of surplus-value. The following is a summary of his conclusions:

> If production be capitalistic in form, so, too, will be reproduction. Just as in the former the labour process figures but as a means towards the

self-expansion of capital, so in the latter it figures but as a means of reproducing as capital, i.e., as self-expanding value – the value advanced'. [I, 531]

In *Das Kapital* the stationary regime, the equations for which have been given above, is called 'simple reproduction', and forms a contrast with regimes of balanced growth, which Marx calls 'extended reproduction'. For Marx the fundamental difference between them is the capitalist attitude to savings:

> As a periodic increment of the capital advanced, or periodic fruit of capital in process, surplus-value acquires the form of a revenue flowing out of capital. If this revenue serves the capitalist only as a fund to provide for his consumption, and be spent as periodically as it is gained, then, *ceteris paribus*, simple reproduction will take place. [I, 531–2]

Marx sees simple reproduction as a 'strange assumption' (II, 399), contradicting the very essence of capitalism, which is accumulation and increasing wealth. He will use it to try and prove that the 'free' worker is in reality in chains, and quite unable to leave his condition as a worker at any time during the economic cycle. This fatality he expresses in a series of striking phrases:

> Capitalist production, therefore, of itself reproduces the separation between labour-power and the means of labour. It thereby reproduces and perpetuates the condition for exploiting the labourer. It incessantly forces him to sell his labour-power in order to live, and enables the capitalist to purchase labour-power in order that he may enrich himself. It is no longer a mere accident that capitalist and labourer confront each other in the market as buyer and seller. It is the process itself that incessantly hurls back the labourer on to the market as a vendor of his labour-power, and that incessantly converts his own product into a means by which another man can purchase him .... Capitalist production therefore, under its aspect of a continuous connected process, of a process of reproduction, produces not only commodities, not only surplus-value, but it also produces and reproduces the capitalist relation; on the one side the capitalist, on the other the wage-labourer. [I, 541–2]

9.3 A numerical example

For the purpose of his demonstration, Marx examines the circulation of money. He reduces the number of productive sectors in the economy to two:

sector I: producing the means of production;
sector II: producing consumer goods.

Capitalists belong to two classes also: KI (those of sector I) and KII (those of sector II). Similarly with the workers, OI working in sector I and OII working in sector II. Starting from a situation where the economic agents hold adequate stocks of goods and money, Marx tries to assure himself that the processes of production and consumption will inevitably recreate a situation identical to the initial situation, from the point of view of capital held.

Table 9.1 is a description of the accounts of the two sectors. The figures are taken from Book Two, Chapter XI of *Das Kapital* (II, 401). Table 9.2 gives the stocks held by each of the four agents KI, KII, OI, OII at the beginning of the period.

TABLE 9.1

	Sector I	Sector II
Constant capital (i.e., means of production)	4000	2000
Variable capital (i.e., wages distributed)	1000	500
Surplus-value (the rate of surplus-value is 100%)	1000	500
Value of goods produced	6000	3000

TABLE 9.2

	KI	KII	OI	OII
Capital goods	6000	0	0	0
Consumer goods	0	3000	0	0
Money				
Variant a	6000	3000	0	0
Variant b	5500	1500	0	0
Variant c	5000	1500	0	0

Figures 9.1 and 9.2 show the flow of money between the four poles of the economy. This flow takes place whenever there is an exchange necessary for the carrying out of the process of consumption and production.

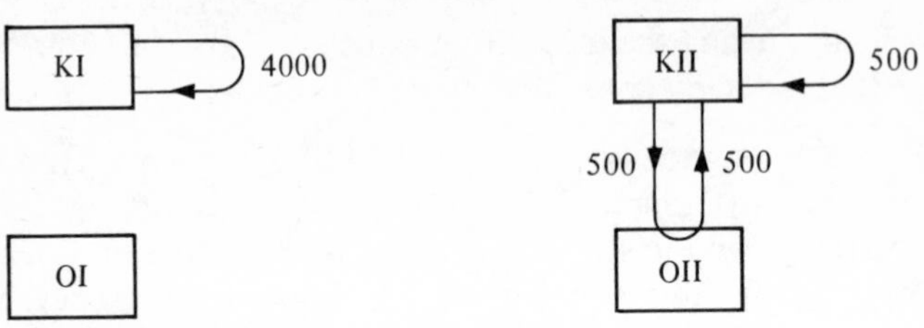

FIGURE 9.1

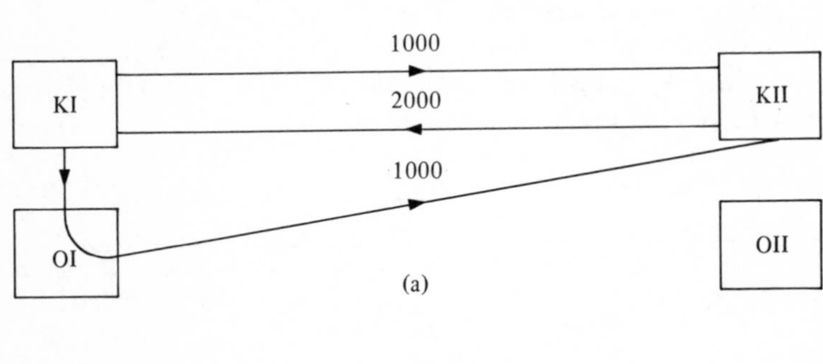

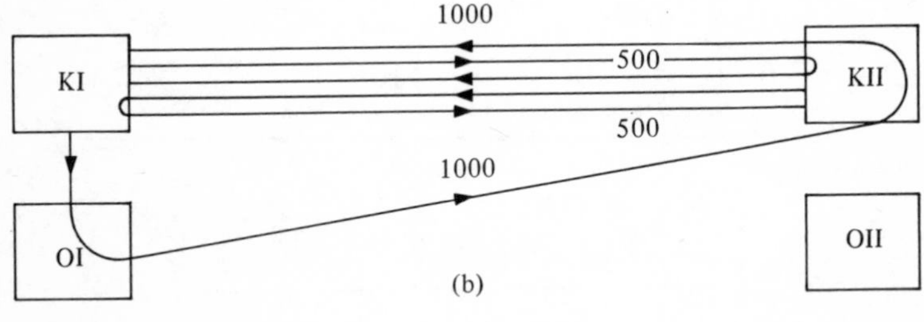

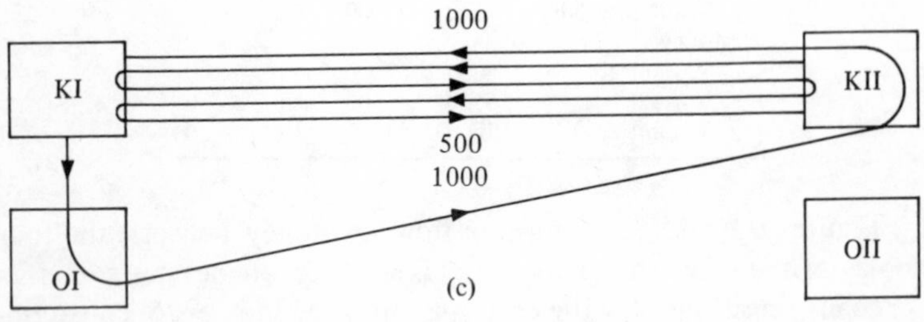

FIGURE 9.2

1. Exchanges carried out within each sector:

Salaries paid by KII to OII:	500
Consumer goods bought by KII:	500
Consumer goods bought by OII:	500
Means of production bought by KI:	4000

On completion of this cycle, KII once more has the 1000 that he had put into circulation, and KI has paid himself the 4000 of means of production that he needs. These internal operations are identical for the three variants a, b, c.

2. Exchanges carried out between one sector and another:

Salaries paid by KI to OI:	1000
Consumer goods bought by OI:	1000
Consumer goods bought by KI from KII:	1000
Means of production bought by KII from KI:	2000

In the three variants, KI and KII recover the amounts of money they originally put into circulation. This money 'oiling' the system has enabled all agents to purchase consumer goods from sector II and at the same time has enabled the means of production, which is the output of sector I, to be distributed between the two sectors according to their needs. The factors of production have been set up in each sector, so the process of production can begin. It will re-create quantities identical to those initially existing in the two sectors. The reproduction of the goods is assured and with it the reproduction of the 'capitalist relationship': *the rich remain rich and the poor remain poor.*

9.4 Some additional comments

In conclusion, we shall formulate three comments on the various schemes of simple reproduction.

First, the variants a, b and c differ only in the amounts of money used to carry out the exchange of means of production and consumer goods between the two sectors.[1]

This exchange is concerned with two quantities with a value equal to 2000. In variant a 4000 are necessary, 2000 being put into circulation by KI (of these 1000 circulate via OI), and 2000 by KII. Each unit of money moves once from the pole KI to KII. With variants b and c the amounts of money used are respectively 2000 and 1500. In the case of b each unit of money moves twice between poles KI and KII. In the case of variant c 1000 units circulate twice between KI and KII, and 500 units circulate four times. (See Figure 9.2) This is summarised in Table 9.3.

TABLE 9.3

	Quantity of money	Number of movements × quantity of money
	(1)	(2)
Variant a	4000	4000 × 1 = 4000
Variant b	2000	2000 × 2 = 4000
Variant c	1500	1000 × 2 + (500 × 4) = 4000

The constant figure 4000 shown in column (2) is equal to the total value of the transaction between the two sectors. This is simply confirmation of the identity $MV = PQ$ of the quantitative theory of money.

Second, simple reproduction has been shown to be possible since the exchanges between the two sectors are in equilibrium. Marx states that:

> It follows that, on the basis of simple reproduction, the sum of the values of $v + s$ of the commodity-capital of I (and therefore a corresponding proportional part of the total commodity-production of I) must be equal to the constant capital IIc, which is likewise taken as a proportional part of the total commodity-production of department II; or $\text{I}(v + s) = \text{IIc}$. [II, 406]

This equation means in fact that those capitalists and workers who work at the production of machines, semi-finished products and various materials exchange part of them for consumer goods, and the fact that this exchange is mediated by a system of money and prices really changes nothing.

This equation is the immediate consequence of equation (27), according to which the value of the social product[2] is equal to the sum of revenues distributed (wages plus surplus-value). This equality leads to:

3000 value of the social product	–	1000 revenue from sector II	=	2000 revenue from sector I

Now:

3000 value of the social product	=	3000 value of production of sector II

3000 value of the production of sector II	–	1000 revenue of sector II	=	2000 constant capital of sector II	=	2000 revenue of sector I

This demonstration is fully treated by Marx (II, 408).

Third, the Marxian model of simple reproduction just analysed is of very slightly theoretical interest today; it describes very inadequately the role of money in real economies, and our only purpose in describing it here is to make Chapter XX of Book II of *Das Kapital* somewhat easier for the reader to understand.

10 The Conversion of Values into Production Prices

10.1 Rate of profit and rate of surplus-value

For Marx the *surplus-value* created by a productive activity represents the excess of receipts over expenditure for wages and means of production (cf. Section 5.1). According to the neoclassical economists, *profit* is arrived at by deducting from receipts not only the cost of wages, and purchases of capital goods and semi-finished products, but also the rent paid for natural non-reproducible factors, such as land, water, minerals, etc. Theoretically, therefore, profit and surplus-value should coincide only if this last category of inputs is neglected (or if they exist in such unlimited quantities that they have no price).

Marx, however, confuses *a priori* the two magnitudes of profit and surplus-value:

> Profit results from the investment of a value as capital. If we designate profit by p we may convert the formula $C = c + v + s$, or $k + s$, into the formula $C = k + p$; in other words, the value of a commodity is equal to the cost price plus the profit. [III, 25]

And further on:

> The surplus-value, or the profit, consists precisely of the excess of the value of the commodity over its cost price; in other words it consists of the excess of the total amount of labour in the commodity over the paid labour contained in it. [III, 29–30]

This identification of surplus-value with profit has greater validity for Marx than for the neoclassical economists, and we know that as long as the Theory functions, i.e., as long as 'commodities are sold at their value', non-reproducible factors other than labour cost nothing and do not enter into the calculation of the cost of production. To avoid unprofitable discussion on this point, we shall assume, as we have throughout this second part, that profit and surplus-value are identical, not because, like Marx, we are convinced of the permanent validity of the Theory, but, quite simply, because we shall disregard non-reproducible factors other than labour.

If, therefore, as Marx states, 'Profit, such as it presents itself here, is the same as surplus-value' (III, 25), why does he immediately add: 'only it has a mystified form' (III, 25)? It will be easier to answer this question if the definitions of the rate of profit and the rate of surplus-value are recalled:

> The transformation of surplus-value into profit must be deduced from the transformation of the rate of surplus-value into the rate of profit and not vice-versa. [III, 30]
> The rate of surplus-value measured by the variable capital is called rate of surplus-value [We saw this in Section 7.3] The rate of surplus-value measured by the total capital is called profit. [III, 30]

Using symbols already familiar from Chapter 7, the rates of profit and surplus-value in firm E_j can be expressed algebraically:

$$h_j = \frac{\pi_j}{\tilde{s}v_j} \qquad j = 1, 2, \ldots, n$$

$$\theta_j = \frac{\pi_j}{\sum_{i=1}^{n} p_i a_{ij} + \tilde{s}v_j} \qquad j = 1, 2, \ldots, n$$

where π_j is the profit (or surplus-value) per unit of goods produced. We have seen that the price system associated with Marxian equilibrium, and which will henceforward be called *system of value-prices*, was such that the same rate of surplus-value was created in all firms; for it was supposed (Section 7.3) that added value is divided in the same proportions between capitalist and worker in all firms.

Since the rates of surplus-value h_j have in common h, the rate of profit in firm E_j is written thus:

$$\theta_j = \frac{h\tilde{s}v_j}{\sum_{i=1}^{n} p_i a_{ij} + \tilde{s}v_j} \qquad j = 1, 2, \ldots, n$$

or again

$$\theta_j = \frac{h}{1 + \dfrac{\sum_{i=1}^{n} p_i a_{ij}}{\tilde{s}v_j}}.$$

The ratio

$$\left(\sum_{i=1}^{n} p_i a_{ij}/\tilde{s}v_j\right)$$

is merely the ratio of constant to variable capital in firm E_j and is called in *Das Kapital* 'value-composition of capital' (I, 574). Marx also uses the expression 'organic composition' when describing it: 'I call the value-composition of capital, in so far as it is determined by its technical composition and mirrors the changes of the latter, the *organic composition* of capital' (I, 574). If, as ordinary observation confirms, these organic compositions vary from firm to firm, then the profit rates as defined above will also vary. But 'capital is, by nature, a leveller' (I, 375), or in the words of Malthus, quoted by Marx: 'The capitalist expects equal returns on all parts of the capital advanced by him' (III, 25); which means that for the capitalist, constant capital, as well as variable capital, must create the same percentage of surplus-value, and that from this point of view, 'one sphere of production is now as good or bad as another' (III, 151–2). It is, therefore, the mechanism of competition between different capitals that will lead to the equalisation of the rate of profit.

Marx sums up discussion on this point in the following terms:

> If the commodities are sold at their values, then,... considerably different rates of profit arise in the various spheres of production, according to the different organic composition of the masses of capital invested in them. But capital withdraws from spheres with low rates of profit and invades others which yield a higher rate. By means of this incessant emigration and immigration, in a word, by its distribution among the various spheres in accord with a rise in the rate of profit there and its fall there, it brings about such a proportion of supply to demand that the average profit in the various spheres of production become the same. [III, 153]

10.2 Production prices

The immediate consequence of this equalisation of the rates of profit is evidently to create disparities in the rates of surplus-value. The added value within each firm is no longer redistributed in a uniform proportion. The price system, which will ensure the financial equilibrium of firms, and which Marx calls 'production-prices', in contrast to 'value-prices', will fail to respect the Theory (cf. Sections 5.1 and 7.3).

A simple example will show why such a revision of the price system is necessary. In the economy being considered, we have separated, as Marx often does, the sector producing means of production (sector I) from the sector producing consumer goods (sector II); within each sector workers OI (alternatively OII) are placed under the control of capitalists KI (alternatively KII).

1. *Production techniques* During each period, KI produces one unit of a productive commodity, using one unit of labour; KII produces one unit of consumer goods, by means of the one unit of productive commodity and one unit of labour (the complementarity hypothesis is taken for granted); two units of labour are available, one being used in sector I and the second in sector II. The social product is finally one unit of consumer goods which now has to be divided among the four poles of the economy, KI, KII, OI, OII.

2. *The distribution of the social product* Let us suppose that the average rate of surplus-value is 100 per cent; OI and OII will receive half a unit of consumer goods, which they will share equally. The half unit remaining may be divided between KI and KII in proportion to the wages (here paid in kind) paid in each sector. KI and KII will each have a quarter unit. The price of the unit of productive commodity (expressed in kind) will therefore be:

Surplus-value of KI	0.25
OI wages	0.25
Total	0.50

This price system is that of value-prices; but one can verify that rates of profit differ from one sector to another:

$$\theta_{\mathrm{I}} = \frac{0.25}{0.25} = 100 \text{ per cent}$$

$$\theta_{\mathrm{II}} = \frac{0.25}{0.75} = 33 \text{ per cent}$$

If a different result is sought, then KI must reduce his profit, and let KII have his output at a price of less than 0.50. Let us call this price x_0. It should be valid for:

$$\theta_{\mathrm{I}} = \frac{x_0 - 0.25}{0.25} = \theta_{\mathrm{II}} = \frac{1 - (0.25 + x_0)}{0.25 + x_0}$$

x_0 is the positive root of the quadratic equation;

$$4x^2 + x - 1 = 0 \qquad \text{or} \qquad x_0 \# 0.39$$

The uniform rate of profit is now

$$\theta = \theta_{\text{I}} = \theta_{\text{II}} = \frac{x_0 - 0.25}{0.25} \quad \# 56 \text{ per cent}$$

in between 33 and 100 per cent. The unit of consumer goods forming the whole of the social product divides up as follows:

OI: 0.25
OII: 0.25
KI: 0.14
KII: 0.36

What can be learned from this elementary arithmetical exercise?

1. The uniform rate of profit is established *after* the average rate of surplus-value has been fixed for the whole of the economy.
2. The social product is still divided between the two social classes in the ratio 50%:50%.
3. The price of each commodity is obtained by adding to the production costs (which are expressed by the same system of prices) a constant profit margin in relative value.

10.3 Simultaneous determination of the uniform rate of profit and production costs

Before applying generally the results thus obtained to an economy with *n* sectors, it should be pointed out that the method that Marx used to calculate the average rate of profit and production-prices is incorrect (cf. III, 120).

First, he lumps together into a single overall capital a series differing in their organic composition; and then, by comparing the total of the surplus-values created by each individual firm to the total capital, he deduces from this an average rate of profit. After which he calculates the production-price of each commodity by adding to its production cost the profit, as calculated by applying the average rate of profit. The basic error is, of course, in working out the rate of profit and the production-price successively and not simultaneously. Marx omits the fact that the organic composition of a capital is in reality a value-composition and that a system of prices is therefore necessary for a valuation of its components. Since such a system can only be the system of production-prices, the average rate of profit cannot be calculated before prices.

Marx was probably aware of this difficulty, but was unable to deal with it because he lacked the necessary algebraic tools; he merely mentions it in passing:

> let us admit an average composition of $80c + 20v$. It may be that in capital composed thus the $80c$ is higher or lower than the value of constant capital c, because this c is made up of commodities whose production price is different from their value. Similarly the $20v$ may vary from their own value if, in the consumer goods purchased by salaries, there are articles whose production price varies from their value. [III, 160]

He makes a similar remark on p. 127 of vol. III, but concludes that it is pointless to pursue the question further. 'Our present analysis does not necessitate a closer examination of this point.'

We shall try to show that, within the two-class model of Chapter 7, there is a uniform rate of profit θ and a system of production-prices $(\bar{p}, \bar{s})$ that achieves equilibrium in the balance sheets of the n firms, and also a distribution of revenues among the two classes that is in conformity with a rate of surplus-value h *given in advance.*

These conditions are reflected in the following system of equations:

$$\bar{p}' = (1 + \theta)(\bar{p}'A + \bar{s}v') \tag{52}$$

$$\bar{p}'y_1 = \bar{s} \cdot \bar{W} \tag{53}$$

$$\bar{p}'y_2 = \pi' \cdot x \tag{54}$$

where y_1 and y_2 are the consumption vectors of the two classes, and π the vector of profit per unit. Quantities are calculated from the equations already used:

$$y_1 = \lambda_1 \alpha_1 N_1 = \frac{k\bar{W}}{v'(I - A)^{-1}\alpha_1 N_1} \cdot \alpha_1 N_1 \tag{28}$$

$$y_2 = \lambda_2 \alpha_2 N_2 = \frac{(1 - k)\bar{W}}{v'(I - A)^{-1}\alpha_2 N_2} \cdot \alpha_2 N_2 \tag{28a}$$

$$x = (I - A)^{-1}(y_1 + y_2). \tag{29}$$

This split is related to the rigidity of the consumer behaviour of the two classes. In general terms, the transformation of value-prices into production-prices modifies relative prices, hence consumption patterns and consequently the whole of the physical equilibrium. We will however limit ourselves to the simple case studied so far.

From the equations above there are three unknowns whose values remain to be found, θ, $\bar{p}$ and $\bar{s}$. Let us suppose for the moment that the matrix $\{I - (1 + \theta)A\}$ is invertible. We then have, according to (52),

$$\bar{p}' = (1 + \theta)\, \bar{s}v'\{I - (1 + \theta)A\}^{-1}.$$

If combined with (53) and (28), this equation produces

$$1 + \theta = \frac{1}{k} \cdot \frac{v'(I - A)^{-1}\alpha_1}{v'\{1 - (1 + \theta)A\}^{-1}\alpha_1} \tag{55}$$

If we posit:

$$z = (1 + \theta) \qquad \text{and} \qquad f(z) = v'(I - zA)^{-1}\alpha_1,$$

it can be seen that equation (55) takes the following form:

$$z = \frac{1}{k}\frac{f(1)}{f(z)}. \tag{56}$$

Here $f(1)$ is the quantity of labour necessary for the production of the consumption of each member of the working class at the level of $\lambda_1 = 1$. The expression $f(z)$ represents the same quantity, but only when the matrix of the technical coefficients is replaced by zA. Since z is greater than unity we can expect $f(z)$ to be greater than $f(1)$, since the technical coefficients are less effective in the second case (the technical coefficients have increased). Indeed, $f(z)$ is probably an increasing function of z for $z \geq 1$.

The root z_0 in equation (56) is obtained as being the abscissa of the point of intersection of the first bisector and the curve C representing the function $(1/k)\cdot\{f(1)/f(z)\}$ which is decreasing. This root can exist, since when $z = 1$ the point $M_1(1, 1/k)$, situated on curve C, is above the first bisector (see Figure 10.1). The existence of this root can be mathematically demonstrated, based upon the following theorem:

Theorem Let A be a productive matrix $(n \times n)$ with positive or zero elements, v a non-negative vector of R^n such that all the coordinates

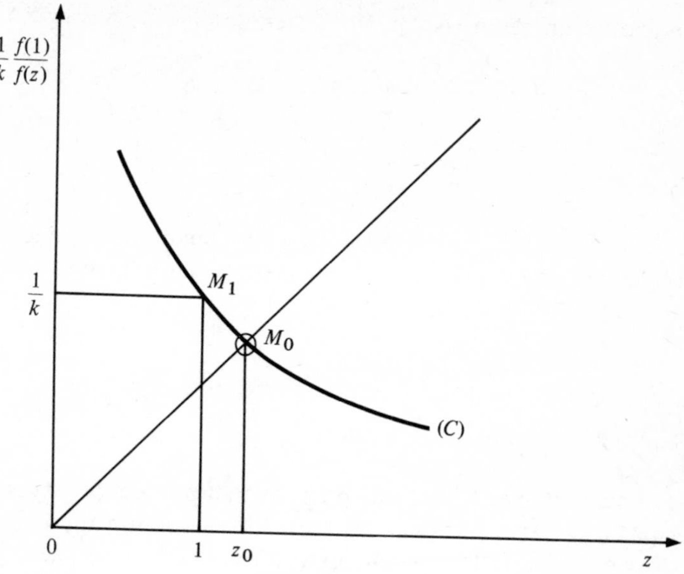

FIGURE 10.1

of $v'(I - A)^{-1}$ are strictly positive, and α_1 a second non-negative vector of R^n and different from the zero vector; then there exists a, $1 < a < +\infty$ such that:

1. $f(z) = v'(I - zA)^{-1}\alpha_1$ is a function of z, defined, continuous and strictly increasing in the interval $[1, a]$;
2. when z tends towards a $(z < a)$, $f(z)$ tends towards $+\infty$.

This theorem is derived from theorems 5, 6, 8 enunciated by Dorfman, Samuelson and Solow ([3], 265).

If this theorem is accepted, it is clearly seen that the function

$$g(z) = z - \frac{1}{k} \cdot \frac{f(1)}{f(z)}$$

is negative for $z = 1$ and positive for $z + a - \varepsilon(\varepsilon > 0)$. Since $g(z)$ is continuous it becomes zero for a value z_0 within the interval $[1, a - \varepsilon]$.

These general formulae allow the immediate solution of the

numerical example in Section 10.2, where

$$A = \begin{bmatrix} 0 & 1 \\ 0 & 0 \end{bmatrix} \qquad v' = [1 \quad 1] \qquad k = \tfrac{1}{2}$$

$$\alpha_1 = \begin{bmatrix} 0 \\ 1 \end{bmatrix} \qquad \alpha_2 = \begin{bmatrix} 0 \\ 1 \end{bmatrix}.$$

This also gives once more $\theta = 0.56$ from equation (55), and the production-prices $\bar{p} = (0.39;\ 1)\,\bar{s} = 0.25$ by substituting this value of θ in equation (52).

10.4 Properties of production-prices

Let us start by mentioning one property that production prices do *not* possess. Generally speaking, they do not confirm the Labour Theory of Value. If they were to do so, it would mean that they were proportionate to value prices and to the rates of profit calculated according to this system of prices, so that the organic compositions would be the same from one branch to another. This would in turn produce

$$\sum_{i=1}^{n} p_i a_{ij}$$

proportional to v_j, whatever the value of j;

$$\sum_{i=1}^{n} p_i a_{ij} + s v_j = p_j$$

proportional to v_j, whatever the value of j: now, since p_j is already proportional to u_j, finally v_j will be proportional to u_j for all values of j.

In economic terms, the amount of labour socially necessary for the production of any commodity is a multiple of the amount of labour directly necessary for its production. Putting it mathematically, it is sufficient that the vector of the employment coefficients v be an eigen vector to the left of matrix A since $u = v'(I - A)^{-1} = \mu v'$ with $\mu \geq 1$, and therefore

$$v' = \left(\frac{\mu - 1}{\mu}\right) v'A$$

where $(\mu - 1)/\mu$ is the corresponding eigen-value. The organic composition γ common to all firms is linked to μ, h and θ by the relationships $\gamma = \mu - 1$ and $\theta = h/(1 + \gamma)$. In this case, which is most unnatural, the 'special case' where surplus-value is proportional to variable capital (cf. Sections 5.1 and 7.3) is compatible with the behaviour of firms.

What are the relationships generally existing between production-prices and value-prices? In this connection, Marx notes that 'The sum of all the prices of production of all commodities in society, comprising the totality of all lines of production, is equal to the sum of all their values' (III, 122–3). Since it is absurd to attempt to add up prices, this remark can only mean that the social product has the same value, whether it be calculated by means of value-prices or by means of production-prices, as can be seen from the equations

$$\bar{p}'y_1 = \bar{s} \cdot \bar{W} \tag{53}$$

$$\bar{p}'y_2 = h\bar{s} \cdot \bar{W} \tag{54}$$

for production-prices, and

$$p'y_1 = \tilde{s} \cdot \bar{W}$$

$$p'y_2 = h\tilde{s} \cdot \bar{W}$$

for value-prices. This combination leads to

$$\bar{p}'(y_1 + y_2) = (1 + h)\,\bar{s} \cdot \bar{W}$$

$$p'(y_1 + y_2) = (1 + h)\,\tilde{s} \cdot \bar{W}$$

$$\frac{\bar{p}'y}{\bar{s}} = \frac{p'y}{\tilde{s}}$$

(the prices used here being the prices expressed in units of labour). The immediate consequence of this equality is that the difference between the two types of evaluation noted at the level of the individual sector of production exactly compensate each other:

$$\sum_{i=1}^{n} \left(\frac{\bar{p}_i}{\bar{s}} - \frac{p_i}{\tilde{s}} \right) y_i = 0.$$

It would seem excessively bold to venture further than this, and especially to affirm, as Marx does, that production-prices exceed values in those sectors having 'capitals of higher composition' (i.e., higher than the average), and conversely in the opposite cases (III, 126).

10.5 The implications of the theory of 'conversion'

Rather late in the day, therefore, in Book III of *Das Kapital*, Marx seems to abandon the Labour Theory of Value. Does this introduction of production-prices imply a readjustment of his initial model: and if there are inconsistencies between the first and last parts of his book, are they the fault of those responsible for the posthumous editions, especially Engels?

The simple answer is no; for as early as Book I (I, 208, 212, n. 1; 368, n. 1), Marx clearly indicates that he intended to treat the subject of production-prices in this way.

This theory of the 'conversion' of values into production-prices does not make Marx a convert to any bourgeois theory of profit; and far from being a new theory of surplus-value, it is only a comparatively unimportant appendix to the Marxian theory of exploitation. This is quite clear from a reading of the equation defining the new system of prices. Equation (55), in particular, shows that, other things being equal, the rate of profit depends simply and solely on the coefficient of redistribution of the social product, i.e., on the rate of surplus-value. This rate of profit becomes nil when exploitation ceases ($\theta = 0$ if and only if $h = 0$). 'Assuming all other conditions, among them the value of the advanced constant capital, to be given, the average rate of profit depends on the intensity of exploitation of the total labour by the total capital' (III, 53). Or again: 'this gap [between production prices and value] suppresses neither the determination of prices by value, nor the limits of profits'.

It seems very probable therefore that the transition from value-prices to production-prices is merely a perfecting of the original model, since its only purpose is to describe more realistically the redistribution of surplus-value. The core of Marx's theory continues to survive, in the form of a highly original attempt to explain the continued existence of surplus-value, quite apart from its method of distribution, in a context where, according to neoclassical theorists, it is doomed to disappear. In fact, the introduction by Marx of production-prices affords his critics but partial satisfaction; they put forward the same objection time and time again: the existence of profits where productivity is constant impels the producer to increase his production, whereupon tensions on the labour market, and the resulting wage increases, wipe out initial profits. We have seen in Chapter 8 how Marx answers these arguments with counter-arguments that will be considered fragile, ambiguous and incomplete, or else highly cogent, according to the amount of sympathy one has for the author.

The same objection can be made if the equations are presented in dynamic terms. To make our model dynamic, we proceed in exactly the same way as in the case of simple reproduction (cf. Section 9.1), at least as far as the physical equilibria (equations (47) and (48)), and the budgetary equilibria of the two classes (equations (50) and (51)), are concerned. The only equation that needs to be re-interpreted is (52), concerning firms:

$$\bar{p}' = (1 + \theta)(\bar{p}'A + \bar{s}v'). \tag{52}$$

This equation is obtained by assuming that the series of vectors of production-prices, salaries and profit rates are stationary:

$$\bar{p}_0 = \bar{p}_1 = \bar{p}_2 = \cdots = \bar{p}_t = \cdots$$

$$\bar{s}_0 = \bar{s}_1 = \bar{s}_2 = \cdots = \bar{s}_t = \cdots$$

$$\theta_0 = \theta_1 = \cdots = \theta_t = \cdots$$

in the interval

$$\bar{p}'_{t+1} = (1 + \theta_t)(\bar{p}'_t A + \bar{s}_t v'). \tag{57}$$

The first half of equation (57) shows the prices of outputs *at the end of the period*, whereas the second half shows the inputs utilised *at the beginning of the* period. The profit rate therefore has here the role of an interest rate; equation (57) expresses the fact that the present discounted value of the profit, calculated with that rate, attached to each activity is nil:

$$\frac{\bar{p}'_{t+1}}{1 + \theta_t} - \bar{p}'_t A - \bar{s}_t v' = 0.$$

The interest yielded by the capital appears to the capitalist, whether he owns it all or not, not as a surplus-value, but as a cost of utilisation; as the remuneration of an independent factor of production.

10.6 Successive redistribution of surplus-value

In *Das Kapital*, the theory of redistribution is presented as a theory of successive distributions of the social product.

First, there is the sharing of the social product between workers and non-workers, i.e., the division into salaries and surplus-value. The determination of the rate of surplus-value is the result of a confrontation between the two classes. Since the capitalists have temporarily suspended their competition and present a united front, they succeed in holding down the consumption of the working class to a level that only just ensures its subsistence and reproduction. The system of prices that sustains such an equilibrium is that of value-prices. The Theory is valid.

Second, the surplus-value is divided up among the capitalists according to the capital invested by each. Surplus-value is transformed into profit, and value-prices into production-prices. The mechanism of the division here is pure competition.

Third, we described how capitalists can be divided into two types: the industrial and the financial capitalist; and we have shown also that Marx based this division of total profit into the *profit from business*, and *interest*, on the working of the Law of Supply and Demand (cf. Book III, Section V).

Fourth, the owner of land and non-reproducible commodities other than labour receives part of the surplus-value in the form of 'rent'. Book III, Section VI, gives a description of the mechanism by which the amounts of this type of revenue are fixed, and therefore of the method by which the prices of those commodities from which it derives are also fixed. Marx's theory of rent is particularly abstruse, and could only have a (polemic) interest if it were confronted with Ricardo's theory. Suffice it to say here that fundamentally it is based upon the competition between those who seek, and those who offer, land.

The definitive equilibrium (cf. Vol. III) is sustained by a new price system, correcting that of production-prices, and for which 'natural' factors of production are evaluated.

It is quite clear that the expression 'successive distributions of the social product' is not to be taken literally; the order in which these distributions are described is purely for the purpose of the demonstration, and does not correspond to any kind of economic reality. Similarly, the price systems are only intermediary calculations, of which only the last corresponds to a real equilibrium.

The neoclassical economist may now be tempted to declare triumphantly that Marx has made this long detour merely to end up with a result that Walras has condensed into a few masterly equations. His definitive price system is none other than the price system announced by the Theory of General Equilibrium. In spite of analogies between the two, such affirmations are quite unjustified.

To describe properly Marx's theory of redistribution and prices, the phrase 'successive divisions of surplus-value' must replace the more abstract notion of 'dichotomy': the model splits into two submodels. The first, which we have tried to explain within the framework of games theory, would fix the rate of surplus-value; the second, re-establishing the traditional mechanisms of competition, would, if the rate of surplus-value is given, make possible the calculation of all the revenue, price and quantity variables. This characteristic of dichotomy is very much in the classical tradition: for Ricardo, for example, the calculation of ground rent must precede the calculation of salaries and profit; and in the monetary field, the absolute level of prices is determined independently of other magnitudes. But, as in Ricardo's case, dichotomy is not the consequence of a scientifically rigorous treatment of an overall model in which all the 'facets' of the economic agents' behaviour was simultaneously taken into consideration.

It was Walras, using mathematical models, who was the pioneer of 'interdependence', with its unified models, in which all the elements were linked to one another. In such models, the different components making up revenue all depend upon each other, and on the structural characteristics of the economy – natural wealth, production techniques, consumer preferences, etc. Such an analysis gained in power, but became less instrumental. It was no doubt a transition through which the economic sciences had to pass in order to achieve the progress they were later to record.

Part III

THE DEVELOPMENT OF THE CAPITALIST ECONOMY ACCORDING TO MARX

Introduction

Its existence denied by the Labour Theory of Value but subsequently affirmed by the theory of exploitation, profit is set in motion in Marx's analysis of the development of the capitalist economic system. As is only to be expected, according to Marx, profit is fated to disappear, caught between these two opposing concepts. However, this third phase is not a mere repetition of the first, but the consequence of the passing of the existing economic system to a later stage of evolution. Chapter 11 will be devoted to unravelling the tangled web of causal relationships that, according to Marx, thus condemn capitalism to extinction.

Das Kapital is a sea of facts and incomplete observations, of unfounded statements and undemonstrated truths which are mercilessly repeated, but now and again small 'islands' of theory emerge, which can quite easily be described with the aid of mathematical models. The *Law of the Falling Tendency of the Rate of Profit* is obviously the most important of these, and in Chapter 13 its significance, and also its weaknesses, will be assessed.

Before that, however, in Chapter 12, dealing with the *General Law of Capitalist Accumulation*, we shall consider how the capitalist class, by increasing its productive capacity and efficiency and by creating an 'industrial reserve army', strives to put off the dreaded day of its disappearance.

Finally, Chapter 14 will present an attempt to see what lies behind Marx's rather enigmatic ideas of 'extended reproduction', and show that they are far closer to the precise miniatures of our present-day linear growth models than the ambitious large-scale frescoes of social dynamics so dear to thinkers of the last century.

11 A Short Description of the Theory of Capitalist Development

11.1 Historical time and economic time

Physical time is a purely formal 'linear container', along which successive changes are recorded, such recording being carried out by reference to changes in some simple system, such as the movement of the stars, stellar oscillations, the movements of a pendulum, etc.

In the realms of pure economics time also passes at regular speeds, and we saw earlier that, if no account is taken of the uneven and intertwined rhythms of the phenomena of production and consumption, we could reduce economic time to physical time. As shown in Section 6.5, this reduction was forced upon Marx, just as it is necessary to the economist of today.

Running parallel with this classical conception of the regular evolution of economic phenomena, based upon the division of time into abstract and arbitrary periods, we find, not so much in *Das Kapital* as in Marx's other writings, an attempt to think out the laws governing the development of the social and cultural 'totality' of a given society, even of all humanity; in short, to define the laws of history. Such an objective is much more ambitious and grandiose than what is usually attempted by the theoretician of growth and economic fluctuations, whose task is limited to finding means of representing how the different economic variables are organised in time, given certain initial circumstances and structural characteristics. The results of his research therefore cover only a very small part of the 'totality', but can theoretically be applied to any historical situation, any society, without exception, provided that its economic structures satisfy the hypotheses formulated at the beginning of the theoretical study. The economic sciences and their dynamic branch are therefore partial and a-historical.

It surely cannot be denied today that Marx failed in his attempt. Like many before him, he succumbed, at the dawn of a new science, to the temptation to discover the philosopher's stone and construct a single all-embracing theoretical system. In 1867, it was as bold as today it is presumptuous to undertake a synthesis of human sciences that were still in their infancy. Since, however, man does not live by bread alone, the great Marxist vision of history, and the prophecies made by the Master in the name of the science of historical development, continue to arouse the enthusiasm of layman and intellectual alike.

Be that as it may, what concerns us here about Marx's theory of history is not so much its perennial topicality as its very close relationship with economic theory. This is because, within the 'totality', Marx considers the economic sphere to be the most important, regarding other aspects as being largely conditioned by the manner in which the satisfaction of social needs is satisfied, or, as Marx puts it, by the 'relationship between production and distribution' that is their consequence. This is the reason why Marx bases his division of historical time on the dominant *modes of production* that succeed each other. *The primacy of the economic sphere* over the others is clearly expressed in various parts of the work; for example: 'To the extent that it seizes control of social production, the technique and social organisation of the labour-process are revolutionised and with them the economico-historical type of society' (II, 57).

When applied to the modern and contemporary periods, Marx's theory of history, seen as a theory of capitalist development, enables us to link together logically various items of economic analysis which appear in *Das Kapital* as quite unrelated.

This theory of capitalist development therefore follows the second principle of the Marxian theory of history (the first being the primacy accorded to economic phenomena), viz. the strict determinism according to which history unfolds. Each period, and therefore each mode of production, contains within itself the seeds of its own destruction, and the means of passing on to a later period, to a superior mode of production. Thus: 'Capitalist production begets, with the inexorability of a law of Nature its own negation' (I, 715). In the same way, the capitalist system will inevitably give rise to a communist society: 'The economic structure of capitalistic society has grown out of the economic structure of feudal society. The dissolution of the latter sets free the elements of the former' (I, 168).

Marx has therefore sought to create a closed model of capitalism, i.e., one where all the variables are endogenous and react upon each other: the capitalist economy, like our stellar and planetary systems, moves forward blindly and inevitably along a road marked out for all eternity. Thus for example, in contradistinction to the theories of the neoclassical economists, nearly all of whom consider technical progress, the accumulation of capital and the growth of the social product to be merely contingent phenomena, these factors are, in Marx's view, induced characteristics, resulting necessarily from the warring presence of the different forces of the economic system. Capitalism is condemned to proliferate, but even as its power increases it is undermined by the endemic ills of excessive centralisation of capital – under-employment, economic crises – which will bring about its overthrow. The age of capitalism will finish in a dying spasm, opening the way to the millenium of the classless society.

Quite apart from the question of whether history has verified these theories, it must be said that at the purely logical level the economic foundations on which these prophecies are built are, to say the least, rather vague and incoherent. For Marxists, the neoclassical theory of technical progress and economic growth is greatly marred by serious shortcomings, but these are perhaps only the signs of an entirely praiseworthy attitude of scientific humulity.

However, before subjecting Marx's theories on this point to detailed criticism, we shall devote the rest of the present chapter to a consideration of their main characteristics.

11.2 Induced technical progress

Competition is what forces the capitalist to improve his technique of production; he will only rarely, of course, himself be an inventor of genius or a brilliant engineer, but his pressing need for new tools and methods stimulates scientific production. Thus the widely held view that scientific discoveries are made by chance, or independently, and are then applied to industry, must be reconsidered. The scientist is also in the pay of the capitalist.

When the capitalist mode of production takes over a given sector, or society, it adopts the techniques that are being used at that moment in that field. But it is implacably impelled to transform and modernise them. This is how Marx describes the process that renders the introduction of new production techniques inevitable:

> Let us suppose that each article costs, on an average, one shilling and represents two hours of social labour ... under the altered mode of production it costs only ninepence and contains only $1\frac{1}{2}$ hours' labour. The real value of a commodity is, however, not in its individual value but its social value; that is to say, the real value is not measured by the labour-time that the article in each individual case costs the producer, but by the labour-time socially required for its production .... He the capitalist will therefore sell them above their individual value but below their social value, say, at tenpence each. By this means he will squeeze an extra surplus-value of one penny out of each .... Thus ... there is a motive for each capitalist to cheapen his commodities by increasing the productiveness of labour. [I, 302]

But this situation can only be temporary:

> This extra surplus-value vanishes as soon as the new mode of production has become general, and has consequently caused the difference between the individual value of the cheapened commodity to vanish. [I, 301]

This ceaseless quest for 'extra surplus-value' benefits the capitalist class overall when the increase in productivity affects, directly or indirectly, those branches of industry producing consumer goods for the working class. The result is indeed a fall in the value of labour, and a consequent increase in the rate of surplus-value. In Marx's words, there is 'production of relative surplus-value' (cf. Section 8.4 for a definition of this term in opposition to 'absolute surplus-value'). If the individual interests of the capitalist and those of his class come together,

> the object of the development of the productiveness of all labour, within the limits of capitalist production, is to shorten that part of the working day, during which the workman must labour for his own benefit, and by that very shortening to lengthen the other part of the day, during which he is at liberty to work gratis for the capitalist. [I, 304]

In the above extracts it can be seen that Marx identifies technical progress and increased productivity, and we find little mention of the neoclassical economists' distinctions about the effect on technical progress of such things as the point of impact of the new technology, human labour, means of production or other non-reproducible factors. Marx is, of course, quite free to neglect these difficult points in his own world, where the Labour Theory of Value is valid, i.e., where the only commodity that deserves to be economised is labour. He is perfectly correct, if there is no rate of interest, in declaring that the social division of labour means that each gain in productivity in the sector of the means of production is reflected without distortion in the costs of the branches utilising such means of production:

> The development of the productive power of labour in any one line of production, for instance in the production of iron, coal, machinery, building, etc., ... appears to be the premise for reduction of the value, and consequently of the cost, of means of production in other lines of industry, for instance in the textile industry, or in agriculture. [III, 59–60]

Marx also notes that an increase in productivity most often takes place when there is an increase in the scale of production. The industrialist – and this is where he differs from the craftsmen and guild members of earlier ages – coordinates and brings under his control the labour of a large number of workers; it is through their scientifically organised co-operation that gains in productivity are achieved (cf. Book I, Chapter XIII). In Chapters XIV and XV of that Book, Marx describes how the capitalist system transformed the production plant; instead of a simple artisan's bench there is now a factory; instead of independent craftsmen, there are now workmen who carry out a skill – or part of a skill – on behalf of a common master. With the harnessing of sources of energy, especially steam, the tool now becomes a machine, acquires a life of its own, and so much power that the worker is reduced to the state of being a mere adjunct of it. The age is reached of 'mechanism and large-scale industry'.

11.3 Induced technical progress (continued)

Thus competition between capitalists is a powerful factor in the transformation and perfecting of the techniques of production. And so is competition between capitalist and worker.

In a dynamic process, if it is desired that strict complementarity of inputs be maintained, all the quantities used must be fed in regularly. In particular, too rapid a growth of stocks of the means of production compared with the availability of labour leads to increased competition among capitalists on the labour market, leading in turn to an overall increase in salaries at the expense of the surplus-value. The only remedy is to increase productivity by technical innovation, a step that, by making many workers unemployed, will increase the size of 'the industrial reserve army'. The permanent existence of a pool of unemployed – and it is difficult to know whether this is the result of structural or of technological circumstances – is absolutely essential for the uninterrupted creation of surplus-value. For Marx, this of course implies that situations providing full employment are quite exceptional in an economic world characterised by technological change; under-employment is the normal situation in capitalist economies.

This tendency to produce 'relative overpopulation' in a capitalist society is called by Marx '*the General Law of Capitalist Accumulation*', and a formalised version of it will be presented in the following chapter. What is of interest to us here is the causal relationship postulated by this law between technical progress and the capitalist's desire to reduce the tension on the labour market.

11.4 Induced growth

In reality, the word 'growth' covers two types of phenomenon, which will be called here 'extensive growth' and 'intensive growth'. The first expression relates to the continuous infiltration into different sectors of production of the capitalist mode of production, i.e., the elimination by the capitalist of direct producers, small-scale employers or craftsmen. The second term relates to the increase in the quantity of goods produced and the means of production utilised in a given branch of the capitalist economy. In Marx's view, 'each self-contained fraction of social capital' tends inevitably to increase, by the transformation of the surplus-value it creates into capital (Book I, Chapter XXIV). Such an increase may be achieved by production on a larger scale in the same sphere of activity as before (intensive growth); or else, the surplus-value may be separated from the original capital that created it and become an independent capital, usually in a sector as yet undeveloped (extensive growth). This description of the two types of growth is really nothing more than the description of the history of capitalist development. Marx devotes the whole of the Eighth Section of

Book I (Chapter XXVI–XXXIII) to extensive growth: using the phrase 'primitive accumulation', he endeavours to define the circumstances in which the first capital and the first groups of 'free' workers, i.e., workers separated from their means of production, appeared, and to show the necessary interrelationships between agriculture and industry at the beginning of the capitalist period, the importance of the role of the State, etc. At the time of writing *Das Kapital* he sees the phase of extensive growth as having come to an end, and merely gives an historical account. As for intensive growth, all he does is propose a theory.

This tendency for each self-contained fraction of capital to increase by the incorporation of surplus-value is made inevitable by competition:

> The development of capitalist production makes it constantly necessary to keep increasing the amount of capital laid out in a given industrial undertaking, and competition causes the immanent laws of capitalist production to be felt by each individual capitalist, as external coercive laws. It compels him to keep constantly extending his capital, in order to preserve it, but extend it he cannot, except by means of progressive accumulation' (I, 555)

Here too, the usually accepted causal sequence is reversed. It is not savings, and its corollary investment, that engender growth: it is growth, induced by competition, that forces the capitalist to invest and therefore to save. But how does competition operate, that it should produce such a result? For the study of equilibria in the Marxian sense showed that a positive surplus-value can indeed be permanently created in a static system, but that it is totally consumed by the capitalist class. Does this then mean that Marx, calling into question the whole basis of his own theory of surplus value, admits that fear of a progressive decrease in profits forces capitalists to increase the volume of their production? But we know that if they did such a thing they would very soon come up against the limited working population, and thus see their profits disappear in increased salaries.

The induced, endogenous and inevitable character of growth comes to light therefore only after a more complex analysis, which may be reconstructed as follows. The break-up of the capitalists' unstable coalition occurs initially not in the sphere of production, but in the sphere of technical progress, because some independent producers, ever on the lookout for extra surplus-value, make a technical breakthrough. All the capitalists working in the same branch are obliged to follow suit and adopt the new technique. This innovation is based upon a new stock of means of production working at a superior level. Such investments create an increased demand for labour, which threatens to endanger the creation of surplus-value, because of the ensuing increases in salaries. This only makes the capitalists all the more determined to adopt the new techniques, which will enable them to economise their use of labour in accordance with the General Law of Capitalist Accumulation. Thanks to these even more capitalistic techniques, the rate of profit is supposed to decline – Marx's Law of the Falling Tendency of the Rate of Profit. The desire to maintain their total profit at its previous level once more leads the capitalists to produce on a larger scale.

Growth and technical progress are therefore two inseparable phenomena which reinforce each other in a series of cumulative processes. However, in the course of its upward movement capitalist development wears itself out. It contains within itself the causes of its own decline, and these causes we will now consider.

11.5 Factors producing instability and the degeneration of capitalism

The capitalist mode of production finds that one of its fundamental characteristics, competition, is weakened by the increasing 'centralisation' of capital; i.e., 'the merging of a greater number of capitals into a lesser number' (I, 586). This centralisation has three causes.

1. 'The battle of competition is fought by the cheapening of commodities. The cheapening of commodities depends, *ceteris paribus*, on the productiveness of labour, and this again on the scale of production. Therefore the larger capitals beat the smaller' (I, 586–7).
2. 'With the development of the capitalist mode of production, there is an increase in the minimum amount of individual capital necessary to carry on a business under normal conditions' (I, 587).
3. 'With capitalist production an altogether new force comes into play – the credit system – which soon becomes a new and terrible weapon in the battle for competition ... and is finally transformed

into an enormous social mechanism for the centralisation of capitals' (I, 587).

These few pages devoted to centralisation pre-figure contemporary Marxist theories about monopoly and state capitalism: 'In a given society the limit of centralisation would be reached only when the entire social capital was united in the hands of either a single capitalist, or a single capitalist company' (I, 588).

The centralisation of capital is not the only reason for the degeneration of competitive capitalism. A very powerful contributory factor is the expansion and contraction of the scale of production, alternating at an ever-increasing speed.

Das Kapital does not offer a single coherent theory of economic cycles; Marx sometimes sees them as a 'mechanical necessity' (I, 593), sometimes as the result of 'commercial vicissitudes' (I, 592), i.e., of over-production in certain areas, or even as the consequences of 'violent fluctuations of price ... in consequence of changing yields' (III, 88). The most novel of Marx's explanations for its time, and the one to which most attention was paid, is probably that which brings monetary factors into play. Speaking of certain joint-stock companies, Marx writes: 'Any disturbance in the money market will therefore paralyse such companies, whilst those companies will create disturbances in the money markets' (II, 420). And there are times when Marx sounds distinctly like a predecessor of Keynes – did not the author of *A General Theory* salute the author of *Das Kapital* as an illustrious forerunner? For example, Marx says:

> The conditions of direct exploitation of the workers and those of the realisation of surplus-value are not identical. They are separated logically, as well as by time and space. The first are only limited by the productive power of society, the last by the proportional relations of the various lines of production, and by the consuming power of society. [II, 191]

Is not this, though clumsily expressed, the principle of effective demand? And Marx vaguely perceives the possibility of the simultaneous under-employment of all the factors of production: 'On this self-contradictory basis it is no contradiction at all that there should be an excess of capital simultaneously with an excess of population' (III, 191).

The 'break-down', the destruction of the capitalist mode of production and its overthrow by socialism, will put an end to all these evils. But how we shall realise when the last crisis is upon us, and how much time will be left before the final apocalyptic end of capitalism, are two points on which Marx remains completely silent – thereby making his prophecy impossible to disprove, but also setting serious problems for generations of Marxists, and being the source of profound dissension among them.

11.6 'Islands' of theory which can be formalised

In reality, the Marxian theory of capitalist development, which we have briefly summarised, is much more an artist's fresco, or an epic poem, than a theory. And the language clothing it is the language of struggle, battle and war. This was also true of the theory of exploitation, but at least that theory could be fitted, even if imperfectly, into the framework of games theory (cf. Sections 8.4 and 8.5); whereas, so complex is the theory of capitalist development, and so imprecisely formulated, that it is surely condemned to remain in metaphorical form.

The difficulties met in formalising the theory are due to the extreme malleability of all those elements generally considered as being structural characteristics (techniques of production, consumption and saving patterns, etc.), to the vast number of interdependences, actions and reactions postulated between the variables, and to the fact that the temporal framework is abandoned. The Marxian dynamic and the pure economy can come together only at one or two points. Two pieces of theory can be formalised, bearing in mind the economic instruments available to us: these are the General Law of Capitalist Accumulation, and the Law of the Falling Tendency of the Rate of Profit, to be discussed in Chapters 12 and 13. A third subject, extended reproduction, can easily be discussed in mathematical terms, as Marx himself tried to do, and this will be the theme of Chapter 14.

12 The General Law of Capitalist Accumulation

12.1 The enunciation and significance of the law

The content of this law has already been indicated (cf. Section 11.3). It states that capitalists, by adopting techniques that achieve greater productivity, avoid the shrinking of the working-class population until it becomes too small for the needs of capital. A certain slackness on the labour market, or, to put it more bluntly, the existence of unemployment, of a 'relative over-population' or of 'an industrial reserve army', to use some of Marx's own expressions, is a factor favourable to the formation of a surplus-value, and to the pursuit of accumulation.

In neoclassical terms, the reproducible means of production are remunerated only if they are 'scarce', i.e., if their marginal productivity is strictly positive. If there is strict complementarity between means of production and labour, this productivity remains positive provided there is a surplus of labour, as it is clearly shown by the production diagram in Figure 12.1. By means of technical progress, the capitalist will concentrate all his efforts on maintaining the scarcity of the means of production, and hence on continuing to create a surplus-value.

Oddly enough, the General Law of Capitalist Accumulation is not completely at odds with the neoclassical theories on capital and interest. Both accept that the means of production receive a remuneration only as long as they are scarce (cf. the right-hand half Mx of the figure), disagreement arising when this is not so, when the means of production and labour exist in adequate proportions (point M of the figure); in such a case surplus-value is still derived, in Marx's view, from the exploitation of the working class, whereas the neoclassicists deny such a possibility. This was, of course, the subject of the discussion that occupied the whole of Part II of the present work.

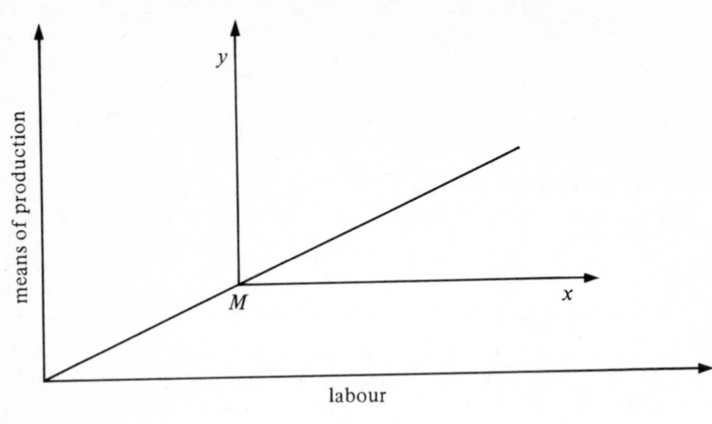

FIGURE 12.1

12.2 General hypotheses

A formalised presentation will first be given of the theoretical framework within which the Law of General Accumulation is set: this will enable us to quantify the relationships that must be observed by the different rates and parameters of behaviour if the capitalist is to obtain regular growth at the rate he desires. The model adopted has three new features compared with those used so far:

1. time is a continuous parameter varying from 0 to $+\infty$;
2. the means of production are of infinite duration; this hypothesis will be abandoned in Section 13.3;
3. the economy consists of only one sector, therefore of only one commodity (apart from labour), which is at the same time a means of production and a consumer commodity.

These hypotheses do not betray the spirit of Book I, Chapter XXV, where the General Law of Capital Accumulation is set out, first because in that chapter Marx for once seems willing to allow the substitution of fixed capital by constant capital (see I, 592, note referring to Jahn Barton); and second because, from the outset, Marx emphasises the macroeconomic nature of the research being undertaken:

> The many individual capitals invested in a particular branch of production have, one with another, more or less different compositions. The

average of their individual compositions gives us the composition of the total capital in this branch of production. Lastly, the average of these averages, in all branches of production, gives us the composition of the total social capital of a country, and with this alone are we, in the last resort, concerned in the following investigation. [I, 574–5]

The other hypotheses of the model will already be familiar to the reader. They are recapitulated below, together with the necessary commentaries.

A state of the economy during the interval of time $(t, t + dt)$ is characterised by:

$Q(t)\,dt$: the flow of the commodity produced between t and $t + dt$
$K(t)$: existing stocks of means of production (fixed capital) at moment t
$N(t)$: the size of the working class at moment t
$W(t)$: the number of workers employed
$\lambda(t)\,dt$: the average working-class consumption per head, between moments t and $t + dt$
$s(t)\,dt$: wages, expressed in physical unities, distributed between moments t and $t + dt$

In situations where there is under-employment, the only ones being considered here, the final output is proportional to the stock of capital, which is the only limiting factor:

$$Q(t) = m \cdot K(t). \qquad (58)$$

The amount of labour necessary for achieving this production is strictly dependent on the stock of capital, and hence on the volume of production. This amount of labour can be calculated from the overall employment coefficient v:

$$W(t) = v \cdot Q(t). \qquad (59)$$

The *workers* consume all their revenue, which as usual is the minimum necessary for the reproduction of the work-force. In *Das Kapital* there is a slight ambiguity between two possible hypotheses:

– real wages can be assumed to be constant ($s(t) = s$, whatever the value of t);
– average *per capita* consumption can be assumed to be constant ($\lambda(t) = \lambda$, whatever the value of t).

Since in the preceding chapters the second of these hypotheses has been assumed, we shall continue to do so here; but $s(t)$ and $\lambda(t)$ are constantly linked by

$$s(t) \cdot W(t) = \lambda(t) \cdot N(t). \tag{60}$$

The result is that, if the work-force employed grows less quickly than the total population – and this is the case below – then real wages must increase, if our hypothesis is to retain its coherence.

The working population grows at a constant rate, assumed to be exogenous:

$$N(t) = N_0 \cdot e^{\nu t}. \tag{61}$$

What this equation shows is Marx's refusal to associate demographic variables with economic variables, and hence to refuse to follow the classical economist in a discussion of these problems. It is in this same Chapter XXV of Book I that Marx's hostility to the teachings of the prophets of the principles of population is seen at its most virulent. This point has already been considered at length (Section 2.5). Equation (61) would seem to apply only to natural growth of the population. However, we shall assume that this formula also embraces the other possibilities of increasing the numbers of the working class, mentioned by Marx:

1. 'progressive expropriation of the direct or indirect producers' (II, 171);
2. the 'expropriation of the smaller capitalists by the movement towards centralisation of capital' (III, 189).

The working population, i.e., capable of working, $\bar{W}(t)$, is a constant fraction of the overall population, and therefore grows at the same rate as it:

$$\bar{W}(t) = \bar{W}_0 \cdot e^{\nu t}. \tag{62}$$

Out of its surplus-value, *the capitalist class* re-invests a fraction α, which for simplicity we shall assume to be constant. We shall also assume (although it takes us away somewhat from the text of *Das Kapital*) that this fraction is re-invested solely in fixed capital. This means that wages and any increase in wages are immediately paid in kind out of production and are instantly consumed, instead of being paid out by the capitalists in the form of variable capital. This hypothesis has only very minor influence on the results given by this model.

12.3 The solution of the model

The behaviour of the capitalists in regard to savings provides us with the differential equation governing the working of the system:

$$\text{Investment} = \text{Rate of Savings} \times \text{Surplus-value}$$

$$K(t+dt) - K(t) = \alpha\{Q(t)\,dt - \lambda \cdot N(t)\,dt\}$$

$$\frac{dK(t)}{dt} = \alpha\{Q(t) - \lambda \cdot N(t)\}$$

or again, by use of the relationships (58) and (61),

$$\frac{dK(t)}{dt} = \alpha\{mK(t) - \lambda N_0 \cdot e^{vt}\}. \tag{63}$$

The solution $K(t)$ for this equation must remain positive, as must its derivative $dK(t)/dt$, since the second half of equation (63) proportional to surplus-value cannot fall to zero.

The results of the calculation are summarised below. The kind of development noted will depend on the initial conditions and the values of the different parameters:

Case I $\alpha m < v$.

The rate of growth of production (equal by definition to the production of αm) is lower than the rate of growth of the population. All further developments can only lead to a degradation of the system, and within a more or less short space of time the capitalist class is eliminated, since surplus-value disappears.

Case Ia $\lambda N_0 > Q_0$, *i.e.*, $(SV)_0 < 0$.

From the very beginning it is impossible to create any surplus-value, so the system cannot even begin to function (Figure 12.2).

Case Ib $\lambda N_0 < Q_0$, *i.e.*, $(SV)_0 > 0$.

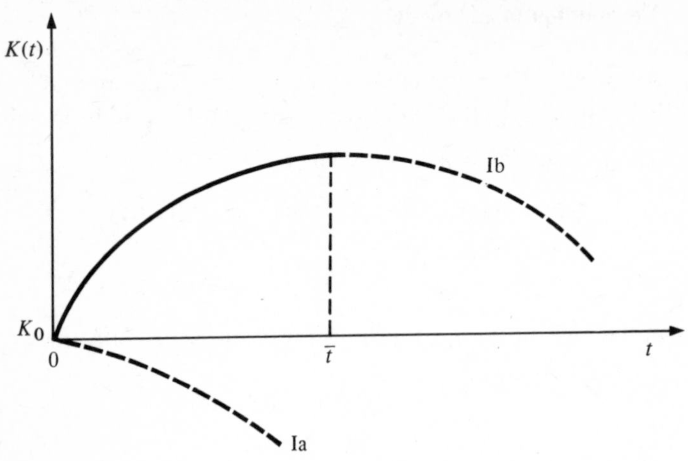

FIGURE 12.2 *Case I: $\alpha m < v$.*

Surplus-value is reduced to nothing at moment

$$\bar{t} = -\frac{1}{v - \alpha m} \cdot \log \frac{v}{\alpha m} \cdot \frac{\alpha \lambda N_0}{K_0 v - \alpha (SV)_0}.$$

Between 0 and $\bar{t}$, capital develops according to

$$K(t) = -\frac{\alpha \lambda N_0}{v - \alpha m} e^{vt} \left\{ 1 - \frac{K_0 v - \alpha (SV)_0}{\alpha \lambda N_0} e^{-(v - \alpha m)t} \right\}. \quad (64)$$

Case II $\alpha m > v$

Here the rate of growth of production exceeds the rate of growth of the population. But this is not sufficient to ensure an expansion of the economy. It may be, for example, that initially the rate of growth of capital is insufficient to counter-balance the rate of growth of the population, and the economy cannot take off (see Figure 12.3).

Case IIa $\lambda N_0 > Q_0$, *i.e.*, $(SV)_0 < 0$.

Surplus-value cannot be formed from the beginning. There is net disinvestment.

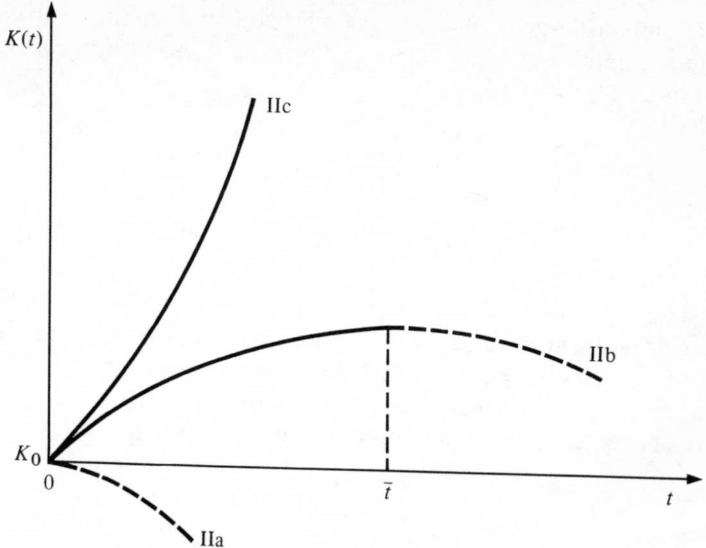

FIGURE 12.3 *Case II*: $\alpha m > v$.

Case IIb $\lambda N_0 < Q_0$, *i.e.*, $(SV)_0 > 0$
and $\alpha(Q_0 - \lambda N_0) < vK_0$, *i.e.*, $\alpha(SV)_0 < vK_0$.

Here, it is true, there is positive surplus-value, but capitalist savings are lower than 'demographic investment', i.e., than the investment considered necessary to ensure a constant standard of living for a population that is expanding at the rate v. This situation resembles that described in Case Ib. The moment at which surplus-value is reduced to nothing is given by:

$$\bar{t} = \frac{1}{\alpha m - v} \cdot \log \frac{v}{\alpha m} \cdot \frac{\alpha \lambda N_0}{K_0 v - \alpha(SV)_0}.$$

For $0 \leq t \leq t$:

$$K(t) = -\frac{K_0 v - \alpha(SV)_0}{\alpha m - v} \cdot e^{\alpha m t} \times \left\{1 - \frac{\alpha \lambda N_0}{K_0 v - \alpha(SV)_0}\, e^{-(\alpha m - v)t}\right\} \tag{64a}$$

Case IIc $\lambda N_0 < Q_0$, i.e., $(SV)_0 > 0$
and $\alpha(Q_0 - \lambda N_0) > vK_0$, i.e., $\alpha(SV)_0 > vK_0$.

The capitalist regime can now take off. And the asymptotic growth rate of capital is precisely the rate of growth of production αm.

For all $t \geq 0$:

$$K(t) = \frac{\alpha(SV)_0 - vK_0}{\alpha m - v} \cdot e^{\alpha mt} \times \left\{1 + \frac{\alpha\lambda N_0}{\alpha(SV)_0 - vK_0} e^{-(\alpha m - v)t}\right\} \qquad (64b)$$

Since cases where one of the strict inequalities indicated above may be replaced by an equality are highly improbable and therefore of no real importance, we shall not examine them here. In the following pages we shall concentrate upon Case IIc, where the economy enters upon a period of indefinite expansion.

12.4 The creation of an industrial reserve army

For the developments described above to occur without causing a *per capita* increase in consumption which would jeopardise the creation of surplus value, care must be taken to ensure that the amount of labour necessary to set capital in motion is at all times less than the amount of labour available. In other words, that the ratio of workers actually employed to the numbers of workers available is less than 1.

In the case of an expanding economy (Case IIc above), this ratio is expressed as:

$$w(t) = \frac{W(t)}{\bar{W}(t)} \qquad (65)$$

$$w(t) = w_0 \cdot \frac{\{\alpha(SV)_0/K_0\} - v}{\alpha m - v} \cdot e^{(\alpha m - v)t} \times \left\{1 + \frac{\alpha\lambda N_0}{\alpha(SV)_0 - vK_0} e^{-(\alpha m - v)t}\right\}$$

obtained by combining (58), (59), (62) and (64b).

It is quite clear that $w(t)$ is greater than w_0 for every value of t, and tends asymptotically towards infinity. The economy will before long find itself in a situation of over-employment, with all the dire consequences for surplus-value that such a state implies.

Using less detailed methods, Marx arrives at the same conclusions:

> If we suppose that the composition of capital also remains constant ... then the demand for labour ... clearly increases in the same proportion as the capital. [I, 575]
>
> For since in each year more labourers are employed than in its predecessor, sooner or later a point must be reached, at which the requirements of accumulation begin to surpass the customary supply of labour. [I, 575]

Or, in a more stereotyped form: 'Accumulation of capital is, therefore, increase of the proletariat' (I, 576).

How can the capitalist extricate himself from this difficult situation?

He can of course moderate his passion for accumulation, by letting the stock of capital increase only at a rate at most equal to the rate of increase of the available working population (reduction of the rate of saving α and, *ipso facto*, of the rate of growth αm). Thus Marx writes:

> Accumulation slackens in consequence of the rise in the price of labour, because the stimulus of gain is blunted. The rate of accumulation lessens; but with its lessening, the primary cause of that lessening vanishes, i.e., the disproportion between capital and exploitable labour-power. [I, 580]

Or again:

> If the quantity of unpaid labour supplied by the working-class, and accumulated by the capitalist class, increases so rapidly that its conversion into capital requires an extraordinary addition of paid labour, then wages rise and, all other circumstances remaining equal, the unpaid labour diminishes in proportion. But as soon as this diminution touches the point at which the surplus-labour that nourishes capital is no longer supplied in normal quantity, a reaction sets in: a smaller part of revenue is capitalised, accumulation lags, and the movement of rise in wages receives a check. [I, 581–2]

Such prudence is probably inconsistent with the psychology of the capitalist, which is why Marx dwells much more on the capitalist's alternative solution, increasing productivity to reduce his demand for labour. New techniques are introduced, says Marx, in successive waves, and mainly when the economic cycle is at a high point:

> But at the same time, as the number of workers attracted by capital reaches its maximum, goods become so abundant that the slightest

obstacle to their commercialisation prevents the social machine from functioning; capital's rejection of labour takes place suddenly, on a huge scale, and in a brutally violent fashion; and this very disarray forces the capitalist into extreme measures to economise on labour. [I, 590]

To illustrate this, but without complicating unduly the mathematical treatment, we shall postulate that the coefficient of overall labour decreases regularly, and not by fits and starts, at a rate η, which will be assumed to be independent of the rate of accumulation of capital:

$$v(t) = v_0 e^{-\eta t}. \tag{66}$$

The proportion of the working class actually employed, $w(t)$, and the rate of growth of that proportion $(1/w) \cdot (dw/dt)$, are given by

$$w(t) = w_0 \cdot \frac{\alpha(SV)_0/K_0 - v}{\alpha m - v} e^{(\alpha m - v - \eta)t} \left\{ 1 + \frac{\alpha\lambda N_0}{\alpha(SV)_0 - K_0 v} e^{-(\alpha m - v)t} \right\} \tag{67}$$

$$\frac{1}{w} \cdot \frac{dw}{dt} = (\alpha m - v - \eta) - \frac{H(\alpha m - v)}{1 + He^{-(\alpha m - v)t}} \tag{68}$$

where

$$H = \frac{\alpha\lambda N_0}{\alpha(SV)_0 - vK_0}.$$

This latter rate varies in constant fashion from $\{\alpha(SV)_0/K_0 - v - \eta\}$ to $\{\alpha m - v - \eta\}$. If full employment occurs at the beginning of the period ($w_0 = 1$), the capitalists will achieve regular growth only if $w(t)$ decreases constantly. The rate of growth at w_0 and the asymptotic rate of growth must both be negative. The conditions necessary for a steady rate of growth are therefore:

$$\begin{gathered} (SV)_0 > 0 \\ vK_0 < \alpha(SV)_0 < (v + \eta)K_0 \\ v < \alpha m < v + \eta \end{gathered} \tag{69}$$

which is expressed as follows.

1. At moment w_0 there must be a rate of saving somewhere between *demographic investment* and *full-employment investment* (i.e., the investment exactly necessary for the maintenance of full employment).

2. The internal rate of growth must exceed the rate of growth of the population by an amount at most equal to the rate of growth of productivity.

Marx, whose aim in life was not exactly to help the capitalist class to achieve a steady rate of growth, takes good care not to mention these conditions, and the result of the model to which he calls attention is evidently the creation of unemployment ($w(t) < 1$) or, as he calls it, 'an industrial reserve army' (I, 592). Not only does unemployment reduce salaries by creating keen competition for jobs available, but it also creates a pool of labour which allows the capitalist to pick the right moment for him to invest. 'This system supplies social capital with a great force for sudden expansion, of marvellous elasticity' (I, 592).

12.5 Technical progress and the unions' struggles

This model once more raises those doubts about the unchanging level of the working class's standard of living, and its maintenance at mere subsistence level, which occupied the central place in the arguments put forward in Part II.

If l denotes the rate of improvement of the standard of living, whether obtained by union efforts or by any other means, it can easily be seen that the growth conditions of (69) must be replaced by

$$\begin{gathered} (SV)_0 > 0 \\ (v + l)K_0 < \alpha(SV)_0 < (v + \eta)K_0 \\ v + l < \alpha m < v + \eta. \end{gathered} \tag{70}$$

The capitalist class must therefore strive by manipulating the different rates of l, η and α to keep the economy on the rails of expansion, expressed by the limits of the inequalities (70). In particular, the rate of growth of productivity must exceed the rate of improvement in the standard of living ($\eta > 1$). Technological change thus becomes a weapon in the hands of the capitalists in the 'game', or rather 'the struggle', which brings them face to face with the working class for the fixing of wage rates.

For by creating unions the workers aim at acquiring a monopoly position in the labour market. When there is 'a regular co-operation between the employed and unemployed' (I, 599), relative over-population loses its capacity to weaken the negotiating position of each individual worker. For the capitalist the answer lies in the increasing use of fixed capital instead of labour. Bringing in new machines, laying men off, and thus momentarily breaking the solid union front are the best means of breaking the workers' wage demands. In the chapter devoted to 'The Strife Between Workmen and Machine', Marx writes:

> But machinery not only acts as a competitor who gets the better of the workman, and is constantly on the point of making him superfluous. It is also a power inimical to him, and as such capital proclaims it from the roof tops, and as such makes use of it. It is the most powerful weapon for suppressing strikes, those periodical revolts of the working class against the autocracy of capital .... It would be possible to write quite a history of the inventions made since 1830, for the sole purpose of supplying capital with weapons against the revolts of the working-class. [I, 410–11]

We have here, therefore, a further stimulant to technological progress, and a fitting companion to those already mentioned as being inherent in the capitalist mode of production (cf. Sections 11.2 and 11.3).

13 The Law of the Falling Tendency of the Rate of Profit

13.1 Marx's demonstration

The Law of the Falling Tendency of the Rate of Profit is an essential element in the Marxian theory of capitalistic development, for it is this law that, entering into conflict with capitalists' desire to maintain the amount of their profits, incites them to accumulation.

The subject of the lowering of the rate of profit has been gone into at great length by the classical economists (cf. Ricardo [16], Chapters VI and VII), and is the nightmare of the early capitalists. Marx in his turn resuscitates this terrifying spectre, and even confers upon it the status of a law (the scientific aura surrounding the law makes it all the more terrifying), providing a demonstration that is at the same time highly original and ... irrefutable. 'Simple as this law appears from the foregoing statements, all of political economy has so far tried in vain to discover it .... The economists cudgelled their brains in tortuous attempts to interpret it' (III, 166).

When applied to Ricardo's *Principles*, such a judgement is surely excessively severe, for his theory on this point is a beautifully constructed piece of logic which Marx finds it impossible to equal.

In Ricardo's opinion the lowering of the rate of profit can come about:

1. in the short term, because of a temporary increase in real wages, caused by an excess of demand on the labour market. But such a reduction cannot continue indefinitely, for, says Ricardo, 'There is nothing more certain than the principle that the number of workers must always, in the long run, be proportional to the means of paying them' ([16], 232);
2. in the long term, because of the consequences of accumulation, i.e., of the combined growth of the volume of capital invested, the population, and the scale of production. The level of real wages is

maintained at a constant level because of the phenomenon of demographic regulation described above. Decreasing yields in the area of agriculture cause ground rents to increase at the cost of profits, and the rate of profit itself to come down, until with the collapse of this source of accumulation the economy enters upon a stationary regime.

Ricardo's propositions are formulated at the end of long and rigorous argument, whereas Marx's demonstration occupies the first few lines of Chapter XIII of Book III, and is the result of a consideration of the mathematical expression of the rate of profit. Such simplicity, such brevity, are surely not a little disquieting?

$$\text{Rate of profit} = \frac{\text{Surplus-value}}{\text{Capital advanced}}$$

$$\text{Rate of profit} = \frac{\text{Surplus-value/Variable capital}}{1 + \dfrac{\text{Constant capital}}{\text{Variable capital}}}$$

$$\text{Rate of profit} = \frac{\text{Rate of surplus-value}}{1 + \text{Organic composition of capital}}$$

We have already seen the very same formula employed in Section 10.1 to denote the rate of profit of the individual firm:

$$\theta_j = \frac{h}{1 + \dfrac{\sum_{i=1}^{n} p_i a_{ij}}{\tilde{s} v_j}}$$

It is of course perfectly legitimate for Marx to extend this formula to the whole of the economy, provided that it is assumed:

1. that the economy is evolving in a dynamic fashion that may become stationary; this assumption is necessary to give substance to the phrase 'social capital' (which would be reduced to nil in an aggregate static economy);
2. that the constant and variable fractions of capital are evaluated by means of the system of production prices, which ensure (by construction) that the rates of profit of different branches are equal.

With the help of the mathematical expressions of Chapter 10, the following equation for the average rate of profit could be obtained, derived from formulae (52), (53), (54):

$$\theta = \frac{h}{1 + \dfrac{\bar{p}'Ax}{\bar{s}v'x}}. \tag{71}$$

The demonstration is based on two premises:

1. that the organic composition of capital (which, it should not be forgotten, is a value-composition) increases;
2. that the rate of surplus-value h is constant.

The conclusion is then inevitable: the rate of profit decreases. Marx expresses the law in these terms:

> The same rate of surplus-value, with the same rate of exploitation, would express itself in a falling rate of profit, because the material growth of the constant capital, and consequently of total capital, implies their growth in value, although not in the same proportion. [III, 164]

We should therefore concentrate our attention not on the deduction, which is perfectly logical, but on the premises.

13.2 Marx's errors

First, what causes the increase in the value-composition of the social capital? Search as one will, no satisfactory answer to this question can be found in *Das Kapital.*

When it comes to using this fact in demonstrating the validity of the Law of the Falling Tendency of the Rate of Profit, Marx merely writes:

> *Now we have seen** that it is one of the laws of capitalist production that its development carries with it a relative decrease of variable as compared with constant capital and consequently as compared to the total capital, which it sets in motion. [III, 165]

Elsewhere he writes:

> ... because *we know** that the growth of capital involves a change in the constitution of its value and that as this change progresses the value of *MP* increases, that of *L* always decreasing relatively and often absolutely. [II, 84]

* Italics added.

Or again:

> This law of the progressive increase in constant capital, in proportion to the variable, is confirmed at every step (*as already shown**) by the comparative analysis of the prices of commodities, whether we compare different economic epochs or different nations in the same epoch. The relative magnitude of the element of price, which represents the value of the means of production only, or the constant part of capital consumed, is in direct, the relative magnitude of the other element of price that pays labour (the variable part of capital) is in inverse, proportion to the advance of accumulation'. [I, 583–4]

In the chapter devoted to 'Machinery and Modern Industry' (Book I, Chapter XV), there are the glimmerings of an explanation when he writes:

> But *we have already seen that**, with every advance in the use of machinery, the constant component of capital, that part which consists of machinery, raw materials, etc., increases, while the variable component, the part laid-out in labour power, decreases. [I, 423]

Unfortunately, these ringing convictions are based upon the very slight proofs adduced when he simply writes that:

> Analysis and comparison of the prices of commodities produced by handicrafts or manufactures, and of the prices of the same commodities produced by machinery, shows generally that, in the product of machinery, the value due to the instruments of labour increases relatively, but decreases absolutely. [I, 368]

The statistics accompanying this statement do not confirm it, and even if they did we would still be deeply disappointed to see Marx build a whole theory upon such fragile statistical observations, and deduce such an important phenomenon without attempting to establish its fundamental causes.

Marx was no doubt persuaded to take up this position by the proposition – quite correct and implied by the Law of Capitalist Accumulation – that states that the volume of material capital grows at a higher rate than that of workers employed. But what is true with regard to technical composition may very well not be so when it comes to value composition. And yet he is too good a logician to commit such a simple error.

After all, he writes:

> This diminution in the variable part of capital, or the altered value-composition of the capital, however, only shows approximately the

* Italics added.

> change in the composition of its material constituents .... The reason is simply that, with the increasing productivity of labour, not only does the mass of the means of production consumed by it increase, but their value compared with their mass diminishes. Their value therefore rises absolutely, but not in proportion to their mass. [I, 584]

Marx also mentions 'the cheapening of the elements of constant capital' as one of 'the causes checking the tendency of the rate of profit to fall' (III, 184).

All these considerations leave one with the feeling that Marx was wrong in coming to such a hasty conclusion regarding the direction in which social capital's value composition was developing, and that a thorough examination of all the changes wrought by all the endogenous variables in the system, including prices, is necessary.

It is difficult to avoid reaching the same conclusion when one goes on to consider the second premise to Marx's demonstration of the validity of the law, i.e., the constant rate of surplus-value. Strictly speaking, Marx tells us that any improvements in productivity give rise to an increase in the relative surplus-value, and therefore in the rate of surplus-value, since the standard of living of the working class remains constant.

Marx is, of course, perfectly aware of this, and his embarrassment is evident in many places. Thus:

> We have seen that on average the same causes, which raise the rate of relative surplus-value, lower the mass of the employed labour-power. It is evident, however, that there will be a 'more or less' in this according to the proportion in which the opposite movements exert themselves. [III, 183]

Even more clearly:

> The rate of profit might even rise, if a rise in the rate of surplus-value were accompanied by a considerable reduction in the value of the elements of constant, and particularly of fixed, capital. [III, 179]

Hence his use of the word 'tendency', which he prudently combines with 'falling' in connection with the rate of profit. In the last analysis, there is very little difference – and that a subjective one – between a 'Law of Falling Tendency' and a 'Law of the Rising Tendency'. Which is why we shall turn to the models used previously to provide more objective evidence on which to form a judgement.

13.3 A first test of the validity of the law

We will first examine the dynamic macroeconomic model within which was established the General Law of Capital Accumulation from which the Law of the Falling Tendency of the Rate of Profit is supposed to derive.

If we follow closely the definitions in *Das Kapital* (implicit in the calculations made in Vol. III, pp. 53–5), and use the same symbols as in Chapter 12, the rate of profit is expressed:

$$\theta(t) = \frac{Q(t) - \lambda N(t)}{\delta K(t) + \lambda N(t)}$$

where part of the numerator consists of the surplus-value created per unit of time, and part of the denominator the capital utilised during the same period, while the parameter δ is the rate of depreciation of the fixed capital, inversely proportional to its useful life. Marx would have said that it defined the number of circulations of fixed capital accomplished in a given unit of time.

In our model in Chapter 12, fixed capital was given an indefinite length of life corresponding to $\delta = 0$. In the case of a rate of depreciation that is not zero, the fixed capital $K(t)$ will evolve according to a differential equation very similar to the one already solved. If we compare

$$\frac{dK(t)}{dt} + \delta K(t) = \alpha\{mK(t) - \lambda N_0 e^{vt}\} \tag{72}$$

with

$$\frac{dK(t)}{dt} = \alpha\{mK(t) - \lambda N_0 e^{vt}\} \tag{63}$$

it will be seen that the solution to the first equation can be obtained by replacing m by $\{m - (\delta/\alpha)\}$ in the solution of the second.

If the conditions for indefinite expansion are present, capital and production increase asymptotically at a greater rate than that of the population; i.e.,

$$\alpha\left(m - \frac{\delta}{\alpha}\right) > v.$$

The rate of profit therefore increases, from

$$\theta(0) = \frac{m - \lambda N_0/K_0}{\delta + \lambda N_0/K_0}$$

to m/δ. The rate of profit noted in individual firms, and which may be assumed to vary in parallel to this overall rate, does not therefore collapse in the way predicted by Marx.

A reconstruction of Marx's demonstration may be attempted within this framework. In the equation expressing the rate of profit:

$$\theta = \frac{\text{Rate of surplus-value}}{1 + \dfrac{\text{Depreciation}}{\text{Wages bill}}}$$

the value-composition of capital, $\delta K(t)/\lambda N(t)$, expressed in terms of the model's only material commodity taken as money, increases, certainly; but it must not be forgotten that logically the same must be true of the rate of surplus-value.

Yet again, it is seen that this formulation of the rate of profit leads us to no clear conclusion as to how it will evolve. Only the use of an overall model showing us the functioning of the economy will enable us to get rid of this area of uncertainty.

13.4 A second test of the validity of the law

The second test to be carried out on the Law of the Falling Tendency of the Rate of Profit comes within the framework of the model of general equilibrium described in Chapters 7, 8 and 9. Compared with the previous model it has the disadvantage of describing only a static economy (or at best a stationary one), but it does enable us to achieve a more refined analysis of the impact of technical progress on the sectorial variables – price, production, consumption, rate of profit, etc.

For Marx, the explanation of the falling of the rate of profit is the result of capitalists adopting new techniques which lead to the use of a smaller work force, since they are beset by the fear of seeing their labour needs exceed the number of workers available.

For the model we are now considering, we may legitimately hesitate regarding which hypothesis to adopt as far as the differential rates of increase in the productivity of different branches are concerned. According to whether technical progress preferentially affects sector I (the producer of means of production), sector IIa (producer of the means of subsistence) or sector IIb (producer of luxury goods), the rates of surplus-value, and therefore the rates of profit, will be different. For an appropriate range of values of rate of growth in productivity, it may be assumed that there will be a reduction in rates of profit.

Marx freely admits that the introduction of new techniques in the production of goods consumed by the working class increases the 'relative surplus-value' (cf. Sections 7.4 and 11.2 above, and Vol. I, pp. 296–304). The volume of profits increases while the rate of profit decreases. On this point he is in disagreement with Ricardo, who considers that it is precisely such gains in productivity that can delay the long-term decline in the rate of profit:

> This gravitation as it were of profits [he writes], is happily checked at repeated intervals by the improvements in machinery, connected with the production of necessaries, as well as by discoveries in the science of agriculture which enable us to relinquish a portion of labour before required, and therefore to lower the price of the prime necessary of the labourer. [[16], 91]

To enable us to decide between these two opposing theses, we can carry out an experiment in comparative statics, to which the economy could be submitted in order to study the behaviour of the rate of profit. Let us suppose that there occurs:

1. a uniform reduction, in relative value, in the coefficients of employment in all branches.

$$dv_j = -\eta v_j$$

Vectorially,

$$dv = -\eta \cdot v. \tag{73}$$

The coefficients relative to inputs other than labour are not affected by technical progress:

$$dA = 0 \text{ (zero matrix).}$$

2. an exogenous increase in the working class population:

$$dN_1 = \nu N_1 \tag{74}$$

and of the working population:

$$d\bar{W} = v\bar{W}. \tag{75}$$

The numbers making up the capitalist class are assumed to be invariable:

$$dN_2 = 0. \tag{76}$$

13.5 Results of the second test

We can see what happens when these combined stimuli act upon the different variables of the equilibrium.

Effect upon the standard of living of the working class

We concluded from our study of the Marxian theory of surplus-value that quite clearly this standard of living was maintained at an unchanging minimum standard:

$$\lambda_1 = \lambda_1^*$$

$$d\lambda_1 = 0. \tag{77}$$

Effect upon the consumption of the working class

The consumption vector, $y_i = \lambda_1 \alpha_1 N_1$, varies from

$$dy_1 = \lambda_1 \alpha_1 \, dN_1 = vy_1 \tag{78}$$

since each of the quantities consumed increases at the same rate as the population.

Effect upon the coefficient of distribution of the social product

The working class's standard of living λ_1 is given by

$$\lambda_1 = \frac{k\bar{W}}{v'(I - A)^{-1}\alpha_1 N_1}. \tag{28}$$

By differentiation, and bearing in mind the equalities already established,

$$\frac{d\bar{W}}{\bar{W}} = \frac{dN_1}{N_1} \qquad \text{and} \qquad d\lambda_1 = 0.$$

We get

$$0 = \frac{dk}{k} - \frac{d\{v'(I-A)^{-1}\alpha_1\}}{v'(I-A)^{-1}\alpha_1}$$

$$0 = \frac{dk}{k} - \frac{dv_j}{v_j}$$

whatever be the value of j. Finally, we get

$$\frac{dk}{k} = -\eta. \tag{79}$$

Effect on the rate of surplus-value

It will be recalled that the rate of surplus-value h is related to the coefficient k by

$$h = \frac{1-k}{k}.$$

Its relative variation can easily be deduced from this:

$$\frac{dh}{h} = \eta \cdot \frac{1}{1-k} \tag{80}$$

or again:

$$\frac{dh}{h} = \eta \cdot \frac{1+h}{h}. \tag{80a}$$

It can be seen from this that the increase in the rate of surplus-value depends solely upon gains in productivity.

Effect upon the standard of living of the capitalist classes

The standard of living of the capitalist classes is given by

$$\lambda_2 = \frac{(1-k)\bar{W}}{v'(I-A)^{-1}\alpha_2 N_2}. \tag{28a}$$

By differentiation, after making all calculations, we get

$$\frac{d\lambda_2}{\lambda_2} = \frac{dh}{h} + v. \tag{81}$$

The rate of improvement of the standard of living of the capitalist class is the sum of the rate of growth of surplus-value and the rate of growth of the labour force. Which is explained by the fact that the working classes are exploited even further.

Effect upon the consumption of the capitalist classes

Since $dN_2 = 0$, it is clear that

$$dy_2 = \frac{d\lambda_2}{\lambda_2} \cdot y_2$$

$$dy_2 = \left(\frac{dh}{h} + v\right) y_2. \tag{82}$$

Effect upon the production vectors

Production vector x is given by equation (29):

$$x = (I - A)^{-1}(y_1 + y_2) \tag{29}$$

where y_1 and y_2 have been transformed into

$$y_1 + dy_1 = y_1(1 + v)$$

according to (78);

$$y_2 + dy_2 = y_2\left(1 + \frac{dh}{h} + v\right)$$

according to (82). The growth of x is not homothetic, since

$$dx = vx + (I - A)^{-1}\frac{dh}{h} \cdot y_2.$$

To the extra production created by the increase in the available labour force (at the rate v), must be added that made necessary by the further demand of the capitalists, arising from the increase in the rate of surplus-value.

Effect on the system of value-prices

The price system p and wages s are related by

$$p' = sv'(I - A)^{-1}. \tag{15}$$

By differentiating this relationship we get

$$dp' = \left(\frac{ds}{s} - \eta\right)p'. \tag{83}$$

If we assume that the level of wages in normal terms (i.e., in units of account) is unchanged, prices (in units of account) will fall at a uniform rate. The behaviour of money-prices based on gold will obviously depend on productivity gains in the sector where 'money material' is reproduced (II, 473) and in the other sectors from which it derives. Our non-monetary model cannot take account of the effects of possible variations in 'the value of money' (the expression used by Marx in III, 60).

Effect on the rate of profit

It is this effect that most concerns us. Equation (71), giving the rate of profit, cannot be used because it contains endogenous price and production variables which are related to each other and also to the rate of profit. The fundamental error of Marx's demonstration is precisely the fact that he neglects these interdependent relationships.

It is therefore on equation (55) that we must base our reasoning, for in this equation the rate of profit has been isolated as being the only unknown:

$$1 + \theta = \frac{1}{k} \cdot \frac{v'(I - A)^{-1}\alpha_1}{v'\{I - (1 + \theta)A\}^{-1}\alpha_1}. \tag{55}$$

This new equilibrium corresponds to a new rate of profit o which, since the vector of employment coefficients v has become $v + dv = v(1 - \eta)$ (equation (73)), and the coefficient of the distribution of the social product k has decreased in the same proportions $k + dk = k(1 - \eta)$ (equation (79)), verifies:

$$1 + \theta = \frac{1}{k(1 - \eta)} \cdot \frac{v'(I - A)^{-1}\alpha_1}{v'\{I - (1 + \theta)A\}^{-1}\alpha_1}. \tag{84}$$

If we use the same symbols as in Section 9.3

$$z = 1 + \theta$$

$$f(z) = v'(I - zA)^{-1}\alpha_1$$

equation (84) is written:

$$z = \frac{1}{k(1-\eta)} \cdot \frac{f(1)}{f(z)}.$$

The curve $(\hat{C})$, representative of the function

$$\frac{1}{k(1-\eta)} \cdot \frac{f(1)}{f(z)}$$

is obtained by displacing the equation curve (C) $(1/k) \cdot \{f(1)/f(z)\}$. The first bisector therefore meets curve (C) before curve $(\hat{C})$ (Figure 13.1).

The rate of profit obtained with this new equilibrium is thus greater than with the old. Hence the theorem below – which contradicts Marx's Law of the Falling Tendency of the Rate of Profit:

Theorem 8 An even growth in the productivity of firms will produce an increase in the rate of profit.

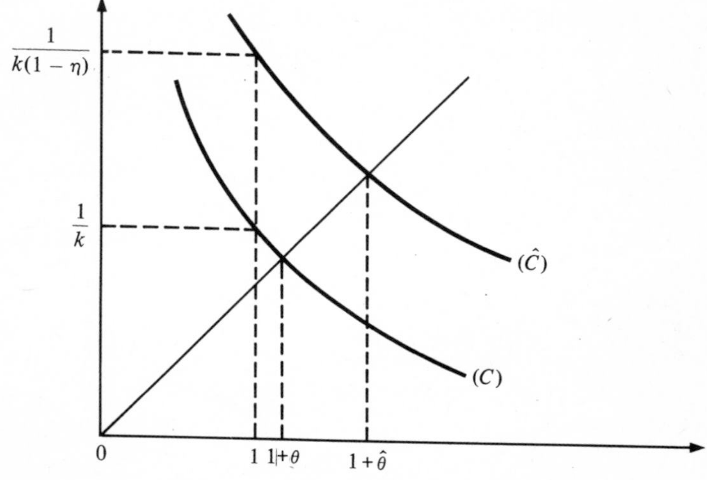

FIGURE 13.1

Effect upon the system of production

Once the new rate of profit has been calculated, its value reinserted into equation (52) gives us the system of prices of production:

$$\bar{p}' = (1 + \hat{\theta})\{\bar{p}'A + \bar{s}v'(1 - \eta)\} \tag{52}$$

from which is obtained:

$$\bar{p}' = (1 + \hat{\theta})\bar{s}v'(1 - \eta)\{I - (1 + \hat{\theta})A\}^{-1}$$

We cannot, on the basis of this equation, make a judgement on whether production-prices (expressed in units of salary) will vary upwards or downwards. The increase in the rate of profit and in all the coefficients of the matrix[1] $[I - (1 + \theta)A]^{-1}$ are counter-balanced by the change in the vector v and $v(1 - \eta)$.

However, given that the social product does not change and that price values are uniformly reduced, one may conclude that there is a falling of the 'general level' in production prices (the average figure for production prices weighted by the components of final output).

14 Extended Reproduction

14.1 Preliminary remarks

This chapter complements Chapter 9, which dealt with simple reproduction; for within the internal structure of *Das Kapital* the study of extended reproduction and the study of simple reproduction play somewhat analogous roles; after convincing himself that exploitation is possible in a stationary economy, Marx then seeks to demonstrate that the same possibility exists when there is growth. In other words, he wishes to show that in an economy characterised by regular expansion the economic situations of the capitalists and the workers respectively are identical from one period to another – the only difference being that, although the workers are just as badly off as before, the capitalists have, in fact, increased the extent of their wealth; capitalist relationships of production are maintained, but on a wider basis.

It will be recalled that whether the economy develops according to a process of extended reproduction or simple reproduction depends upon the capitalists' decision to consume either a part of their surplus value or all of it. It will be remembered also that for Marx only the process of extended reproduction can be observed in reality, simple reproduction being simply an abstract hypothesis. For capitalist accumulation is inevitable for the many reasons put forward in the short description of the theory of capitalistic development in Chapter 11.

However, it has already been pointed out that the study of extended reproduction is only a small part of the theory, a part of which has already been formalised, and which in any case does not fit in very well with the arguments by which Marx shows the irresistible development of capitalism and its no less inevitable and apocalyptic disappearance. It is perhaps the comparative independence of Marx's working out of schemes of extended reproduction that has most value and interest from the point of view of the history of economic thought; the close relationship existing between Marx's models and the growth models of Von Neumann and Leontief were noted many years ago.

Unfortunately, the quality of these schemes is considerably diminished by the particularly arid commentary that accompanies them in *Das Kapital*, and by the needlessly complicated numerical examples chosen by the author. In this connection Mrs Joan Robinson notes that 'at his death, the growth models were nothing but a chaotic mass of notes', and she goes on to add: 'May Heaven preserve us from posterity deciding to take as subjects of study all the old envelopes on which economists have scribbled numerical examples to illustrate some point of theory' ([17]).

We shall therefore confine ourselves in this chapter to providing a literal expression of the schemes of extended reproduction, which we shall then use to 'decipher' the many numerical examples worked out by Marx. Finally we shall propose a general study of these growth systems, as Marx himself would have done had he had at his command more complex algebraic instruments. This will also provide us with the opportunity of reconsidering some of the results achieved by the modern theory of growth, already described in Section 5.6.

14.2 A literal expression of the formulae of extended reproduction

We shall give here only a non-monetary version of these formulae, which means that we shall not attempt to follow Marx in the development of ideas concerning the circulation and hoarding of metallic money during the process of extended reproduction. The economy is seen by Marx to be like some vast hydraulic system where a network of flows of real goods is superimposed upon a network of monetary flows. The development is identical to that adopted for the study of simple reproduction (cf. Section 9.3). Any theoretical interest such ideas might have is greatly reduced by Marx's maintaining the hypothesis of the absence of any system of credit. 'When we drew up our scheme ... neither merchants, nor money-changers, nor bankers ... exist here' (II, 508).

Like the previous one, Marx's model here also comprises the two sectors:

1. sector I, producing the means of production;
2. sector II, producing the consumer goods.

Within each sector capitalists and workers co-exist (KI and OI on the one hand, and KII and OII on the other hand).

Time is divided into equal periods as is the usual practice. The different operations are linked together so as to conform to the general hypotheses formulated in Chapter 6, and already used on several occasions (cf. Sections 9.1 and 10.4) (synchronism, periods of production of the same length as the periods being analysed, etc.). All goods necessary both for the individual consumption of capitalists and workers and for productive consumption during the period are available as from the beginning of this period. The result of the workers' labour as far as means of production is concerned will be such that at the end of the period the stock of consumer goods will be more than replaced, and the stock of means of production will be increased, allowing the same process to be repeated, but on a wider basis.

Table 14.1 describes the current accounts of both sectors' figures for the initial period. The way in which the capital of both sectors is organically constituted is a structural fact:

$$V_1 = r_1 \cdot C_1$$

$$V_2 = r_2 \cdot C_2.$$

The average rate of surplus-value h applied to the variable capital gives us the amount of surplus-value in each sector:

$$(SV)_1 = h \cdot V_1$$

$$(SV)_2 = h \cdot V_2$$

TABLE 14.1

	Sector I	Sector II
Purchases of means of production (constant capital C)	C_1	C_2
Wages (variable capital V)	V_1	V_2
Surplus-value (SV)	$(SV)_1$	$(SV)_2$
Total: value of production	Q_1	Q_2

The equilibrium of the two series of accounts produces the equations

$$C_1(1 + r_1 + r_1 h) = Q_1 \tag{85}$$

$$C_2(1 + r_2 + r_2 h) = Q_2. \tag{85a}$$

The uses to which the surplus-value is put are of three kinds. One part $(1 - \alpha)$ is used by the capitalist class for their consumption. A second part α is reinvested in each sector in the form of increases in variable capital and constant capital; such increases must be reflected physically in the form of means of consumption and means of production, in the production of the period. It is assumed that the organic composition of this increased capital is not altered; so that increases in both variable and constant capital are in the ratio of $V_i : C_i = r_i$ ($i = 1$ or 2 according to whether it is sector I or II that is being considered).

Finally, surplus-value is broken down according to the formula:

$$hr_i C_i = \underbrace{(1 - \alpha)hr_i C_i}_{\text{capitalists' consumption}} + \underbrace{\frac{\alpha hr_i{}^2}{1 + r_i} C_i}_{\text{increase in variable capital}} + \underbrace{\frac{\alpha hri}{1 + r_i} C_i}_{\text{increase in constant capital}} \qquad (i = 1, 2). \tag{86}$$

To equations (85) must now be added the equations expressing the equality in numbers of jobs and in resources, of each type of output.

In means of production,

$$Q_1 = C_1 + C_2 + \frac{\alpha hr_1}{1 + r_1} C_1 + \frac{\alpha hr_2}{1 + r_2} C_2. \tag{87}$$

In consumer commodities,

$$Q_2 = r_1 C_1 + r_2 C_2 + (1 - \alpha)hr_1 C_1 + (1 - \alpha)hr_2 C_2 + \frac{\alpha hr_1{}^2}{1 + r_1} C_1 + \frac{\alpha hr_2{}^2}{1 + r_1} C_2. \tag{87a}$$

The elimination of the variables Q_1 and Q_2 from the equations (85), (85a) and (87), (87a) leads to

$$\frac{C_1}{C_1 + C_2} = \frac{1 + \dfrac{\alpha hr_2}{1 + r_2}}{1 + r_1 + hr_2 + \alpha h \left\{ \dfrac{r_2}{1 + r_2} - \dfrac{r_1}{1 + r_1} \right\}} \tag{88}$$

$$\frac{C_2}{C_1 + C_2} = \frac{r_1 + (1-\alpha)hr_1 + \dfrac{\alpha hr_1^2}{1+r_1}}{1 + r_1 + hr_1 + \alpha h\left\{\dfrac{r_2}{1+r_2} - \dfrac{r_1}{1+r_1}\right\}}. \quad (88a)$$

The compatibility of these equations can be easily verified: the sum of the two right-hand parts is equal to unity. For extended reproduction to be possible according to the hypotheses adopted so far, the constant capital must therefore be distributed between the two sectors in the ratios indicated by one or other of the two equations (88) and (88a). This ratio, which is a function of the structural parameters (organic composition of capital, the rate of saving, the rate of surplus-value), is also constant in time.

In what circumstances can the model be made dynamic? The constant capital C_i $(i = 1, 2)$ grows by

$$\frac{\alpha hr_i}{1 + r_i} C_i$$

between successive moments. Output Q_i, and also all the other variables of sector i which are proportional to constant capital, grow therefore in the same ratio, $\alpha hr_i/(1 + r_i)$. The fact that $C_i/(C_1 + C_2)$ $(i = 1, 2)$ is invariable in time implies that in the two sectors the rate of growth is equal, and indeed, that the growth throughout the economy is homothetic. If our hypotheses are accepted, such a programme of balanced growth is possible only if;

1. $$\frac{hr_1}{1 + r_1} = \frac{hr_2}{1 + r_2}.$$

Therefore:

$$r_1 = r_2$$

in other words, only if the capital in both sectors has the same organic composition;[1]

2. constant capital is distributed between the two sectors in adequate proportions (equations (88) and (88a)).

The first of these conditions is, on Marx's own admission, unrealistic (cf. Section 10.2). As for the second, it can be realised from moment one only as the result of pure chance. Marx, of course, did not pursue the discussion in these terms, and imposed only one condition – a much less severe one – for the process of extended reproduction to begin [see the inequality (91) in the following section]; it could only be continued with, at least in the form described in the numerical examples, if at least one of the structural hypotheses posited above were broken.

14.3 The equilibrium of exchanges between the two sectors

Let us continue to assume that the organic composition of capital in both sectors is distinct, and further that the capitalists now consume all the surplus-value, giving us a rate of saving that is nil ($\alpha = 0$). The extended reproduction model degenerates into one of simple reproduction. Condition (88) becomes

$$\frac{C_1}{C_1 + C_2} = \frac{1}{1 + r_1 + hr_1}$$

which can also be written

$$C_1(r_1 + hr_1) = C_2.$$

We have here one of the most familiar properties of models of simple reproduction, demonstrated in Section 9.4:

$$V_1 + (SV)_1 = C_2$$

$I(v + pl) = \text{II}c$ (using the symbols found in *Das Kapital*). (89)

If there is simple reproduction, the constant capital in sector II is equal to the variable capital, increased by the surplus-value, in sector I. This equality reflects the equilibrium of the exchanges taking place between the two sectors.

In the case of extended reproduction, these two quantities are different, as can be seen if we rewrite the equation of equality of jobs and resources in terms of constant capital:

$$Q_1 = C_1(1 + r_1 + hr_1) = C_1(1 + \gamma_1) + C_2(1 + \gamma_2) \qquad (87)$$

where

$$\gamma_1 = \frac{\alpha hr_1}{1 + r_1} \quad \text{and} \quad \gamma_2 = \frac{\alpha hr_2}{1 + r_1}$$

are the rates of growth of the two sectors.

Simplifying:

$$C_1(r_1 + hr_1) - C_1\gamma_1 = C_2(1 + \gamma_2). \qquad (90)$$

The *left-hand part of the equation* represents the amounts of goods purchased by sector I from sector II (variable capital + surplus-value – the increase in constant capital deducted from the surplus-value, but bought by sector I from itself). *The right-hand part* represents the amount of goods purchased by sector II from sector I, expressed in terms of constant capital. The transactions between sectors I and II balance, but the revenues distributed (variable capital + surplus-value) in I must be greater than the constant capital in II:

$V_1 + (SV)_1 > C_2$

$I(v + pl) > \text{II}c$ (using the symbols found in *Das Kapital*) (91)

The difference between the two quantities is accounted for by the increases in constant capital which are necessary for both I and II, as is clearly shown by the equation

$$C_1(r_1 + hr_1) - C_2 = C_1\gamma_1 + C_2\gamma_2.$$

In this connection, Marx writes:

> In production on the basis of increasing capital, $I_{(v+s)}$ must be equal to IIc plus that portion of the surplus-product which is re-incorporated as capital, plus the additional portion of constant capital required for the expansion of the production in II. [II, 521]

In one sense, there are the beginnings of extended reproduction in sector I, since surplus-labour 'has been expended in means of production Ic, instead of IIc, in means of production of means of production instead of means of production of articles of consumption' (II, 500).

14.4 The decoding of some of the numerical examples contained in *Das Kapital*

The starting point of the first example is Table 14.2 (II, 510). The structural parameters can be calculated from the table, and give:

$$r_1 = \tfrac{1}{4}$$

$$r_2 = \tfrac{1}{2}$$

$$h = 1.$$

TABLE 14.2

Sector	C	V	SV	Total
I	4000	1000	1000	6000
II	1500	750	750	3000

The rate of saving of the capitalists in sector I is taken as being equal to $\frac{1}{2}$. Finally, $V_1 + (SV)_1 > C_2$. Reproduction on an extended basis seems to be possible. But it cannot be achieved on the basis of the structural relationships posited at the beginning of Section 14.2, for the initial distribution of constant capital between the two sectors does not conform to that laid down by the theoretical formula (88) (the reader can verify this for himself), and the organic compositions differ from one sector to another ($r_1 \neq r_2$).

Marx considers savings in sector II as being a residue. The capitalists in this sector adapt their behaviour to the demands of the other sector, and their rate of saving is no longer equal to $\frac{1}{2}$. Such a hypothesis is, of course, quite unjustified. And Marx could have freed himself from it by permitting the capitalists to transfer their savings from one sector to another within the framework of a financial market. But we know that he refused to consider any such hypothesis.

Marx works out his calculations in the following way; the passing from the situation in year t to that of year $(t + 1)$ is achieved by the following formulae:

$$\left.\begin{aligned} C_{1,t+1} &= C_{1,t}(1 + \gamma_1) \\ V_{1,t+1} &= r_1 C_{1,t+1} \\ (SV)_{1,t+1} &= hV_{1,t+1} \end{aligned}\right\} \quad (92)$$

$$\left.\begin{aligned} C_{2,t+1} &= C_{1,t} + V_{1,t} + (SV)_{1,t} - C_{1,t+1} \\ V_{2,t+1} &= r_2 C_{2,t+1} \\ (SV)_{2,t+1} &= hV_{2,t+1}. \end{aligned}\right\} \quad (92a)$$

It can quite easily be verified that the equilibria of the economy succeed each other as shown in Table 14.3 (cf. II, 510–14). This table also enables us to calculate the rates of saving and the rates of growth for each sector at each period.

TABLE 14.3

Sector	C	V	SV	Total
		(Period 0)		
I	4000	1000	1000	6000
II	1500	750	750	3000
		(Period 1)		
I	4400	1100	1100	6600
II	1600	800	800	3200
		(Period 2)		
I	4840	1210	1210	7260
II	1760	880	880	3520
		(Period 3)		
I	5324	1331	1331	7986
II	1936	968	968	3872
		(Period 4)		
I	5856	1464	1464	8784
II	2130	1065	1065	4260
		(Period 5)		
I	6442	1610	1610	9662
II	2342	1172	1172	4686

The numerical values chosen by Marx are such that the rate of saving and the rates of growth of sector II become stabilised after period 1 at $\frac{3}{10}$ and 10% respectively (see Table 14.4) – not surprisingly, since this is the result of the recurring system to be found in equation (92) and (92a); since $\{C_{1,t}\}$ form a geometric progression of ratio $(1 + \gamma_1)$, this also applies to $\{C_{2,t}\}$, since

$$C_{2,t+2} = (r_1 + hr_1 - \gamma_1)C_{1,t+1} = (1 + \gamma_1)C_{2,t+1}.$$

Only the first $C_{2,0}$ has an arbitrary value but has no influence on the values of the terms in the series. After period 2, sector II therefore grows at the same rate as sector I.

Thus, when the organic composition of capital differs from one sector to another, balanced growth (i.e., growth where all the quantities involved increase at the same rate) can be obtained only if the rates of savings of the capitalists in sectors I and II, and noted as α_1 and α_2, bear out the equation

$$\gamma_1 = \frac{\alpha_1 hr_1}{1 + r_1} = \frac{\alpha_2 hr_2}{1 + r_2} = \gamma_2.$$

TABLE 14.4

Period	Rates of saving I	Rates of saving II	Rates of growth I	Rates of growth II
			%	%
0	$\frac{1}{2}$	$\frac{2}{10}$	10	6.5
1	$\frac{1}{2}$	$\frac{3}{10}$	10	10
2	$\frac{1}{2}$	$\frac{3}{10}$	10	10
3	$\frac{1}{2}$	$\frac{3}{10}$	10	10
4	$\frac{1}{2}$	$\frac{3}{10}$	10	10
5	$\frac{1}{2}$	$\frac{3}{10}$	10	10

γ_1 and γ_2 being constant beyond period 0, the same will be true of α_1 and α_2. In the numerical example given above, it can be seen that $\alpha_2 = \frac{3}{10}$ is the rate of saving in sector II which is compatible with

$$\alpha_1 = \tfrac{1}{2},\quad r_1 = \tfrac{1}{4},\quad r_2 = \tfrac{1}{2},\quad h = 1 \qquad \text{and} \qquad \gamma_1 = \gamma_2 = 10\%.$$

Whatever he says, and at this point his remarks are particularly unclear, Marx in fact applies to his second numerical example precisely the same treatment as that given to the first (cf. II, 518). And yet, in this case, the organic compositions of the capitals involved are equal, which also presupposes equality in the rate of saving in each of the two sectors as soon as balanced growth is achieved, i.e., as soon as we reach period 2.

TABLE 14.5

Sector	*C*	*V*	*SV*	Total
		(Period 0)		
I	5000	1000	1000	7000
II	1430	285	285	3000
		(Period 1)		
I	5417	1083	1083	7583
II	1583	316	316	2215
		(Period 2)		
I	5869	1173	1173	8215
II	1715	342	342	2399
		(Period 3)		
I	6358	1271	1271	8900
II	1858	371	371	2600

The systematic application of formulae (92) and (92a) give the same equilibria as they did for Marx, except for slight rounding-up differences. They are set out in Table 14.5 (cf. II, 522–3). The rates of growth and of saving for each sector and each period come out as shown in Table 14.6.

TABLE 14.6

	Savings rate		Rate of growth	
Period	I	II	I	II
0	$\frac{1}{2}$	$\simeq \frac{6}{10}$	–	–
1	$\frac{1}{2}$	$\frac{1}{2}$	$\frac{1}{12}$	$\frac{1}{9}$
2	$\frac{1}{2}$	$\frac{1}{2}$	$\frac{1}{12}$	$\frac{1}{12}$
3	$\frac{1}{2}$	$\frac{1}{2}$	$\frac{1}{12}$	$\frac{1}{12}$

14.5 The shortcomings of the schemes of extended reproduction

This examination of the numerical examples given in *Das Kapital* has surely shown quite clearly how imprecise and devoid of economic significance are Marx's schemes of extended reproduction.

The reason for these shortcomings is that Marx neglected to explain many variables necessarily included in his model. Thus he makes no distinction between prices and quantities, the only variables he considers being 'values' in the Marxian sense of the word (the amount of labour-time socially necessary). This position was forced upon him by his decision to defer consideration of the concepts of rate of profit and production-prices until Book III (Chapter I–XII), i.e., *after* the study of extended reproduction, which is found in Book II, Chapter XXI. This is the real source of the difficulty experienced in trying to reconcile within a system of balanced growth homogeneous savings behaviour as between the two sectors, and the organic compositions of heterogeneous capitals. The existence of equal rates of profit in all branches unifies the capital market. It is the entire class comprising the owners of the means of production which saves a fraction of the surplus-value; and these savings are invested in production activities, in proportions that maintain the equality of sectorial profit rates. The act of saving is disassociated from the act of investing. Such an approach reproduces real behaviour much more faithfully.

Just as Marx's study of extended reproduction neglects prices, so too does it disregard the total amount of labour utilised in production. Yet it is evident that the increase in production of which Marx speaks must come from either (a) an increase in the labour force employed, or (b) an increase in the productivity of the existing labour force.

This second factor is mentioned only incidentally: 'We have explained at great length in Book I ... that more labour can be rendered fluent, if necessary, without increasing the number of labourers or the quantity of labour-power employed' (II, 505). Nor does the absolute increase in the number of workers employed pose any problem, since, in Marx's view, this arises either because of 'the natural annual increase in population' (II, 524), or because there is a 'relative surplus-population among the working-class' (II, 518), or even because these two causes exist simultaneously. The expansion of the social product is, in theory, governed by the increase in the available working population, and only spectacular technical progress, and the consequent creation of an 'industrial reserve army', can remove this constraint.

We are thus once more faced with the whole series of problems raised by the General Law of Capitalist Accumulation. It is only by this very thin thread that the theory of extended reproduction is linked to the general theme of the Marxian theory of capitalist development. It is worth noting here that Marx persists in committing the error of making variable capital, and therefore wages, increase at the same rate as the social product, thus flying in the face of his own theory on wages as the cost of subsistence (for a given total population, wages must remain constant, irrespective of the number of those employed). If there is an improvement in the productivity of the means of subsistence, then in strict logic the overall wages total, expressed in 'value', must go down, and the rate of surplus-value must go up (cf. Section 13.4).

14.6 The neoclassical version of extended reproduction

It is possible to modify the Marxian schemes of extended reproduction in such a way that they take account of the criticisms made above and the observations made in previous chapters. We shall see how a simplified economy applying the hypotheses contained in the static models used in Chapters 2 and 3 can be used to initiate a regime of balanced growth. Since this section will be more normative than descriptive, the whole population will be brought together in a single class, N in number, and having the same consumer preferences.

The process of making the model dynamic is similar to the one studied in Section 9.1.

All quantities are now dated, whether they refer to a whole period, t ($t = \cdots, -1, 0, 1, 2, 3$) or to the first and last moments of a period (t and $t+1$).

x_{t+1} is the vector of goods produced at the end of period t.

x_t is the vector of initial stocks available at the beginning of period t, and which are none other than what was produced in period $(t-1)$.

N_t is the total population at moment t.

W_t is the total population available for employment at the same moment.

Consumption recorded during period t will be related to N_t, and $\bar{W}_t$ will be the labour-power available during the same period. N_t and $\bar{W}_t$ grow in parallel at a constant rate v:

$$N_t = N_0(1+v)^t$$

$$\bar{W}_t = W_0(1+v)^t.$$

The proportion of workers actually employed is also constant, and will be given the same symbols as previously:

$$a = \frac{\bar{W}_0}{N_0} = \frac{\bar{W}_t}{N_t}.$$

λ_t is the standard of living reached through consumption during period t, but deducted from the quantity available x_t.

(p_t, s_t) is the system of prices existing at moment t. If i is the rate of interest, then the prices obtaining at moment $(t+1)$ will count in any balance sheet set out at moment t, reduced by the coefficient $1/(1+i)$.[2]

Equations (10), (11), (12), defining static equilibrium, now become for the same structural characteristics:

$$Ax_{t+1} + \lambda_t \alpha N_t = x_t$$

$$v' x_{t+1} = \bar{W}_t$$

$$\frac{p'_{t+1}}{1+i} = p'_t A + s_t v'.$$

This recurring system can have as a solution a balanced growth regime of rate v, characterised by:

$$x_t = (1 + v)^t x_0 \qquad \lambda_t = \lambda_0$$

$$p_t = p_0 \qquad \text{and} \qquad s_t = s_0$$

The values for these variables relating to any period verify

$$(1 + v)Ax + \lambda\alpha N = x \tag{93}$$

$$(1 + v)\upsilon' x = \bar{W} \tag{94}$$

$$p' = p'(1 + i)A + s(1 + i)\upsilon' \tag{95}$$

The 'budget' equation which was seen to be redundant in a static system (cf. Section 3.1) now takes on the form

$$v(p'Ax) + v(s\upsilon'x) + p'\lambda\alpha N = i(p'Ax) + i(s\upsilon'x) + s\bar{W} \tag{96}$$

which is to be interpreted as follows:

$v(p'Ax)$:	investment in means of production (constant capital)
$+ v(s\upsilon'x)$:	investment in wages (variable capital)
$+ p'\lambda\alpha N$:	consumption
$= i(p'Ax + s\upsilon'x)$:	revenue from capital invested
$+ s\bar{W}$:	revenue from labour.

What value can be assigned to the index of the standard of living λ, assumed constant, which is associated with such a system? Since, apart from the fact that A and υ are replaced by $(1 + v)A$ and $(1 + v)\upsilon$, equations (93) and (94) have the same structure as equations (10) and (11) of the static equilibrium model, the value of λ is obtained by carrying out the same substitution as in formula (14). Hence:

$$\lambda = \frac{\bar{W}}{(1 + v)\upsilon'\{I - (1 + v)A\}^{-1}\alpha N}. \tag{97}$$

The price system is deduced directly from equation (95):

$$p' = s(1 + i)\upsilon'\{I - (1 + i)A\}^{-1}. \tag{98}$$

The last three formulae yield a number of consequences which, in extremely concentrated form, reproduce the essential points of the results achieved throughout this study.

1. The growth system here being considered is 'maximal', since λ attains its maximum value consistent with resources available, technology and the rate of growth of the population. To verify such a result it is sufficient to repeat the demonstration of Section 3.2 regarding the optimality of static equilibrium (but with A and v being changed into $(1 + \nu)A$ and $(1 + \nu)v$. Proposition 4 of Section 5.6 is proved.

2. One question still remains: can this maximal standard of living be associated with any interest rate, as formula (97) would have us believe? The answer is no, for the physical equilibrium corresponding to this value of λ, is 'sustained'[3] only by a rate of interest i equal to the rate of growth ν of the population and a system of prices p which is given by (98) (where i would have been given the same value as ν).

It is, in fact, only in this situation that the marginal efficiency of capital (whose value is precisely ν, since a capital of 100 becomes $100(1 + \nu)$, thanks to the rate of growth) is at all times equal to the rate of interest. Equation (96) shows that, furthermore, investment (i.e., savings) coincides with the revenue from capital, and consumption coincides with wages. The capitalist class has been deprived of its material base.

Thus, if the rate of interest i is permanently to exceed the rate of growth ν of the population, leaving the capitalists with the wherewithal for consumption, it must be supposed that the mechanisms of free competition of both capitalists and workers function only imperfectly. The 'class struggle', this time taking place within an expanding economy, encourages a certain amount of exploitation.

3. When the population is stationary ($\nu = 0$), the rate of interest which must be associated with it is also nil ($i = 0$) (see proposition 10, in Section 5.6). It is once again a case of static equilibrium, or more precisely, of simple reproduction (cf. Section 11.1).

As we saw in the case of an expanding economy, a rate of interest superior to the rate of growth, and therefore strictly positive ($i > 0$), implies a distribution of the social product between those who possess capital and the workers, the same distribution as that described in Chapter 10, devoted to production prices. The rate of interest i coincides with a rate of profit of θ.

Notes

PREFACE

1. 'The Transformation of Values: What Marx "Really" Meant,' *Journal of Economic Literature* XII (March 1974), 51–62.

2. It may be useful to try to examine formally just what a perfectly rigid version of the reserve army argument can be made to imply about wages. If the level of employment were determined exclusively by wages we would have an unemployment relationship

(1) $$u_t = f(w_t), \qquad f' > 0,$$

where u_t and w_t represent, respectively, unemployment and wages in period t. If, in addition, we posit a lagged inverse relationship between unemployment and wages, we have another equation

(2) $$w_{t+1} = g(u_t), \qquad g' < 0.$$

Clearly, (1) and (2) together do constitute a difference equation model whose time path will be oscillatory since $f'g' < 0$. It will be stable if $f'g' > -1$. Its equilibrium wage is given by the solution to

$$w = g[f(w)],$$

obtained by substituting (1) into (2) and setting $w_t = w_{t+1} = w$, as equilibrium requires.

Note, however, that there is nothing built into the process which makes w in any way approximate the physical subsistence wage. More important, as we will see, Marx clearly rejected *any* such deterministic model of wages. Presumably, he would have argued against the realism of both equations (1) and (2) since they provide no room for the role of 'the respective power of the combatants' (i.e., the workers and the capitalists, whose struggle, in his view, determines the actual level of wages).

3. See 'On the Folklore of Marxism', *Proceedings of the American Philosophical Society* (forthcoming).

FOREWORD

1. The quotations given in this translation are taken from the three-volume translation of *Das Kapital* published by Lawrence & Wishart, London, in 1954.

2. Numbers within square brackets refer to works listed in Appendix 3.

3. *Das Kapital* is composed of three books, entitled, respectively, I. 'The Development of Capitalist Production' (33 chapters); II. 'The Process of Circulation of Capital' (21 chapters); III. 'Capitalist Production as a Whole' (52 chapters). Only the first book was published in Marx's lifetime, in 1867. The second and third books were written by Engels, on the basis of manuscript notes left by Marx at his death. The first editions of these are 1885 and 1894 respectively.

INTRODUCTION

1. 'bourgeois' textbooks, of course.

CHAPTER 2

1. If x is a magnitude that is a function of time t, then $x = x(t)$, $x(t)$ being the derivative of x in relation to time: $x(t) = (dx/dt)(t)$.

2. It should be noted here that this model assumes the availability of labour $\bar{W}$ to be exogenous and completely inelastic.

CHAPTER 3

1. The symbols signifying inequalities between vectors mean, evidently:

$$a \geq b \text{ means } a^i \geq b^i \text{ for } i = 1, 2, \ldots, n$$

$$a > b \text{ means } a^i > b^i \text{ for } i = 1, 2, \ldots, n.$$

2. This term is used by the American economist D. Gale in [4].

3. R^n_+ is the sub-set of the points with positive coordinates of R^n, a space with n dimensions.

4. We have used as the title of the section an expression that Marx considered 'irrational'; he greatly preferred the phrase 'value of labour-power', (I, 503). We shall only make this distinction between the two expressions in Section 6.2.

5. By using the expression due to Frobenius of the determinant of a squared matrix M for form

$$M = \left(\begin{array}{c|c} A & B \\ \hline C & D \end{array}\right)$$

(where A is square and regular):

$$\det M = \det A. \det (D - CA^{-1}B).$$

6. Malthus goes into particularly great detail over this macabre aspect of the question.

7. For example, Malthus writes: 'Improvement in the quality of sterile land can only come from work and time; as cultivation spreads, annual increases decline regularly' ([11], 22).

8. In reality, they attached little importance to this (cf. Ricardo [16], Chapter V, and Malthus [10], Chapter IV).

CHAPTER 4

1. That is, in static analysis.

2. In an economy where the means of production are in private hands, each consumer can calculate his revenue by adding together his various sources of income. In a collectivist economy, it will be assumed (a) that each consumer knows *a priori* what his share of the national income is, and (b) that prices are calculated in such a way as to confer upon this aggregate income a constant conventional value.

CHAPTER 5

1. By 'pure profit' is meant that which does not remunerate any 'forgotten' factor of production. Bourgeois economists usually keep this expression to describe the profit remaining once interest on capital has been paid. In order to remain faithful to Marx's conception, we shall not use the term in this sense, so as to show that, within the framework of our hypothesis, profit and interest are one and the same thing (see Section 5.3).

2. For the sake of simplicity it will be supposed throughout this chapter that the structure of current prices does not change with time.

3. If there is at least one commodity within the economy – means of exchange, for example – that can be kept without expense, then the rate of interest cannot fall below zero.

4. This argument is based upon that put forward by Malinvaud in [9], 195.

5. The case of 'living labour', paid for only after it has been used, is also envisaged by Marx (cf I, 170).

6. i.e., compatible with the behaviour adopted by economic agents.

7. $U = \sum_0^\infty \delta^t u(C_t/N_t)$ where δ is the rate of future depreciation, u the *per capita* consumption utility C_t/N_t at period t ('current' utility).

8. This result is arrived at intuitively. The simple growth of the population depreciates the future value of a unit of consumption. If there is no 'impatience', this phenomenon alone prevents the reduction of the rate of interest to zero.

9. In reality, these results would seem to be independent of the formalism adopted and the degree of neoclassic orthodoxy of the discoverers. Thus we have Von Neumann, the first to have opened up this line of research, and so close to Marx in certain respects.

CHAPTER 6

1. Any salaries paid to staff who replace him as 'exploiters' should be deducted from this pure profit.

CHAPTER 7

1. We make no mention of rent here, since labour is the only useful non-reproducible commodity.

CHAPTER 9

1. We disregard here money necessary for exchanges within sectors.

2. For Marx the term '*social revenue*' (II, 414) coincides with the value of goods produced by sector II (here = 3000 units). Marx reserves the expression *social product* for the sum of all commodities produced (here 3000 + 6000 = 9000 (II, 413)). Bearing in mind the hypothesis put forward in Chapter 7, this *social product* is also *social wealth*, and exceeds *social capital* by the amount of individual capitalist consumption (I, 560).

CHAPTER 13

1. See Dorfman, Samuelson and Solow [3], theorem 8, 261.

CHAPTER 14

1. Joan Robinson has made a detailed study of this particular case in [17].

2. It should be noted that, as regards the evolution of any system of prices, the rate of interest depends upon what is chosen as money. One can however talk of the rate of interest (without further detail) when the price structure is not altered in time, as is the case in a system of balanced growth.

3. Meaning here 'compatible with the behaviour of the economic agents'; in this case, maximisation of the standard of living by the worker–consumer; maximisation of the present value of profit by the capitalist–entrepreneur.

Appendix 1 Correspondence Between the Present Work and the Text of *Das Kapital*

Marx almost certainly developed his arguments according to a logical plan, which is probably the result of didactic considerations and of the views regarding the 'economic discourse', philosophical and literary in style, that dominated his period.

Our own hypothetic–deductive presentation of the theories contained in *Das Kapital* has meant a departure from such a plan, and a reconstitution of the theories by searching for their elements through the work.

This is why there are very few examples of a close correspondence between our commentary and the relevant chapters of *Das Kapital.*

In this appendix we shall, whenever possible, indicate the chief passages of *Das Kapital* that have given rise to the various chapters of our study.

Conversely, we shall also point out, in Appendix 2, the sections of our study that the reader may find useful for an understanding of some of Marx's chapters.

Introduction

Epistemological considerations are not systematically formulated in *Das Kapital*, no doubt because they had already figured prominently in Marx's earlier works.

Chapter 1. The Concept of Value

Chapter 1 of Book I presents the main aspects of this concept, which is absolutely basic to our understanding of Marx's ideas; the reader cannot be too strongly urged to read it. The celebrated definition of use-values and exchange-values, and the would-be demonstration of the Labour Theory of Value, are to be found therein.

Chapter 2. The Concept of Equilibrium

Although he did not provide a precise definition of this concept, Marx uses it continually, as the many quotations taken from Book I, stressing the notion of equilibrium, make abundantly clear.

In Book III, Chapter X, are developed the notions of individual values and prices, and market values and prices, which refer to the exchange relationships observed outside a state of equilibrium.

Similarly, the hypotheses of constant productivity, and of strict complementarity, of the factors of production are never formally presented; but all the numerical examples, especially in Book I, are systematically based on them.

Chapter 3. A First Validation of the Theory

Marx is at odds with the classical economists, because he contests the validity of Malthus's 'Principles of Population', according to which the size of the population is determined by the volume of its means of subsistence.

His reasoning on this point is to be found in Chapter XXV of Book I, the very important chapter dealing with the General Law of Capitalist Accumulation.

Unlike the neoclassical economists, he believes however that 'the value of labour-power' is equal to the time necessary for the production of its means of subsistence, a belief clearly stated in Book I, Chapter VI; although Marx hastens to add that the norm varies from period to period and civilisation to civilisation.

Chapter 4. Limitation of the Field of Validity of the Theory: A Static Analysis

In a static economy, the existence of non-reproducible goods is the main obstacle to the application of the Labour Theory of Value. Yet at no time does Marx bring up this problem. He merely proposes an obscure and unconvincing theory of ground rent in Book III, Chapters XXXVII–XLVII – after he has developed the main principles of his theory.

The famous condemnation of the 'fetishism of commodities' is contained in the fourth part of Chapter I, Book I. Such a condemnation may have been valid when applied to the 'vulgar economists' of his day, but they are certainly out of date today. Chapter L of Book III, 'The Semblance of Competition', contains a very good synthesis of Marx's thinking on this subject.

Chapter 5. Limitation of the Field of Validity of the Theory: A Dynamic Analysis

In Section V of Book III, Marx proposes a theory for determining interest and the profits of a business, but only a brief summary of this is given in our study, attention being principally concentrated on 'pure profit'. This section also contains a few ideas on the banking and credit mechanism.

'Bourgeois' explanations of profit are disputed by Marx in Chapter XXIV of Book I, devoted to 'The Conversion of Surplus-Value into Capital'. This chapter is particularly critical of the theory of 'abstinence'.

Chapter 6. The Main Hypotheses

The distinction – essential in Marx's view – between 'labour' and 'labour-power' is set forth in Chapter XIX of Book I: 'The Transformation of the Value (and Respectively the Price) of Labour-Power into Wages'. Chapter XVII of Book I analyses the factors characterising each type of labour.

A 'General Formula for Capital' is presented in Book I, Chapter IV. The whole of Book II, developing the consequences of the formula, consists of a detailed analysis of the 'Process of Circulation of Capital', based on ideas like the length of period of work, circulation time, etc. (cf. Section II).

In Book II, Marx gives his own definition of 'fixed' and 'circulating' capital (Chapter VIII), proceeding in the next two chapters to criticise those of his predecessors.

In his view, however, this distinction has less relevance than the one existing between 'constant' and 'variable' capital, and proposed in Book I, Chapter VIII.

Chapter 7. Marxian Equilibria

In Section III of Book I, 'The Production of Absolute Surplus-Value', the main items of Marxian vocabulary (surplus-value, rate of surplus-value, constant capital, variable capital, etc.) are brought together. Chapter X of this section, in particular, shows the logical and historical limits within which the length of the working day can, and has, varied.

Once absolute surplus-value reaches a peak, capitalism tries to create a relative surplus-value by lowering the labour-time necessary for the reproduction of labour-power. Section IV of Book I ('The Production of Relative Surplus-Value') describes in detailed and lyrical terms how industrial capitalism has tried to increase this relative surplus-value.

Chapter 8. Materials for a Theory of Exploitation

The popular – but apparently pleonastic – form of the theory of exploitation is given in Book I, Chapter XIX.

As we have already stated, the very high degree of interdependence between wages and the cost of subsistence is clearly indicated in Chapter VI of Book I, 'The Buying and Selling of Labour-Power'.

On the important question of the resemblances and differences between the situation of the wage-earner and the situation of the slave, there are however only some scattered notes. Chapter XXII of Book I, which forms an introduction to the concept of simple reproduction, contains a few key sentences on this subject.

The emergence of the idea of imperfect competition is only lightly touched on, for example in Chapters X and XV of Book III, where Marx deals with the behaviour of the capitalist towards his fellow men.

The fact that capital is indivisible, and so slows down the disappearance of profit, is mentioned in Chapter II of Book II, in the section devoted to 'The Accumulation of Money'.

Chapter 9. Simple Reproduction

This chapter is a faithful commentary of Chapter XX of Book II. As stated, this study of simple reproduction was already announced in Chapter XXIII of Book I, and bears the same title.

Chapter 10. The Conversion of Values into Production Prices

This chapter follows very closely the second section of Book III, dealing with 'The Conversion of Profit into Average Profit'. Section I had already defined the concept of the rate of profit and analysed carefully the various factors affecting this rate.

The conversion into prices is only the first of the changes suffered by values. In Chapter XLV of Book III Marx goes on to define a new price system, after taking ground rent into consideration.

Chapter 11. A Short Description of the Theory of Capitalist Development

The incessant search for extra surplus-value leads the capitalist to introduce technical innovations, which directly or indirectly produce relative surplus-value. The theoretical analysis of Chapter XI in Book I is borne out by the historical study which takes up the following four chapters. Marx the historian is also to be seen in Section VIII of Book I, devoted to 'Primitive Accumulation', i.e., the transition from feudalism to capitalism.

Similarly, the transformations that capitalism has never stopped undergoing are prefigured in the very suggestive Chapter XXV of Book I ('The Centralisation of Capital'), and Chapter XV of Book III ('Crises of Overproduction').

Chapter 12. The General Law of Capitalist Accumulation

This chapter consists of a formalisation of Chapter XXV of Book I, already mentioned. In addition, Marx illustrates the theoretical analysis contained in this chapter with a highly documented factual and statistical study.

Chapter 13. The Law of the Falling Tendency of the Rate of Profit

Our chapter corresponds basically to Section III, Book III, which has the same title; i.e., Chapter XIII, 'The Nature of the Law', and Chapter XIV, 'Counteracting Causes'.

Chapter 14. Extended Reproduction

This chapter consists of putting into algebraic form the schemes presented by Marx in Chapter XXI (Section III) of Book II.

Appendix 2
Examination of Topics Treated in *Das Kapital*

	Das Kapital Topics	Main chapters dealing with	*Present work* Chapters and sections dealing with
VOLUME ONE			
The Process of Production of Capital			
Book I			
Part One	Commodities and Money (Chapters I–III)	I	Chapter 1 Section 4.2
Part Two	The Transformation of Capital into Money (Chapters IV–VI)	VI	Section 2.5
		IV	Section 6.4
Part Three	The Production of Absolute Surplus-Value (Chapters VII–XI)	VIII	Chapter 7 Section 6.6 Section 7.3
		X, XI	Section 7.4
Book II			
Part Four	The Production of Relative Surplus-Value (Chapters XII–XV)	XII	Section 7.4
		XIII XIV XV	Section 11.2

Part Five	The Production of Absolute and of Relative Surplus-Value (Chapters XVI–XVIII)	XVII	Section 6.2
Part Six	Wages (Chapters XIX–XXII)	XIX	Section 6.2 Section 8.1
Book III			
Part Seven	The Accumulation of Capital (Chapters XXIII–XXV)	XXV	Chapter 12 Section 11.5
		XXIV	Section 2.5 Section 5.4 Section 5.5
		XXIII	Section 8.3 Chapter 9
Part Eight	Primitive Accumulation (Chapters XXVI–XXXIII)		Section 11.4

VOLUME TWO

The Process of Circulation of Capital

Book IV			
Part One	The Metamorphoses of Capital and their Circuits (Chapters I–VI)	II	Section 8.6
		V	Section 6.5
Part Two	The Turnover of Capital (Chapters VII–XVII)	VIII XI XII	Section 6.5
Book V			
Part Three	The Reproduction and Circulation of the Aggregate Social Capital (Chapters XVIII–XXI)	XX	Section 6.6 Chapter 9
		XXI	Chapter 14

VOLUME THREE

The Process of Capitalist Production as a Whole

Book VI

Part	Title	Chapter	Reference
Part One	The Conversion of Surplus-Value into Profit and the Rate of Surplus-Value into the Rate of Profit (Chapters I–VII)	I, II, III	Section 10.1
Part Two	Conversion of Profit into Average Profit (Chapters VIII–XII)	X	Section 2.6 Section 8.5
		IX	Section 10.2 Section 10.3
		XII	Section 10.3
Part Three	The Law of the Falling Tendency of the Rate of Profit (Chapters XIII–XV)	XV	Section 8.5 Section 9.5
		XIII, XIV	Chapter 13
Part Four	The Transformation of Commodity-Capital and Money-Capital into Commercial Capital and Financial Capital (Chapters XVI–XX)		

Book VII

Part	Title	Chapter	Reference
Part Five	Division of Profit into Interest and Profits of Enterprise (Chapters XXI–XXXVI)	XXIII	Section 5.2
		XXVII	Section 5.5

Book VIII

Part	Title	Chapter	Reference
Part Six	The Conversion of Surplus-Profit into Ground Rent (Chapters XXXVII–XLVII)		Section 4.8
Part Seven	Revenues and their Sources (Chapters XLVIII–LII)	L	Section 4.3

References

[1] Baran, P. A., *The Political Economy of Growth* (Penguin, 1973).

[2] Debreu, G., *Theory of Value* (Yale University Press, 1972).

[3] Dorfman, R., Samuelson, P., Solow, R., *Linear Programming and Economic Analysis* (McGraw-Hill, 1958).

[4] Gale, D., *Theory of Linear Economic Models* (McGraw-Hill, 1960).

[5] Hicks, J. R., *Value and Capital* (new edition, Oxford University Press, 1975).

[6] Keynes, J. M., *The General Theory of Employment, Interest and Money* (Macmillan, 1936).

[7] Koopmans, T. C., *Activity Analysis of Production and Allocation* (Cowles Commission, Wiley and Son, n.d.).

[8] Leontief, W., *The Structure of the American Economy* (Oxford University Press, 1951).

[9] Malinvaud, E., *Lectures on Microeconomic Theory* (trans. Silvey, North Holland, Amsterdam, 1972).

[10] Malthus, T., *Principles of Political Economy* (1820; reprinted by Kelly, U.S.A., 1970).

[11] — *Essay on the Principle of Population* (1798; reprinted in Everyman's Library, 1973).

[12] Marx, K., *Das Kapital* (trans. published by Lawrence and Wishart, 1959).

[13] — *The Poverty of Philosophy* (trans. published in 1900).

[14] — *A Contribution to the Critique of Political Economy* (1859; trans. published by Lawrence and Wishart, 1971).

[15] — *A History of Economic Doctrines.*

[16] Ricardo, D., *Principles of Political Economy and Taxation* (1817; reprinted in Everyman's Library, 1973).

[17] Robinson, J., *Collected Economic Papers*, Volumes I–V (Basil Blackwell, Oxford, Volume V, 1979).

[18] Say, J. B., *Textes Choisis*, ed. P. L. Reynaud (Dalloz, Paris, 1953).

[19] Stoleru, L., *Equilibre et Croissance Economique* (Dunod, Paris, 1967).

[20] Walras, L., *Elements of Pure Economy* (trans. Jaffé, Allen and Unwin, 1954).

Index

Abstinence, 73.
Accumulation, 169, 173; primitive —, 169; general law of capitalist —, 168, 173.
Activity, rate of —, 37.
Administrator, 89; salary of —, 66.
Agents, 12.
Allais, 79.
Aristotle, 8.
Army; industrial reserve —, 168, 173, 180.
Association of capital and labour, 108.
Atomicity; hypothesis of —, 23, 130.

Bailey, 7.
Baran, 120.
Boisguillebert, 7.
Branch, 63.
Break-down, 171.
Budget surplus, 18.

Capital, 94; circulating —, 96; commodity —, 95; constant —, 98, 107; constant — consumed, 99; fixed —, 96; money —, 94; material —, 70; money — cycle, 94; productive —, 95, 97; social —, 142; variable —, 98, 107.
Capitalist, 87; financial —, 69; industrial —, 66, 69.
Centralisation of capital, 171.
Class, 87.
Classical economy, XIV, 7; neo— economy, 7; the — economists, 34, 35; the neo— economists, 35.
Coalition, 130; — of capitalists, 170.
Coefficient of distribution of social capital, 104.
Commodity, 5, 12; reproducible —, 47; non-reproducible —, 47, 64; luxury —, 93.
Competition, 156; semblance of —, 46.
Complementarity; strict —, 14.
Composition; organic — of capital, 146, 187; technical — of capital, 188; value — of capital, 146.
Consumption; individual —, 94; productive —, 94; — habits, 15; sphere of —, 47.
Contradiction, XIV.
Conversion of values into production prices, 144.
Co-operation, 167.
Credit, XV, 75, 170, 200.
Crises, 99, 172.
Cycles; economic —, 171.

Day; length of working —, 92, 109.
De Gaulle, 108.
Demand, 48; correspondence in —, 48; effective —, 171; excess —, 15; law of supply and —, 22, 130; present —, 42.
Depreciation, 97; rate of —, 190.
Development; theory of capitalist —, 164.
Division; social — of labour, 167.
Dorfman, 14, 198.

Economy; vulgar political —, XVII; static —, 17; state of the —, 17.
Efficiency frontier, 30, 104; marginal — of capital, 70.
Engels, XII, XIV, 73, 154.
Equilibrium, 21, 45; Marxian —, 101; temporary —, 80; state of —, 21; theory of general —, 44.
Exploitation, 73; popular form of the theory of —, 144.

Fetichism of commodities, 46.
Firm, 13.
Franklin, 7.

Gale, 27.
Growth, 76; extensive and intensive —, 168; — programme, 77, 137; — regime, 77, 137; rate of —, 242.

Hansen, XVI.
Hicks, 80.
Households, 13.

Impatience, 78.
Index of the standard of living, 16.
Indivisibility, 133.
Inputs, 13.
Intensity of labour, 92.
Interest, 67, 70, 73, 155; — in a socialist economy, 76; theories of —, 67.
Investment; demographic —, 179; full employment —, 182.

Kernel, 128.
Keynes, 70, 71, 72, 171.
Koopmans, 14.

Labour, 90; — power, 90; price of — power, 91; price of —, 33; socially necessary — time, 54; abstract, concrete —, 91; direct and indirect —, 5; dead, living —, 73.
Land; value of —, 61, 91.
Law, of the falling tendency of the rate of profit, 170, 185; — of supply and demand, 22, 130; — of labour-value, 5; general — of capitalist accumulation, 170, 173, 210.
Leontief, 12.
Liquidity; preference for —, 70.
Lock-out, 129.

MacCulloch, XVIII, 73.
Machinism and large-scale industry, 167.
Malinvaud, 74, 128.
Malthus, XIV, XVIII, 37.
Means of subsistence, 93.
Method; dialectical —, XIV.
Mill, J. S., 7.
Mobility of labour, 131.
Mode of production, XV, 164; capitalist —, XV, 61.
Monetary laws, XV; — matter, 196; — theory, XVII.
Money; quantitative theory of —, 142.
Monopoly; bilateral —, 128.

Obsolescence, 98
Occupation; rate of — of the working population, 179.
Optimal growth programme, 78.
Optimality, 29.
Output, 13.
Overpopulation; relative —, 168, 173.

Period of circulation, 95; — of production, 71, 95.
Petty, 7.
Phelps, 79.
Plan, 107.
Preference for the present, 70, 137.
Prices, 9; — system, 47; production —, 9, 146; individual —, 23; money —, 10, 196.
Principle of population, 42, 176.
Production, 12; absence of free —, 28; — function, XIV; linked —, 62; sphere of —, 46; — techniques, 14.
Productive matrix, 27.
Productivity, 14, 92, 210.
Product; social —, 102.
Profit; law of the falling tendency of the rate of —, 187; pure —, 65; unit —, 19; uniform rate of —, 148.
Progress; technical —, 165, 167, 183.

Quesnay, XIV.

Realisable state, 16.
Relationship; capitalist —, 138, 141; exchange —, 5, 11; social —, 46.
Rent; ground —, 156.
Reproduction of capitalist relationships, 138, 141; extended —, 199; simple —, 135.
Revenue; social —, 142.
Ricardo, XI, 6, 7, 37, 96, 185, 192.
Robinson (Joan), 200, 203.

Samuelson, 14, 198.
Savings; capitalist —, 89, 177; workers' —, 90; rate of —, 177.
Say, XIV, XVIII, 37.
Scarcity, 46.
Senior, 7.
Slavery, 120.
Smith (Adam), XI, XIV, 7.
Solow, 14, 198.
Sphere, 63; — of circulation, 65; — of consumption, 46; — of production, 46.
Standard commodity, 11.
State, XV, 111.
Stationary regime, 78, 135, 137.
Steuart, 7.
Stoleru, 76.
Strikes; workers' —, 129, 184.
Structural characteristics of the economy, 12.

Subsistence; cost of —, 117; means of —, 93.
Supply, 48; — correspondence, 48; excess of —, 15; law of — and demand, 22, 130.
Surplus, 120.
Surplus labour, 116.
Surplus value, 64; absolute —, 109, 111; extra —, 166; relative —, 109, 111, 192; unit —, 107; rate of —, 107, 145.

Technical processes, 52.
Theory of general equilibrium, 44; — of exploitation, 114; — of interest, 67, 70, 73; games —, 125; quantitative — of money, 144.
Time of turnover of capital, 95.
Trade unions, 131, 183.

Unemployment, 19, 173.
Unit of account, 11.
Updating, 69, 155.
Utility, 46; — function, 58.

Value, 6, 10; theory of labour —, 5; exchange —, 5; individual —, 23; use —, 5; — of labour, 91; changes in —, 81; — prices, 9, 46.
Von Neumann, 200.

Wages, 19.
Wage-earners, 87.
Wage-earning class, 87.
Waste, 106.
Wealth; social —, 142.

Yield; constant —s, 15, 59; increasing, decreasing —, 59.